ALL STAR CAST

Books by STEPHEN LONGSTREET

The General
Chicago 1860—1919
We All Went to Paris
Yoshiwara
War Cries on Horseback
Young Men of Paris
Canvas Falcons
The Pedlocks
Sporting House
A Treasury of the World's Great Prints
The Real Jazz, Old and New
The Burning Man
Man of Montmartre
City on Two Rivers: Profiles of New York—Yesterday and Today
All Star Cast: An Anecdotal History of Los Angeles

ALL STAR CAST

An Anecdotal History of Los Angeles

STEPHEN LONGSTREET

Drawings by the Author

Thomas Y. Crowell Company
New York / Established 1834

Copyright © 1977 by Stephen Longstreet

Designed by Lynn Braswell

Library of Congress Cataloging in Publication Data

Longstreet, Stephen, 1907—
   All star cast.
   Bibliography: p.
   Includes index.
   1. Los Angeles—History. I. Title.
F869.L857L66 1977   979.4'94   76-43337
ISBN 0-690-01194-6

1 2 3 4 5 6 7 8 9 10

This book is dedicated to
a friendship
with
W. C. Fields
who advised me
"Even if you trust your friends,
always cut the cards . . ."

Contents

viii

CONTENTS

CONTENTS

Introduction

When I became a resident of Los Angeles more than thirty years ago, I started to collect, as an amused citizen, those remarks made about the city that, finally, with added years of research among journals, unpublished texts, printed documents, old letters, newspaper files and interviews, resulted in this story of a strange yet remarkable city. The game of insulting and complimenting Los Angeles—

almost on a paranoiac level—has become nearly an industry. A few samples:

"It's a great place to live, but I wouldn't want to visit there" (Mark Twain, in a 1907 letter).

"God's great blueprint for man's abode on earth" (Aimee Semple McPherson).

"A great place to live if you're an orange" (Fred Allen).

"No man could find a better spot on earth, if only he had some intelligent person to talk to" (Aldous Huxley, in conversation).

"The plastic ass-hole of the world" (William Faulkner).

One soon senses an eerie sensitivity here, wandering between improbable and delicate nuances.

Historian Kevin Starr, a fourth generation Californian, sounded like a poet about the city in an interview in the *Los Angeles Times* of May 22, 1973:

Just look around you—the same dream that propelled the pioneers to California is still a reality. Here is a region of still incredible abundance, of smiling nature, good weather, beautiful surroundings, an area of vast grandeur and size where a man can feel free, unrestrained. Los Angeles is quintessentially California, a city of [A.D.] 2050, decades ahead of the rest of the country, a place where everything is naturally larger than life, from the kooks to the technology. . . . I love Los Angeles because it is a city patterned after no model. It is unique, developed through its own energy and creativity.

To many, the city has remained more mundane, crossed with lingering parochialism. As a genre storyteller, I have for a long time felt the need for a fuller narrative of Los Angeles. There have been many gossipy books of exacerbated licentiousness, but, on close study, they contain mainly legends and unverified stories passed on as "told to." There are, of course, many volumes by specialists who have been analyzing the very stones, computerizing historic documents on the economics, weather and tidal drifts, adding speculations of the future of southern California and its dilemmas. But these are mainly read by students and other specialists.

INTRODUCTION

What I have tried to portray are the human elements—the changeover from a Hispanic mission age to the Protestant ethic, and the games, joys, sorrows, crimes and even vices of more than 200 years of one culture replacing another—always an upward mobility, but with little reverence for tradition. Who, and what they did, and how they did it has, for me, the true flavor of this odd and fabulous city. I don't wonder that Kevin Starr calls California "a mixed blessing, a divided fable."

For any writer there is here, first of all, the vast growth to bewilder him; the city limits take in 454 square miles, but no one pays much attention to these boundaries, for greater Los Angeles, including dominating satellites, is 4,000 square miles, not all given to marijuana, barbiturates, astrology and sunbathing.

Los Angeles has always been the goal of the footloose and the curious, the polymorphous hustler. But its two greatest periods of influx of new citizens were a national drought and a depression, which drove hordes of the dispossessed and despairing west during *The Grapes of Wrath* thirties. World War II offered well-paying jobs to produce vast armaments, airplanes and supplies, creating a migration that has not yet stopped.

It is a city in which nearly everyone drives a car, and has to, for it has the most miserable public transportation of any major metropolis; it is a population on wheels, and living in the resulting exhausts which, mixed with other pollutants, is called smog.

The metropolitan area, always swallowing real estate, contains ninety towns and cities and is dependent on the automobile more than any other city on the globe. Los Angeles exists on a narrow coastal plain, spread out north and south, a conglomeration of captive or independent districts (Beverly Hills is a good example of independence—buried like a plum in the huge pie that is Los Angeles, it is *not* a part of the city). The shoreline is sandy (and often oil-stained), the beaches are like Gauguin's dreams, with some headlands. There are natural harbors aided by breakwaters. The center of the city is twenty-one miles from its harbor area at San Pedro. But that is just a hop and a skip in southern California where people will drive thirty miles to see a movie.

INTRODUCTION

In the northwest section of the city are the Santa Monica Mountains, eroded hills which look as if they were drawn by Doré and Dali. The bulldozer has cut them up and on their precipitous ravines, cliffs and canyons are the most spectacular and expensive homes built by native-born or imported folk. These same encircling mountains, with a layer of hot air on top, keep a golden-brown fog hanging over the city.

The climate is still splendid; the rains rarely fall on these coastal plains. The water supply comes from far away, carried by 300- or 400-mile-long viaducts. Swimming pools indicate not only social status—most of the population think they are a natural need. They are being built at the rate of 1,000 a month. Barbecue pits are also an adjunct to Los Angeles living.

Each district—the city has been moving westward for a hundred years—can be dated by its type of home. Few original mud-and-straw adobes exist of the true Spanish-Mexican era. There are still a few treasured, protected "Steamboat Gothic" Victorian mansions, but most have gone down to rubble, to the bulldozer and the wreckers' ball. Fifty years ago, "Spanish" was the fashionable style, with red-tile roofs and iron-grilled windows. Tracts of thousands of structures took on the title "ranch house" but were, and are, a mockery of the true native ranch-house style. After World War II Los Angeles went mindlessly into modern forms—box-like shapes, houses like spider nests on stilts or cantilevered over yucca and canyon.

In developments like Truesdale Estate, the style of homes has been called "Metro-Goldwyn-Mayer Modern" and "blasé pretence." As for high-rise building, very basic functional forms and lots of renting space carry the day, rather than truly original concepts. "Buildings here are mimeographed, not designed" (a tourist first seeing Century City).

Los Angeles, like California, has always been promises, but it is also a real flesh and blood city and has been the home of some of the century's most modern talents, from Igor Stravinsky to Christopher Isherwood, Frank Lloyd Wright to D. W. Griffith. It is also the home of such irrelevant items as the Manson family, and, as John Barrymore insisted, "the

INTRODUCTION

most beautiful women—the best legs in the world." It is the capital of the Gay Liberation Revolution, "foot-long hot dogs," the Dodgers, Cal Tech, the Rand Corporation and contains a Chinatown with two places serving the best food this side of Peking (not to mention tong wars and Fan Tan gambling dens).

More is the key word to the city: *More* self-assurance, welfare, grotesque creeds, reverence for John Wayne and gurus; *more* sunshine and call girls; *more* colleges and universities; *more* abused Chicanos (Mexican-Americans) and Indians than any other big city; the largest Jewish population—600,000—next to New York (the Hasidic poor on Fairfax Avenue, the rich temple members in Beverly Hills); the Sunset Strip hippies, porno shops, blue movies; sixteen Nobel Prize winners in residence, 2,000 writers (including the basic Irvings, Wallace, Schulman and Stone); more scenery, forty miles of Pacific Ocean; more banks per mile than Wall Street; more cooking-sherry-drinking down-and-outers than the Bowery; the most dangerous freeway and murderous highway system in the United States; more crackbrained politicians and self-made popes, God-drenched messiahs and cults than in all other recorded U.S.A. history; Walt Disney-styled funerals at Forest Lawn, more bottles of Château Rothschild's best years.

The natives are white, red, yellow, brown and all tones in between—from Sioux chiefs to jazz kings (Kid Orey, Jelly Roll, Ben Pollock). Los Angeles has everything from gourmet Spanish chefs to smokers of grass and takers of H and LSD; in Beverly Hills, the schoolchildren with some of the highest IQ's in the nation, in Watts, the lowest reading rate. More crime. Only one morning newspaper, one evening paper, ninety-eight radio and TV stations; a Roman Catholic Cardinal and six Satan cults ("black mass available").

In this story of a city expanding too rapidly I have found and used basic human material as an intoxicated historical writer picking up bits passed by, or neglected by others. I have searched out some of the core of existence of Los Angeles, hunted down its ability to keep swallowing more and more of California. What may have begun as a blind, almost thoughtless, process of growth has today become a kind of unified, yet unwritten, plan to take over as much as possible of the state until Los Angeles is California—not by occupying territory, but through its wealth in oil, shipping, manufacturing, the film and television industry, as headquarters for huge insurance companies, banks, computer and airplane corporations, the powerful, often corrupt, unions. It dominates by money, by political control, the use of lobbies, and has a stranglehold on the state. It controls much state legislation, decides elections by the millions of votes it can throw behind a candidate or a bill.

There are no invented scenes in this book, no imagined dialogues. I have gone to original documented records, and gone through many unpublished journals and letters as well as the remaining files of old newspapers. In the past, California journalism had a wild and often hilarious flavor, but was often careless of facts. I have used it as color, but have rechecked for facts, passed articles by when they seemed myth. The bibliography lists sources and authorities that were invaluable in checking details, dates and personalities and in providing information to correct some early errors in texts now out of print. The Ross collection of Americana has been especially helpful, as have been Rita Norton of the library staff of Los Angeles County; Helen Wurdermann, director of the Los Angeles Art Association; Silvia Roth, who brought order to the original manuscipt; and many in wrangler's jeans or driving Jaguars whom I interviewed and who desired to remain unnamed.

I have not taken sides in the complexity that is a city's human relationship. Nor is this a book of exposés, although some of its contents may astonish some. In letting people tell their own stories, there is a heightened perception and one avoids the style of commemorative plaques.

Nothing will stop the swallowing of the state by Los Angeles, one Dr. Strangelove at Cal Tech told me, *"Unless* the city's lifeblood, water and gasoline, depart from its veins." It remains a fascinating city, senseless at times, ill-served, but cheerful and with a delight in its own virtues, while just offshore frolic shoals of whale and porpoise.

I have tried to follow the advice of Dr. Andrew Rolle in his *California*

INTRODUCTION

History Reappraised: "History represents the impact of the past on the present. . . . The study of history, by illuminating the past, should give us a better sense not only of our origins but of our present and future. . . ."

Stephen Longstreet

Beverly Hills
California
1977

BOOK I

THERE WERE TIGERS THERE

1 Saber-Toothed Tigers, Indians, Spaniards

The first citizen of greater Los Angeles of which we have any physical evidence prowled—during the Pleistocene age—what were to become Hollywood, Sunset and Wilshire boulevards. He was *Smilodon* (from the Greek words for *knife* and *tooth*), the saber-toothed tiger with the amazing crushing jaws and nearly foot-long fangs, who preyed on the plant-eating mastodons, sloths, camels, giant bison

Sir Francis Drake, who reached California on the Golden Hind *in 1579, is thought to be the first European to visit the area. This map, based on his claims, shows the future site of Los Angeles near the lettering "Tigues." (British Museum)*

and bear of the dawn age. They died by the hundreds in the sticky pitch of the La Brea Tar Pits (on Wilshire Boulevard), near which they had come to drink or to attack other drinkers 100,000 years ago. The fossils were first observed scientifically in 1901 by a geologist of the Union Oil Company.

Smilodon died out about 13,000 years ago when the elephant-like mastodons vanished, as did the ancient tiny horse, the peccary and the prehistoric bison—most likely in some catastrophic change of climate.

There is a period of thousands of years after that, the scientists tell us, before man came over from Asia with his dog and his longbow on a land bridge that once existed on the Bering Strait between Siberia and Alaska. But he didn't head at once for what was to be called California. Man in the New World was slow-moving. The best guess (and it is only a guess) is that the Los Angeles Indians, found by the first Spaniards living in what was to be the city, were the Yang-na, who had drifted down into southern California about 1,500 years before by way of Cajon Pass in what is

SABER-TOOTHED TIGERS, INDIANS, SPANIARDS

today called San Bernardino County. They had come down from Owens Valley, and before that from Nevada and even earlier from farther east, retreating from more warlike tribes. This movement could have taken centuries. So there they were—California's first humans—speaking a Shoshonean dialect. They were peace-loving, fat endomorphic types, living in bowl-shaped brush huts, some settling on offshore islands like Santa Catalina. They all left signs—even if only clamshells and fish bones—strewn over what was to become Los Angeles and Orange counties.

The rivers and streams were waterways in those days, not the series of drying puddles of the present dry age. The natives lived on live-oak acorns, which was their staple food, crushed, ground and baked. Those who reached blue water ate the clams and other tidal-pool fish life that could be trapped. Chaparral, a forest growth made up of greasewood, scrub oak, sumac, sage, elderberry and poison oak, furnished material for weapons and medical remedies of great bitterness. The Yang-na chased small game and wore almost no clothing. Some historians see them as naked and dull. But some bolder Indians made pine-plank canoes, and besides discovering the delights of shellfish, they became deep-sea fishers. They believed in the necessity of what they did and in its usefulness to survival.

When the Spanish first came, there were about twenty-five aboriginal villages of Yang-na, scattered over what would one day be Los Angeles County, and they hardly ever numbered more than 300 to 500 people; this is asserted by those who have studied their remains—campsites, graves and fire-marked stones. They lacked the arts, the cruelty and the excitement of the Aztec and the Inca; they were merely expert makers of cooking pots from soapstone brought over from Catalina Island. They wove remarkably good baskets, but remained low on the scale of Indian culture, not approaching the amazing Mayan progress, nor even the crafts of the Indians of the Great Plains. The Yang-na did no farming and made no terra-cotta pottery, wove no blankets. They lacked a later Los Angeles idea that one's share of a culture is definitive progress.

In remote areas being bulldozed for supermarkets or gas stations, one

Los Angeles was founded on orders of this Mission of San Gabriel to grow food and raise cattle for the fathers.

An old print dating from the era when Mexico ruled California and cattle were raised only for their hides and tallow on vast Spanish land grants. Americans managed to seize most of these holdings, usually illegally.

can still turn up their *malcajetes* and *metates* of stone used for the grinding and baking of their acorn food. They readily adopted the maize culture brought by the first explorers from Mexico. And they took to whiskey with the zeal that a Los Angeles Chamber of Commerce meeting takes to dry martinis.

The Yang-na never became a warlike people and they did not seem to have had any idea of mounting war parties against the first white men rimmed in iron, who claimed their land for their own God and King. The Indians, what few there were of them, held on to the land of southern California until the middle of the eighteenth century. They were on the last areas of the earth, outside of polar ice, that had not been claimed by the white empires, mapped and given by the Pope (or by fire power) to nations far away. The covert jealousies of empires began to press in on California. The Russians were moving down from their northwest trading posts. The British were spreading into the Valley of the Ohio, eying the Mississippi and what was beyond for their German Hanoverians on the throne. The Spanish in Mexico, subjects of the royal Ferdinands, had approved of Don José de Gálvez when he claimed that Louisiana, Texas and California were needed as Spanish buffer territory against the moving Russians and British. Don José ordered Governor Gaspar de Portolá and Father Junípero Serra to push forward new Spanish frontiers to the Sacramento River. Alta California came into being in July 1769 with the founding of Mission San Diego de Alcala. Twenty-one missions were to be built on the Camino Real, the King's Highway. In 1771 the largest and most wealthy, the Mission San Gabriel, was set up with Indian muscle by the Franciscan order that controlled all the missions.

It was just ten years later that an area nine miles across the valley was decided on as the spot on which to found the Pueblo of Los Angeles. California was by then an eight-year-old province, and eight of the missions were built. We have a record of how the site was first seen in 1769 by an expedition heading for Monterey Bay under Gaspar de Portolá. A priest, Father Crespi, who went along kept a journal. His is the first mention in history of what was to be Los Angeles:

SABER-TOOTHED TIGERS, INDIANS, SPANIARDS

Tuesday, August 1.—This day was one of rest, for the purpose of exploring and especially to celebrate the jubilee of Our Lady of Los Angeles de Porciuncula.

Wednesday, August 2.—We set out from the valley in the morning and followed the same plain in a westerly direction. After traveling about a league and a half through a pass between low hills, we entered a very spacious valley, well grown with cotton woods and alders, among which ran a beautiful river from the north-northwest, and then, doubling the point of a steep hill, it went on afterward to the south. Toward the north-northeast there is another riverbed which forms a spacious water course, but we found it dry. This bed unites with that of the river, giving a clear indication of great floods in the rainy season, for we saw that it had many trunks of trees on the banks. We halted not very far from the river, which we named Porciuncula.

(This was, of course, today's Los Angeles River and the dry riverbed noted to the north—still dry today—is the Arroyo Seco, now bridged by a structure favored by suicides. The camp could have been set up, if the text is carefully studied, on the river where it would meet present North Broadway.) Father Crespi continues:

This plain where the river runs is very extensive. It has good land for planting all kinds of grain and seeds, and is the most suitable site of all that we have seen for a mission. As soon as we arrived, about eight heathen from a good village came to visit us; they live in this delightful place among the trees on the river. They presented us with some baskets of pinole made from seeds of sage and other grasses. Their chief brought some strings of beads made of shells, and they threw us three handfuls of them. Some of the old men were smoking pipes. We gave them tobacco and glass beads, and they went away.

Thursday, August 3.—At half past six, we left the camp . . . . After crossing the river we entered a large vineyard of wild grapes and an infinity of rosebushes in full bloom. All the soil is black and loamy and is capable of producing every kind of grain and fruit which may be planted.

THERE WERE TIGERS THERE

With Father Crespi's description as a guide, Felipe de Neve, governor of the province, laid his plans for the settlement of Los Angeles before the viceroy. After that, there was only the task of recruiting settlers.

As the sun went down on the west bank of a southern California river on September 4, 1781, forty-four men, women and children prepared to camp out. They neither looked nor felt like founders of a great city. The river had been named by the Spanish exlorer Gaspar de Portolá, as noted, *Nuestra Señora la Reina de los Angeles de Porciuncula*—Our Lady the Queen of the Angels of Porciuncula—for the Jubilee Day of the Lady which was celebrated the day before. The Lady was a sacred image in a church in the Italian town of Porciuncula, where Saint Francis, the bird man, once got remission from the venal consequences of sin. There are other explanations of the naming of Los Angeles, but they are myths.

The settlers sent to found El Pueblo de Nuestra Señora la Reina de los Angeles de Porciuncula found it a long name, so it soon was shortened to El Pueblo by the Spanish and the Mexicans who ruled there. Later, the Americans who seized it from the Latins called it Los Angeles. And today, of course, it is nationally recognized by the two letters L.A.

The settlers were *paisanos,* or country folk, having come up from Mexico after being recruited. At first they had been quartered at the Mission San Gabriel, but on September 4th, they had been sent on, after an early mass, to found the settlement four leagues from the mission. The men, women and children rode mules and horses and were escorted by Christian Indians and four soldiers who cursed the heat in their leather armor and rusty helmets.

Even if it may dampen the pride of some of today's families claiming royal or noble blood among the first settlers, a close look at them will do away with myths. Of the first eleven families who established the Pueblo of Los Angeles, only two men were actually Spanish, and they brought along their Indian wives. Two were black, two were mestizo (half-Indian, half-Spanish), four were pure Indian, and all came with Indian or mulatto wives. There were twenty-two children whose birth lines would have baffled an IBM computer.

SABER-TOOTHED TIGERS, INDIANS, SPANIARDS

Getting there hadn't been easy. It had been good to get under way for they had been quarantined for seventeen days at the mission when smallpox was suspected. The soldiers were under the command of a corporal, José Vicente Feliz. (Los Feliz roads, streets and heights are named for him today.) He was a man who had been on other expeditions, once overland—a dreadful journey—from Sonora across California. We know little else about him, as to character and background.

It had been a dusty trip down an Indian trail (today, Mission Road) to found Los Angeles. It was no splendid Arcadian landscape they had traveled—across sandy wastes, past tule and willow growths—and when they arrived at the river, they picked as a gathering site a huge sycamore which gave them shelter and became a landmark as "El Aliso." When the vicinity became a thoroughfare, it was called Aliso Street. There were also cottonwoods all around, flinging their seeds about, and the black soil looked fertile. On all sides were spreads of sparse grass, flats of cacti and chaparral, as it was the dry season and the landscape was burned to sepia and umber colors. To the north was a range, the San Gabriel Mountains, topped by an incredibly blue sky.

Later historians could make a pattern of all this new California, perhaps because in many ways this settlement was a success. In *California History Reappraised*, Rodman Paul states: "Viewed in their totality, early California characteristics were as distinctive as one could ask for: a bizarre natural environment dominated by an arid climate; an Hispanic heritage that suggested possible ways of living with that environment; a cosmopolitan and speculatively minded crowd of new farmers, some of whom were expert and some ignorant; a large local market and geographic isolation. The sum of all these seemed to prophesy an unusual history."

The settlers, the *pobladores*, remembered they had come a far bit from their original homes in Sinaloa and Sonora. There was no wild pioneer spirit of hunting for a paradise or a fabulous wilderness. They knew that they had been recruited only to set up a farming settlement in this arid region, to grow crops to relieve California's full dependence on ships moving supplies from San Blas to the California missions. Carrying the faith to far places and to pagan savages depended on logistics, and it seemed a settlement could shorten the line of supplies.

They settled down, these first Angelenos, over their tortillas and beans in a spot they planned as a Plaza (just a bit northeast of the present Plaza). There were to be pasturelands, seven-acre farms for each family and fifty-foot house lots for building around the Plaza.

The place was actually already inhabited. But they were only Indians, the Yang-na, naked people innocent of sin, the women in deerskin skirts and beads. The sight of Mexicans and Spaniards was not strange to the Indians, for they had seen people like them at the Mission San Gabriel when it was founded in 1771, and some had listened to the preaching by Franciscan missionaries. Also, they were sometimes pressed into serfdom once their souls had been saved. Even before that they had seen Gaspar de Portolá, who had come along the coast from San Diego and marched all the long way to Monterey Bay.

The Indians lived on the site of the present City Hall and an early Los Angeles hotel, the Bella Union. Corporal Feliz was the natural leader. Neither government officials nor priests seem to have been present.

The settlers waited to see if promises would be kept. When recruited, they had been told they would receive ten pesos a month and daily rations, as well as tools, utensils, cattle, horses and mules, and a five-year moratorium from taxes if the new pueblo was a success—which meant if they survived.

To set this event in its proper chronological perspective it must be pointed out that Los Angeles was founded just six weeks before the British lobsterbacks marched out of Yorktown in Virginia, playing "The World Turned Upside Down," to surrender His Majesty's forces under Cornwallis to General Washington, and a decade before Washington, D.C., was set up as the Capital of the United States. The Americans, themselves, were not to officially cross the continent until Lewis and Clark led their expedition west twenty-four years later.

Charles III accepted all the plans of his adviser, José de Gálvez, for the expansion of Spanish holdings in California by the establishment of missions, *presidios* (forts) and pueblos.

The Reglamento of 1781 gave royal approval (by the Grace of God and occupation) to maintaining the Pueblo of Los Angeles and to providing supplies for the sustenance of its citizens until they were self-sustaining.

By November there were huts with earth roofs for protection as the winter rains and winds were coming. The little puddles were to become raging rivers in flood. A report shows that each family had two fields for corn (it was a maize culture like the Aztec and Mayan), a rough plow, an axe and a hoe. Horses and mules were distributed; some few carts and wagons existed, not many; and there were breeding animals to beget their kind, as well as some fowl with brood hens and a rooster or two to crow on the dung heaps. Some time then, or later, a dam was put up to divert the water needed for irrigation along a sort of canal called a *zanja-madre*.

If it all seemed idyllic and hard *hard* working, there was always the pious worry that man is born in original sin, and the flesh is weak. As twilight fell on March 18, 1782, spiritual and physical power rode into the new settlement on a tom mule. Father Junípero Serra, the zealous founder and head of all the missions of California, was a stern and godly man. He stayed but for the night and moved on in the morning to San Gabriel. He must have put his thoughts together with those of Corporal Feliz over moral conditions at the pueblo, for the heads of three families were run out of town and their land and cattle taken from them. There is no indication as to *what* their crimes had been—seduction of virgins, leading of wives into adultery, drunkenness, too slack in attendance at mass, stealing or just plain laziness. But go they did, just where in the wilderness is not recorded.

2   The Wild Pueblo

B y the middle of the 1780s Los Angeles was in appearance, and in its way of life, a typical Mexican village. There was a chapel and the houses were of adobe, that marvelous building material, cheap and easy to produce, giving thick walls which kept homes cool in summer and held heat in during bad weather. The dwellings had beaten earth floors, timbers holding up roofs of sod or planks, later to be re-

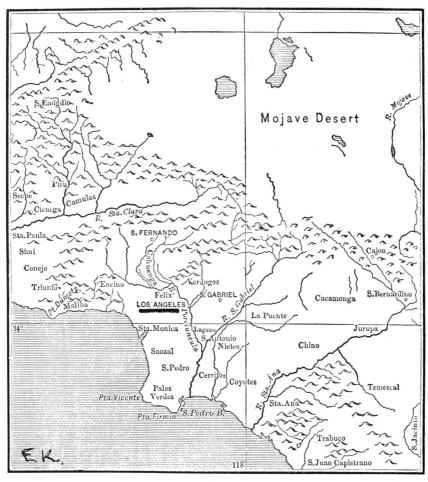

Map of the Los Angeles
district around 1810.
There was even a settle-
ment called Cucamonga.
(Bancroft)

placed and waterproofed by tar from the La Brea pits. The pits, twenty-eight miles from the sea, still held their fossil bones of prehistoric animals. Cattle were beginning to move out beyond the borders of the town and already some people could see the beginnings of what were to become the *ranchos,* or outposts, of the future—vast landholdings where wild long-horned cattle, slaughtered for their hides and tallow, ran in the thousands.

In 1786 the landholdings were officially turned over to those settlers who had made them green and put them into cultivation. Only eight of the original male heads of families had survived, and these were rewarded with a branding iron with which they could mark their kine differently from those of their neighbors. (Barbed wire, however, was still a century away.) The men signed for the land grants and the branding irons with an "X." Writing and reading was usually reserved for those who didn't plant or plow, mostly the clergy.

Corporal Feliz was rewarded by being made *comisionado,* or town manager, who oversaw the *alcalde* and other people who ran the town. Wine had been brought down from the mission at San Gabriel, since the vines of Los Angeles were not yet producing sufficient grapes for the trampling and filling of kegs. Kids and oxen were roasted and string music provided when the town was five years old. The settlers had the credulous optimism of most pioneers.

The Santa Barbara *comandante* was their court of appeal and Comisionado Feliz had to report to him as to the state of justice, law and morality in the Pueblo. In ten years, he could report that the population (human) was 139, families numbered 28 and farms 29, suggesting the presence of a bachelor. There was a *calabozo* (jail), also called in time a calaboose; a chapel, of course, a town hall, a barracks, a storage building, all with walls of rubble, clay and wattle and tarred roofs. Not at all impressive, but practical. Its granary held more grain than most of the missions, and so it had successfully done its job of becoming a source of supply to the Spanish Empire's far-off Pacific holdings. It produced no dazzling careerists, nor too shocking crimes.

THE WILD PUEBLO

The new Plaza was begun in 1818, and a church raised. The Plaza was the center of life, faith and town feeling. A dozen trails, paths and lanes (one could hardly call them roads) led in all directions from the Calle Principal (Main Street) to the San Gabriel mission, to the San Fernando Valley, to the beginning and to the already established ranchos, at least fifty of them. As for Eternity Street (now North Broadway), it led as it did for all mortals to the Campo Santo (the cemetery.) There was also a dusty road to San Pedro Bay, which would in time become the harbor of the city. There wasn't much in trade, but some Yankee ship captains came around the Horn to buy cattle hides for New England shoe leather, and some small dealings in corn were transacted. Salt came from near the Redondo beaches, so there was a road in that direction too. North to Santa Barbara and south to San Diego there were roads. But all these were in the main crude, based on Indian trails or the expanded boundaries of ranchos.

Commerce, small as it was, meant progress. All this led to a life in the town, when the ranchero, his hands, the carters, came to drink wine and brandy in the liquor shops, play *monte* in a gambling house, sport with a woman in some back-room brothel. Los Angeles was becoming a center of sporting life, of pleasuring and "one could frown on some of its morals, but one could not resist nature," as one early letter writer put it. "There is horse racing, bull fighting, more like bull baiting, the bull is rarely killed, it is too costly, and I saw a bear and a bull fight staged. The bear tore up the bull fearfully. They celebrate everything with gaiety, be it a wedding, baptism, a burying. The screaming of ungreased carreta wheels, as they call their carts, is fearful, as bad as the dogs howling at night. The stink of hides shows there are many cattle about, the hides of which we have come for . . . ."

More and more ships came to pick up these hides, and Richard Dana's *Two Years Before the Mast* was to give a true and colorful picture of the contact between Yankee sailors and Spanish town and rancho people.

The ships brought New England tinware and clocks. There were beads from China and silk shawls, tools, furniture, small items of comfort (like pressing irons). From Mazatlán, Acapulco, San Blas, came shoes, sara-pes, sombreros, rebozos, the hottest peppers, dried herbs, silver plate, little figures of the Virgin, the Son, some popular household saints.

The town dealt in trade and bought needed goods, but as the ranchos grew in size, and land grants became bigger, each rancho became a kind of small dukedom of its own. Several hundred people could live on a big spread, the lord and owner and his huge family, freeloading relatives, craftsmen, horseshoers, herdsmen, overseers, leatherworkers, harness makers, wool combers and sheepshearers, tanners and a retinue of half wild half-Indians—all were a community. Add house servants, field hands, a few black slaves, half-breed hangers-on being ruined by alcohol, and you had a small town.

Going to town by horse and cart, or even by a carriage imported from Spain or Mexico City, was an event. It meant social visiting, attending a *fandango,* the burial of a failed duelist or just to a party and to drink or to gamble, to fornicate, to visit the confessional in Church. Night did not stop festivities. Lanterns lit up grogshops, sporting and gambling houses. Whole families, their friends, under clusters of candles, held fêtes. Widows lost their lacerating grievances and matches were made among the adolescents.

All of society was moving forward, at least at the top. The tiller of corn-fields, the worker with the crude plow, remained as always the muscle. But with the rancheros moving more toward cattle raising, there was a kind of new wealth, even if not too many gold coins.

A good example of grit and enterprise was Juan José Domingues, at sixty-five, driving before him a horse herd and 200 head of cattle to set up a rancho along San Pedro Bay. The measuring off of land was vague, and among the first settlers, his Rancho San Pedro took in (in its claims) 75,000 acres. Rancho San Rafael was a mere 36,000 acres, claimed by José Maria Verdugo (today part of the cities of Glendale and Burbank). Manuel Nieto's holdings covered 167,000 acres. Most of these early rancheros were ex-soldiers who settled down, bred families and cattle and lied about old battles and scars.

As for Feliz himself, he took on landholdings that are today inside Los Angeles. He at one time held most of what is now Griffith Park.

All this progress had to be rewarded, and El Pueblo de los Angeles, in 1845, became the capital of Alta California. The governor, Pio Pico, took over an adobe store on Calle Principal as the Governor's House. This would become, much expanded, the celebrated Bella Union Hotel. ("Finest hotel south of San Francisco." No great accolade, for one guest wrote: "Bedbugs so big, two can drug [sic] you out of bed, and four can out wrestle a grizzly.")

The *ayuntamiento* (city council) decided to celebrate capital status by whitewashing all public buildings. On record is the notice of one visitor, "I have seen the City of Los Angeles. I have seen its police and all demonstrated that it is the Mexican paradise." There is no clue as to the writer's trade, but he sounds like a land salesman. The women, as fitting a capital, added froufrou and furbelows to their costumes, and there was talk of the minuet and quadrille. The rustle of taffeta met the creak of buckskin.

In the 1820s there was trouble with the mother country, Spain, in Mexico. Imbued with new political philosophies, by 1822 there was a successful revolution that ended the Spanish regime, not only in Mexico but also in California. Latin ideas of a ruling class and a church in politics made little real change. Changes by revolution, that merely enriched the leaders, were to become a habit in Mexican politics right into the twentieth century. Los Angeles, by April 1822, swore allegiance to the new nation and an assembly was talked of, but not too seriously. The new Church was formally dedicated that year and from the lists of gifts offered up, besides the cattle and other items, there are records of barrels of grape brandy "as deadly as taking two dueling pistols fired into your gizzard" (attributed to Kit Carson).

No matter what calculated strategies of revolution, it was clear from the names of people involved in trade or scandal that Americans were appearing on the scene in growing numbers, and often merged with Californios by marriage. It was a long sea journey home to Salem's or New Bedford's Puritan spinsters.

There was even a Yankee pirate. At least, several early historians called Joseph Chapman a pirate, and one "a regenerated pirate." But modern historians doubt that Chapman was a member of an outlaw group led by a Hypolyte Bourchard that raided, looted and burned Monterey in 1818. In any event, it is outside the range of our story to get involved with *that* part of Joe Chapman's life. What is pertinent is that Joe had the makings of a pilgrim patriarch. Shanghaied in the Sandwich Islands (later called Hawaii) and placed aboard the *Santa Rosa,* outward bound from the islands, Joe planned an escape. He and two sailors came ashore in California and were arrested. But Blond Joe, as he was called, impressed a priest by his jack-of-all-trades skill. He could, as one text puts it, "build a grist mill, cut trees, make a schooner, set broken bones, oversee Indian field gangs, pull teeth, manufacture farm tools, boil soap." Cutting timber for the Los Angeles Church with a gang of Indian loggers, he had downed trees in what is now Pasadena. Father Sanchez looked in, sorry to see such a gifted young man sunk in the "darkness of the Baptist faith." But Blond Joe was admired and "saved" by Guadalupe Ortega, whose father was a rancher. Joe was not only naturalized as a Mexican, but he also entered the Catholic faith and married Guadalupe. He bought a house in Los Angeles and planted a vineyard of 4,000 grapevines. No zealot about laws, he may have done some smuggling. One rumor said he also studied law, but gave it up, claiming, "Don't come to God as a lawyer—he prefers honest sinners."

As more and more American ships came into the harbors of southern California it seemed best to avoid the excessive customs duties and also to get around the ban on the importation at times of tools, cloth and furniture. Women were demanding gold and silk thread and men growing wealthy demanded suits embroidered in gold. Calicos were in demand, as were cottons, white muslin, percale, bows and ribbons, pins, combs and mirrors—anything to do away with the gaucheries of the past. Van-

THE WILD PUEBLO

ity, as the town and countryside progressed, demanded a society that looked better, smelled less gamy, had time to show off. This called for building new homes with ballrooms and dining rooms. Social status, it became clear, could be bought and not inherited from generations of grandees. A rearrangement of sensibilities and social attitudes was taking place.

By the 1830s, packtrains were finding their way to Los Angeles from Santa Fe, New Mexico, to trade goods in exchange for coast-bred mules. A moralist wrote of "the search for the sufficient self." Mountain men, too, would drift in, big, and hairy and hard, and given to celebrating the long cantankerous months behind them in the beaver runs. So drinking, gambling, dancing, the pleasure of women and song were products of the town. Gambling became a curse as Mexicans joined in the fun, and ranchos were in danger when the big gambling palace and monte bank was built on the north side of the Plaza. Other gamester halls followed.

Everyone carried arms in an atmosphere cloaked with close intimations of death. Knives, pistols, Kentucky rifles, the deadly bowie knife brought in by the mountain men were potent male décor. Killings and woundings were common, with "justice not blind but cockeyed," as one letter writer put it, and "everyone bristly, all edge and challenge."

The first of the mountain men were led to Los Angeles by Jedediah Smith, who brought his trappers to the Plaza looking for fun and frolic in 1826. Others came, traders from St. Joe, pelt hunters from the Gila, prospectors, outlaws, runaways from New Mexico and Colorado. Shaggy men in skins, often in Indian gear with capfire-smoked fringed shirts, sometimes followed by a squaw bought from her tribe, Sioux, Blackfeet, Comanche, often carrying a half-breed papoose.

Gold had been discovered in 1842, north of Mission San Fernando (the '49 rush got a better press), and miners trekking to Los Angeles from Sonora stopped over for a snort and a plate of chili beans on their way to Placerita Canyon. Outlaws were many—wary, watching men who talked of no past, and either settled in or passed by, or died in some muddy street or over a hand of greasy cards.

THERE WERE TIGERS THERE

It had a wild side this town, and there had to be law and order and a place of punishment. If not the jail, then the Plaza. "For scandalous conduct," two women had their heads shaved and were forced to stand at the Church doors. There were speed laws; one couldn't ride a horse at too fast a pace—wild and fancy horseplay, mounted or not, was forbidden, and misbehavior could cause arrest and a fine. There were public whippings in the Plaza for vagrancy, swindling, whoring, pimping. And, of course, in the shadow of the Church, blasphemy could bring a whip against one's naked hide. Within limits, the town offered a totality of physical existence.

On Sundays the Plaza was fenced in for bullfights. The rule was first to Church for a hasty mass, *then* a pouring out into the Plaza to watch the play of capes and gestures against some puzzled bull, while the more respectable watched from their windows or verandas. The bull was not very often killed, and no sword was used, as in Spain, but a mere knife tied to a yard-long stick to produce the overwritten "moment of truth." Tail-grabbing was favored, and usually the bull broke out and headed for high grass. Later, a bullring was built beyond the Plaza on Calle del Toro. Gambling and fighting between humans remained in the Plaza, which also delighted in saints' fêtes, fiestas and civic parading. The physical and spiritual structures of the era were very much closer then.

There were civil wars from time to time between the northern and southern Californians. But they never reached a Shiloh or a Gettysburg. "The Latin temperament is too cynical," wrote one sea captain. The civil wars did have a comic-opera flavor that smelled of gunpowder, but they were relatively free of too much harm.

The civil war of 1837 sent troops into town one night, seizing the Plaza under Captain Espinoza (of the North). Prisoners were taken but released, and then the men marched home. The grandiose moment was enough. In 1845 Don Pico collected 400 men to listen to some cannon shots and called a war. American soldiers of fortune were active on both sides but took care not to expose themselves to any danger beyond the brothel bed and the brandy bottle.

In the battle of Cahuenga, with arbitrary inconsistency, one horse was killed and one valuable jenny mule wounded. The enemy sent up a white flag and Pio Pico became governor of a united California. But the Americans were not to react to the logic of wars as fun. In October 1843 United States armed forces, acting on a false rumor that the United States had declared war on Mexico, raised the American flag over Monterey. This was before the age of Vietnam and Cambodia when one disregarded native sensitivity about such things, so Commodore Thomas Catesby Jones, U.S. Navy, who had raised the banner, came down to Los Angeles to apologize. He was given a banquet in the big gambling building on the Plaza. Both sides toasted each other as peace lovers, and there was music and dancing. Denial was made that the United States had designs on Mexican territories in the Southwest.

Three years later, on August 13, 1846, Major John C. Frémont and Commodore Robert F. Stockton marched invading forces into the Pueblo of Los Angeles with a full band playing "Hail Columbia" and "Yankee Doodle." This was a real war; the United States was in the Mexican Southwest for good—no apologizing this time.

3 The United States Takes California

T alking with Adlai Stevenson in the 1940s, when I was an editor
on a newsmagazine, he said, "We have always as a nation been
able to find the proper excuses for the evil deeds we have done
by armed violence. The best example I know of is forcing a war on Mexico and seizing the splendid Southwest. The reason is someplace in a history book."

THE UNITED STATES TAKES CALIFORNIA

Certainly Mexican California was—ignoring moral commitments—easy picking, and the Pueblo of Los Angeles on August 13, 1846, an easy conquest. Commodore Robert F. Stockton had marched his men up from San Pedro harbor, and Major John C. Frémont had come up with his soldiers from San Diego. The two invading forces had made junction in the cornfields and vineyards outside the town, and the people prayed to the image of Nuestra Señora de Guadalupe hanging in the *retablo*. The Americans were part of a plan to seize the towns and ports of California, begun on July 7th, when Commodore John Sloat *again* raised an American flag at Monterey. (*"Ay Dios, Dios, Nada"*—a note on an 1846 Spanish newspaper.)

The forces invading Los Angeles were a sort of panzer force, its guns and ammo, baggage and dress uniforms drawn by *carretas,* each cart held down to the speed of the four plodding oxen teams that drew them. Moving into the Pueblo against no opposition, Stockton's sailors and marines captured at a walk Pio Pico's official building on Calle Principal, while Major Frémont set up camp just outside the Plaza where the Calle de los Angeles met Aliso Street. The natives—were they now *los de abjo?* (the oppressed?)—kept indoors. But they were lured out when the Navy band, in the cool of the evening, began a concert in the Plaza. They played lovely toe-tapping tunes, and as the town had never really had a true band, or one in such splendid uniforms, a crowd—in spontaneous approval—soon collected, and there were *vivas* (according to the Americans) for the invaders. The concerts became a daily event. One old priest was so touched, he told an American officer, "I haven't heard a band since leaving Spain more than fifty years ago. Ah, the music will do more service to the conquest of California than a thousand bayonets."

But the Americans weren't depending on music to hold the town. Guns were set up on a height to command the streets. A proclamation had been issued signifying that the United States in a war with Mexico held this territory. It was signed: "Commodore Robert F. Stockton, Commander-in-Chief and Governor of the Territory of California."

It was a change, the townspeople people admitted, for Governor Pio

The two men who seized Los Angeles for the United States—Major John C. (the Pathfinder) Frémont and Commodore Robert F. (the Sailor) Stockton. (National Archives)

The last and greatest Mexican governor of California, Don Pio Pico, with his wife and nieces, circa 1855. He remained governor of California under the Americans. Today Pico Boulevard is named for him. (Los Angeles County Museum of Natural History)

Pico. The Mexican military commander, General José Castro, had quietly left Los Angeles a week before the Americans came. "It appeared an easy victory and the natives are cheerful and grateful," as one soldier letter writer put it.

After two weeks of music, fraternizing, drinking, dancing and the sports of soldiers, Stockton and Frémont decided to move on, leaving in command an officer named Archibald Gillespie, with fifty men to hold the town, while the rest of the Army and Navy moved on to Monterey. There had been no gratuitous cruelty, no public resistance.

Gillespie proved to be the worst choice that could have been made to put in charge of an occupied town. One soldier wrote home: "An overbearing bully, a martinet, and so blown up with his own importance that he turned the people against the Americans." Gillespie issued an order forbidding two citizens to be together on the streets. No groups were to gather in homes for any reason at all. No galloping of horses in the streets, trotting and pacing only. Shops to close as the sun sank. Liquor and light wines were to be sold only when and where Archibald Gillespie permitted. He lacked heartiness, but was blown up with intolerance.

He began to send search parties into private houses, to arrest and hold in jail important townspeople on no evidence but mere suspicion. Given power, his reasoning seemed to have oxidized away.

Resistance began with the women. He was presented with a basket of peaches in which were imbedded long cactus thorns. In secret meetings, the citizens began to plan a revolt to drive out the Americans. A rebel camp was set up on the heights of Paredon Blanco (now Boyle Heights, the poorer Jewish district of twentieth-century Los Angeles). Here, squatting among the chaparral, Captain Flores as Commandante-General of the revolt, along with José Carrillo and Andres Pico, issued a proclamation, a call to arms: "Arise, throw out the Estado Unidenses" (the North Americans). Talk turned to gunpowder and a bold attack.

Soon Gillespie's forces—taken by surprise—were under siege, potshots and snipers began to dent the walls of the Pio Pico house where the garrison was trapped. Moving out in apprehension to a better position, they hoped, they took over a hill overlooking the Plaza. But it was hopeless. The population in tumultuous imprudence felt a full victory, while for the Americans, a lack of supplies—food, water, gunpowder and other ammunition—prevailed. Time to lower the flag again.

Captain Flores offered humane terms of surrender. After a sad look at the situation, the Americans in abasement gave up. They were permitted to march out of town, flag flying, their drummer setting the march step. The Americans were heading for San Pedro in hopes of a ship to carry them away.

It was an unexpected defeat for United States strategy designed to seize southern California; although most historians agree that Gillespie set off the spark, the tinder of Latin pride was ready, in any event, to blaze up. Not only was Los Angeles recaptured by the Californios, but also San Diego and Santa Barbara. The people felt sure now *esta tierra es nuestra* (this land is ours).

The strategy, as the rebels saw it, was for the Californios to use a series of guerrilla attacks to keep the Americans from marching into the interior and coordinating their forces. As the Americans moved to counterattack, Carrillo raised a group of fifty horsemen who boldly attacked and badly defeated a combined force made up of Gillespie's footloose men (still seeking shipping) and Captain William Mervine's heat-hazed men. It was a quick hot fight at the Rancho San Pedro. The deciding factor in the battle was a four-pound Mexican brass cannon, which was made mobile by drag ropes of hide *reatas;* these were attached to the saddles of a few Californios who then dragged the fieldpiece to wherever it was most needed.

The new war—the audacity of the Californios—was not making events go well for the Americans. General Stephen W. Kearny marched out of Santa Fe with his dragoons to take up position at San Pascual (in what is today San Diego County). He was attacked by Mexican lancers under Andres Pico, handling nine-foot spears. It was a bloody frog-spearing contest, and to the Americans a humiliating defeat. Survivors of both lost battles staggered back into recaptured San Diego to regroup, reflecting on the shallow certainties of conquest gone wrong. Once the situation was clearly seen by the Americans, they reorganized quickly and the Californios' cause was hopeless. Stockton's and Kearny's forces marched out to serious war, and two small battles were fought: at Paso de Bartolo among the willows on the banks of the San Gabriel River and at La Mesa on the Los Angeles River. The white smoke of gunpowder proved superior; firepower usually decided battles. The battles are remembered mainly in American legend because Kit Carson, trapper, guide, Army scout, was on the scene; Carson was to be elevated to an American folk hero by those who hunted something glamorous to excite the folks back East.

The citizens of Los Angeles—aware now that revolts are not won by hope alone—sent out a committee of acquiescence to offer surrender on January 10th—and the Americans marched back into the Plaza of the Pueblo of Los Angeles. The band again took up the tooting of its tunes in public concert. The citizens seemed pleased it was all over, drink was provided for the conquering soldiers, sailors and marines.

Frémont, not to be left out of the final victory, was leading 400 leather-fringed riflemen on horseback south from Monterey. The day *after* Los Angeles capitulated, he occupied the San Fernando Valley mission. A man with an odd, disjointed ego, driven by a brusque wife, he had hopes of the White House.

On January 13, 1847, Frémont, representing the Army, and Andres Pico signed the official ducument of capitulation, called the Treaty of Cahuenga, at a ranch house (the site is today on Lankershim Boulevard in North Hollywood, where "Universal Studios stupefies the world with its assembly line of banal television shows").

The full cession of California to the United States came about when Mexicon, in defeat, plundered of its southwestern territories, signed in resignation the Treaty of Guadalupe Hidalgo. One Mexican officer later quoted Proudhon, *"La propriété c'est le vol"* (property is theft).

Frémont, like most Americans, feeling this was all to the good, took command of the town and soon the fort begun on the hill overlooking

The treaty of July 4, 1849, giving California to the United States. (National Archives) the Plaza was completed by the Mormon Battalion. They had been sold by Brigham Young into the American service, their pay to go into the Mormon Treasury of the Latter-Day Saints in Salt Lake City. They finished the fort and took up garrison duty alongside a New York volunteer regiment. The fort was dedicated on July 4, 1847, as Fort Moors, after an obscure captain who was unlucky enough to be speared through and through by a nine-foot lance at the battle of San Pascual.

The town retained its ayuntamiento and alcalde and its American status with bullfights, gambling, dancing, drinking. So Los Angeles was made for all time an American city.

But the old ways of life were changed, disjointed, by more than the Americans taking over California. A worldwide intensification of hope and greed was about to occur. In January 1848 gold was discovered in a millrace at Coloma. This resulted in a gold rush, of which Los Angeles became for thousands a prosperous way station to the diggings. An army of Mexican miners poured into Los Angeles from Sonora, beating the great gold rush of '49. Many stayed on in the oldest part of the settlement, and their section of Los Angeles became known as Sonora Town. Business was brisk for wagonmakers, blacksmiths, hardware merchants. Even the poorest miner needed a pan, pick and shovel, and if he could afford it, a wheelbarrow, besides a sack of beans, a sack of flour—and a dream that he would soon be able to "shake out solid gold nuggets, big as eyeballs, from the grass roots."

It all made for a lively town and a tough population that grew tougher when the New York Volunteers were turned out 3,000 miles from home to make their own way. The disbanded and soon penniless soldiers mixed with Mexican gold seekers, often also low in funds; this soon produced crimes, violence and a general lawlessness that was hard to control. Many of the ex-soldiers were Bowery toughs and hoodlums, recruited from the notorious Five Points section of New York City.

Spanish-America was like a faded fragrance. Vice and crime took over its own section, the Calle de los Negros, called by the ex-soldiers Nigger Street (or alley) because of the dark complexion of many of the people who had come from Sonora. "A pandemonium of races," one writer called it. Brothels, gambling hells, rowdy saloons, low dives, gave the district a distinct sound and color. Knives and firearms were worn openly in case they had to be reached for quickly. "As for the Americans—a gathering of eagles is usually at a carrion pit." Prices rose for beef cattle needed to feed the miners, bean field crops had a market. There was wealth flowing back from the goldfields, as well as a lack of respect for the law.

As with most city treasuries, there was little money on hand. Parkinson's law, long before he set it down, existed every place politicians were in power—they could spend or get rid of any sums taxes brought in. But Los Angeles had one asset that the city fathers knew could be exploited: land. Land was taxable. Taxes would refill the till for the politicians. The first Los Angeles land boom was about to dawn.

Strange events—a gold rush, annexation, a land boom—all at once. As Wallace Stegner was to write in the *L.A. Times*: "California from the time when it was an island floating vaguely in the seas of fantasy and romance to the time, day before yesterday or so. . . . One can see the whole curve. The present is here to reassure or dismay us with its evidence of what the past has come to!"

The past had been Spanish-Mexican, and the present was to be a growth no one could have imagined when the Americans moved in.

4 A Tough Town Grows Tougher

Now the former Pueblo of Los Angeles was ready to go into the real estate business, for it was entitled to "four square leagues of land," inherited from its Spanish grant as a pueblo. Sales were good in November—as if the fulfillment of some divine ordinance framed in dollars—when land worth $2,490 was sold; all but the space that was the Plaza and the space that was to become Pershing and Elysian parks.

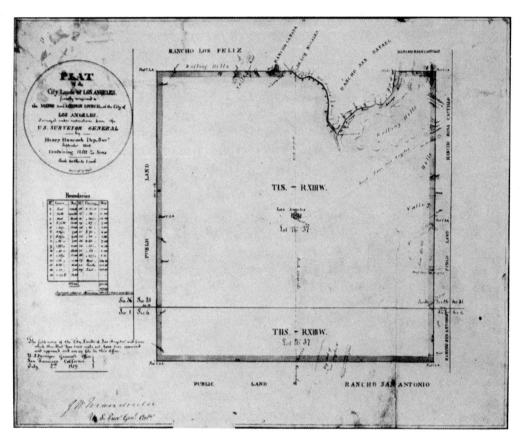

In 1858 a congressional commission created this map to define the four square leagues of land which were to constitute the City of Los Angeles, regardless of rancho claims established under Spanish rule. (National Archives)

Later, the site of the present City Hall had to be bought back from private owners.

On April 4, 1850, Los Angeles was incorporated as one more American city. It elected a mayor, not an alcalde, and a city council, not an ayuntamiento. This called for drinking and celebrating, as did the admitting of California into the Union as a state. This meant more taxes. But the gold rush still growing in the north created a demand for what the south had to sell, mostly meat on the hoof. Cattle drives went north long before the more famous ones moved up from Texas on the Chisholm Trail to Abilene and Dodge City. The California drives cost $2, $3 or $4 a head to get each steer to the minefields. But there they would be grabbed up for as much as $50 to $75 each during the years 1853 and 1854—much better than in the days when all that was produced from huge herds was a hide worth $2 and tallow at 6 cents a pound. Los Angeles and its surrounding ranchos were producing cattle kings.

American Los Angeles, if not romantic and even casual about life, was practical, not evasive as to its possibilities. The town had never been surveyed and no accurate maps existed as to boundaries. The people had accepted, as to be honored, whatever line drawn in the dust, or staked out at corners, existed. But the United States ruled no land could be sold without a proper map. However, as no such person as a surveyor existed in Los Angeles, Army men were assigned to the job, and someone made drawings of the pueblos, streets and buildings in the hot summer of 1849.

It also seemed proper to the Americans to convert the names of the streets into English, listing both the Spanish and the English names on their maps. Calle Principal became Main Street; Calle Fortin, Fort Street (later changed to Broadway); Calle Loma, Hill Street; Calle Primavera, Spring Street. Other streets whose Spanish names now are lost were Street of the Virgin, Street of the Hornets, Bull Street, Street of the Grasshoppers, Eternity Street. Some disrespectful and vulgar names were not listed on the map. Nigger Alley (Calle de los Negros) hung as a name. In a fragment of a letter there is mention of Horseshit Lane (loca-

A TOUGH TOWN GROWS TOUGHER

tion unknown) and Cunt Alley (no other source appears to list these two).

The boom times in beef and supplies shipped to the minefields brought on a rash of building, of adding second stories to houses. Ships stopping off at San Pedro, either from around the stormy Horn or from the treaty ports and tea estuaries of China, unloaded shawls, four-poster beds, Tang and Sung porcelain (or at least copies of them), lace curtains, bedpans and chamber pots of silver, silver-mounted pistols and shotguns. Methodist ladies and Indian concubines practiced the quadrille.

Racehorses were bred finer and more was bet on them. Gambling houses began to hang up fringed whale-oil lamps with crystal shades. Bars were of teak or golden oak. The whores smelled better and "the tin or zinc bathtub is favored by the ladies of the night, and if you can't get a bath in a hotel, go try any agringado cat-house with lace curtains. Sure to find a tub and plenty of hot water."

The town was flooded with northern outlaws, whores and gamblers. As Bret Harte was to write about these types, they were driven out by towns which considered themselves respectable. Vigilance committees pointed them out of town after town, and San Francisco and Los Angeles got a great many of them. An old dance program has this poem written on it:

> O lady, we recline
> But what we give . . .
> Only on ourselves
> Doth nature live . . .

Killings became the expected events of day and night as gold changed hands, bodies were bought and music grew frantic in the late hours in Nigger Alley. The most notorious place was La Aquile de Ora (The Golden Eagle), where the play was for gold and the gambling tables ran at all hours, guarded by musclemen. They took care to drub any clients who claimed they were cheated. A few blows, and men were tossed out into the alley. There Indians, demoralized by their craving for drink, stripped the victims and went hunting a bottle of rotgut whiskey in ex-

THERE WERE TIGERS THERE

change for whatever hat, coat or boots they had taken from their prey.

King of the gamblers was Jack Powers, one of the hoodlums who had come west with the regiment of New York Volunteers. Out of the service, he set up a gambling house, but also worked as a cattle rustler. A killer with several notches on his gun, Jack was soon to be the pattern for many of those who were outside the law. He was a political power with influence and had friends in the right places up and down the state, all a result of his ability to deliver votes at the polls. Ward-heeling, imported from New York's Tammany, was soon present and active in southern California. Whoever controlled the votes, controlled the city. And it was favor for favor. Gunplay backed votes; "the unarmed prophet is destroyed."

Jack Powers was a daring dresser, sporting well-cut hammer-tailed coats, a high gray topper and a handsome silk cravat drawn through a gold ring. He smoothed down his rough edges, at least in public, and acted the gentleman. Jack was an amazingly good rider and of course kept racehorses. "Some of his races were even honestly run sometimes." He liked beautiful harlots, and what the popular press called "actresses." He never appeared in public without at least two bodyguards. There is no record he was ever brought to justice for killing, card cheating, stealing cattle or wives or for crimes unlisted. An irrelevant life in a kinetic society, he represented one aspect of the life in early Los Angeles.

Jack Powers was but one of a couple hundred dangerous men who made their home in the city. Records list murder, arson, blackmail, ransoming of kidnap victims, rape, plain violence for no reason, highway holdups, stagecoach stoppings and the frisking of passengers for their valuables, the use of knockout drops to drug men to ship them to sea with captains at San Pedro as shanghaied sailors. All these crimes were common. Respectable society only took action when it affected the doing of business. At such times some citizens who may have been making a good thing of rents to these types, or selling them their supplies, would be overcome with fear and a Committee of Public Safety would be organized. In July 1853 a group of good solid citizens met in the El Dorado Saloon on Main Street—a fine well-lighted place with a mahog-

This early print of a saloon/gambling house shows Mexican rancheros on the left, Chinese on the right, a minstrel show onstage—and a ruined gambler cursing the playing cards on the floor. (Wells Fargo)

A woodcut of a Chinese gambling house—even the coolies gambled desperately. (Rose collection)

A print of a high old time. Clearly, in California of the 1860s there was no short-age of females. (Ross collection)

any bar, a brass rail, clean spittoons, no hoodlum dive—to form a Vigilance Committee called the Los Angeles Rangers. (*Reminiscences of a Ranger,* by one of them, Horace Bell, makes good reading for many details of the period.)

Other rival law-and-order groups sprang into action, and "Judge Lynch" became active, usually after dark, but often in broad daylight. Fully kept records are few, but in two years, 1854 and 1855, the Rangers had twenty-two men executed, more or less legally; no record exists of those they, or other groups, lynched, ran out of town, horsewhipped or even castrated; racial feeling was heated against non-Anglo Saxon stock "acting up." It was not a time when one said of outlaws, "they only kill their own."

5   Indian Uprising

Anthropologists have never thought too much of the coastal Indians of southern California. They gave little trouble, not being of a warlike nature. They were not the wild Comanches, Sioux, Cherokees of the Plains, nor the cruel and fearful desert warriors of the Apache. No great battles were fought, no Little Big Horn took place, no figures comparable to Sitting Bull, Crazy Horse, Chief Joseph, emerged.

The southern California Indians were destroyed, but mainly by disease, drink and semi-slavery. They were shunted aside into the worst possible corners of the counties or permitted to drift around, destitute, prostituting their women, cadging drinks.

But southern California did have an Indian uprising. Not a true war such as that carried on against the United States Army by Geronimo, Roman Nose and Satanta. The Indians of southern California who went to war had, among other grievances, the fact that they were being exploited by traders and frontier ruffians and taxed by the sheriff, even if not under county jurisdiction. The Indians of the interior included the Cahuillas.

The uprising happened at Warner Hot Springs and resulted in the deaths of nine white men and more Indians. It was the last attempt of southern California Indians to break free of the Americans' grip. Some of them, Cupeños, were Mission San Luis Rey Indians who had left the coast to live in inland villages near the present Warner Hot Springs in 1833.

The leader of the revolt in 1851, Antonio Garra, was chief of the Cupeños. He planned to kill the Americans in southern California, but the descendants of the Spanish would not be harmed. It was a foolish plan.

Several prominent Californians sympathized with Garra, and the Indian chief expected help from them. A former San Luis Rey mission Indian, Garra had gone to live in the village of Kupa at Warner Hot Springs.

He sent couriers to Indians living on the Colorado and Tía Juana rivers, and to the San Gabriel, San Fernando and San Diego mission Indians to come and join the fight. The Quechuan Indians were to attack the military outpost at the junction of the Gila and Colorado rivers, and this would be the signal for full revolt at San Diego, Santa Barbara and Los Angeles.

The village of Kupa lay on the road to San Diego, Los Angeles, Stockton and Sacramento, near the Mother Lode. Garra and his people were exposed to rough, cruel miners harassing them as they poured into California by the southern route, even in winter, particularly when the northern routes were closed. Garra was only moderately successful in getting the help of other Indian leaders.

The Quechuan and Yumas supported Garra at first, as did a section of the Cahuilla nation led by a chief called Chapuli. The help Garra needed was that of Juan Antonio, the most powerful Indian leader and chief of the main branch of the Cahuilla nation. So the uprising began with no full support of the strongest tribes.

The Quechuans attacked an outpost, but it did not fall. Five American sheepherders were killed in the Yuma attack, and their sheep driven off. Hardly a great enough victory to drive the Americans from the country.

Garra, disappointed in the Quechuans' failure and believing the time not ripe, went to a Cupeño village called Wilakal, a few miles from the hot springs. He wrote letters to Don José Antonio Estudillo and Juan Joaquin Ortega, two prominent California leaders, and said he expected their help in his insurrection against the Americans. They ignored him.

On November 21, 1851, Young Garra, son of Garra, attacked Americans taking hot baths at the springs and killed four of them. The Cahuilla chief Chapuli burned the ranch buildings at Warner Hot Springs and made off with the cattle. It was clear these Indians had no idea of how to fight a war against the Americans.

Chapuli and Young Garra holed up in Los Coyotes Canyon. Garra joined them there to escape the soldiers sent out to capture him. He received a message from Juan Antonio, chief of the main body of Cahuillas, asking for a meeting at a village called Razon in the Indian Wells area. Antonio was an Indian Uncle Tom. When Garra arrived, Juan Antonio took him prisoner and turned him over to the American soldiers. Garra was court-martialed on charges of treason, murder and robbery. The treason charge was dropped, as he had never taken an oath of allegiance to the United States. He was executed by a firing squad on the other counts.

Chapuli was killed in a fight in Los Coyotes Canyon. Other Indian leaders were executed more or less fairly—less by the records.

Estudillo and Ortega, the two Californians to whom Garra had written letters, were absolved of complicity.

Being "good" or "bad" Indians didn't matter—in twenty years all were on the reservations at Morongo and Pala that they still occupy today. The Gabrielenos of Los Angeles and Orange counties became extinct.

At the time of the uprising an Indian commission from Washington was in northern California making treaties with Indians. The fighting turned their attention to southern California, where treaties were made with the Indians that guaranteed them land and provisions. The treaties were, of course, rejected by the U.S. Senate.

BOOK II

BOOM TIMES AND LAND AGENTS

6   The Changing Scene

No one was safe from dangerous and unruly living. Don Abel Stearns was a great landowner, owning more acres and controlling more ranchos than anybody in southern California. He lived in lordly style in a big mansion named El Palacio on Main Street near the Plaza. To be invited to El Palacio meant social acceptance; Mrs. Stearns, the former Arcadia Bandini, "his lovely young wife" (no plain or ugly hostess is ever mentioned in memoirs or letters), was from a prominent local family. The Stearnses had a 100-foot ballroom, all gilt and crystal, and a waxed dance floor. Here, in proud serenity, on Washington's birthday 1853, they gave a great gala. Guests were carefully picked. The wearers of satin, taffeta mantuas, watered tabbies, figured velvet and brocades came. Among the accepted were two gamblers, but the rest of the card handlers were ignored. They felt demeaned; this was an insult against a group. It could not be ignored. They decided to crash the ball in a group. When the dancing was at its height, the gamblers' mob attacked El Palacio with a small cannon and a hefty battering ram.

It was an unpleasant surprise more than offensively brusque. The mob got past the posted guards and through solid doors. They burst gleefully into the ballroom among the spinning figures. One of the dancers—a triggerman perhaps—reacted quickly, got out a pistol and shot the first invader. "The firing became general," so many of the male guests must have been armed and able to draw quickly. The raiders outnumbered—their firepower weaker—withdrew. The victims seem to have been of no great number, and the experience not traumatic to the Stearnses, who continued to give parties with more guards.

Mrs. Stearns' half-brother, Arturo Bandini, lived outside the vulgar range of American party-crashing and violence. On his rancho he existed in "the daily pageant of adobe days—silver-saddled horses suddenly reined in before the patio entrance . . ." (wrote Susanna Bryant Dakin) ". . . calico padded *carretas* carrying those who were too young or too old, or too fat, to ride. . . . Within high adobe walls Indian servants were continually at work—preparing for a gala dinner, an evening fête, or an afternoon *cha* (tea) served from a huge silver service. Laughter, chatter, snatches of song . . . ." (There is a suggestion about the scene of the life of an English country squire in *Tom Jones.*)

Mexican Los Angeles, the great days of the ranchos, the original families of *campesinos* (peasants), were mostly gone by the 1860s. There were various schemes to strip the original owners of their land grants, those acres, by sudden sales, holding up the legal acceptance of the

A print of a typical early California ranch, this one owned by Ben (Don Benito)
Wilson. The large mountain in the background, named Mount Wilson after Don
Benito, is today covered with TV transmitting towers.

OVERLEAF:
The original Los Angeles landowners: some members of the Mexican-American
Lugo family about a hundred years ago in their Sunday or fête-day best. (Los
Angeles County Museum of Natural History)

Spanish land grants just long enough to deny the family its rights. So the Californio *compadres'* lands moved mostly into the hands of the Americans. It must also be admitted that the original owners were mad spenders and shrugged off their debts.

The gold rush had petered out by 1857, at least for the ordinary prospector with tin basin, pick and shovel. Boom times tapered off in Los Angeles. Beef prices fell below the cost of raising cattle. The panic which grew did have the effect of closing many gambling houses as cash grew tight and credit went out of sight. Bullfighting almost stopped. The rancheros, as land claimants, were desperately pressing federal courts and any commissioner—*"hijo de la gran puta"*—to give them justice, a legal right to hold their acres under the Land Act of 1852. Somehow, American courts found the original grants very often "abominably flawed." The great droughts in the early 1860s and the small incentive of beef prices prompted most rancheros to give up cattle raising. The vast acres once heavy with grazing steers gave way to smaller plots sold as farms or were laid out as new towns around Los Angeles. Their shop signs were mostly in English now on Main Street and around the Plaza. Mexican-Americans were retreating into a sort of slum, the *barrio,* to cook their native dishes in a *cazuelo,* to speak Spanish and to be seen in the eyes of the Yankee *gueros chingados* as second-class citizens, "lazy, lousy corn-eaters."

The Chinese were crowding in, taking over part of the Nigger Alley area. They not only opened eating places but seemed to find no problem in becoming part of the vice scene. It was time for the old families to leave. Such a dandy as Don Vicente Lugo moved out of town, and his town house, in time, became part of Chinatown, owned by the Hop Sing tong.

One catches a glimpse in the memoirs of Harris Newmark, an early merchant, of the tragic change in the last years of the onetime wealthy wellborn Francisco O'Campo, once one of the town's early and most successful merchants. Newmark describes O'Campo as "he used to sit on the curbstone near the Plaza . . . quite forlorn, utterly dejected in appearance, and despondently recalling the bygone days of his prosperity." There was little left for him, and many like him, but to look forward to a

A rare lithograph of Los Angeles in the mid-1850s. Main Street is at the left.

BOOM TIMES AND LAND AGENTS

bit of land in the burying ground of the Campo Santo—*Gracias a Dios*—at the end of Eternity Street. Very little survived but here and there an old Spanish name on a street or a district, a hill, a road.

While letters and journals give us a great deal of fine information, an official census of the city and county of Los Angeles in 1850 is pure gold for a genre historian. The county had 8,300 residents of which half were "domesticated Indians." In the city itself lived 3,530 people in 518 dwellings; a bit crowded one must admit. Of the townsfolk, 512 claimed to come from 29 states and 699 were born in 28 countries. As for trade: 650 were laborers, 138 farmers, 65 ranchers and overseers and 32 listed themselves as merchants. There were also 8 Jews in the census listing. It is interesting to see one admitting to be a tailor, the other seven "merchants," a label that could include peddling door to door from a basket, collecting old bones and iron or keeping a dry goods and notions shop. Most observed *Masha* and the laws of *kashruth* (kosher dietary rules).

The tailor Jacob Frankfort was the first Jew on record to reach Los Angeles, coming west with the Workman-Rowland wagon train. All of the new non-Christian settlers were under thirty and had come west without wives, mostly from Germany, only two from Poland.

The Newmark brothers, Harris and Joseph, were typical of the Jews in California: hardworking members of the middle class. Harris who wrote (or had written from his notes) *Sixty Years in Southern California,* a remarkable and detailed picture of early Los Angeles, was commended as being a man of "honesty and strict attention to business."

In 1854 a lawyer got off the stagecoach, Meyer Newmark, who was admitted to the California Bar in 1859 and later became City Attorney. Another prominent addition to the Jewish community was Solomon Carvalho, Colonel John Frémont's cameraman, called a daguerreotypist, who had crossed the continent with Frémont in 1853.

We catch best the local color of the period in an early newspaper advertisement:

THE CHANGING SCENE

LAZARD AND KREMER, BELL ROW, wholesale and retail dealers in Dry Goods, Clothing, Boots and Shoes, Groceries of all kinds etc., which will always sell at the lowest market prices for Cash. N.B. The highest prices always paid for gold dust . . . .

California Jews were classed, by some, with the Indians and the Mexicans as second-class citizens. William Stow, speaker of the House in the state Capitol, rose in debate, on a Sunday closing bill, to attack Jews as undesirable Californians who had come to the state for gain. (Who hadn't?) His idea was to tax them above and beyond taxes placed on others, taxes so high that they would be driven out of the community.

The *Los Angeles Daily Star* responded: "Such bigoted views show an intolerance entirely adverse to the spirit and character of our institutions. . . . (Our) just tribute to our Jewish fellow citizens will be read with admiration by every person possessing the enlarging ideas, the generous impulses that constitute a true American. . . ."

Remarkably fine sentiments but hardly in keeping with the newspapers' encouragement of lynchings that was so often expressed by the editors.

7   Mr. Lincoln's War, and After

The Civil War in some ways divided southern California, shifted it a bit from its main purpose—getting ahead. Los Angeles County in the Presidential election of 1860 gave John Breckinridge double the votes it cast for Abraham Lincoln and for Stephen Douglas. However, in electing John Downey of Los Angeles governor of California, it had hoped to keep the state loyal to the Union. (Downey actually favored the South.) The city sent young men to fight for both the United States and for the Confederacy. Loyalties ran from flawed idealism to romantic cant. It was a partisan town, and bolder citizens showed their colors. General Beauregard, C.S.A., had his picture hung on the wall of the Bella Union Hotel, for a while anyway. At El Monte, there was sly maneuvering at a jolly camp that was training the young for the rebel cause under the Bear flag of the State of California.

Union men, loyal to Lincoln and against cession, formed counter groups and there were conflicts and often killings between those who advocated the North and those ardent for the South.

The actual war was far away from the mesquite and western juniper, far off with Grant battling along the Mississippi, and Lincoln trying to get a general who would fight and take Richmond. Excessive excitability and grief filled the Plaza at news of Shiloh and Sherman in Georgia.

Judge Hastings of Los Angeles actually went all the way to Richmond in 1863 to offer himself to Jefferson Davis as one who needed only funds to recruit for the Confederacy 30,000 Californians. The South could have used the men *if* it could have clothed, armed and fed them, for Lee was moving north in three columns toward a town named Gettysburg, where, one of his generals had heard, there was a shoe factory and Lee's army was in the main barefooted. California's 30,000, if they existed, never took the first step to war: the Confederate transport system hardly existed.

Grant would soon move into the Wilderness and hammer Lee to a final meeting. And so Judge Hastings' scheme came to nothing; it failed to produce a mass of Californians ready to fight for the breaking of the Union and for slavery.

Los Angeles did have two generals in the war. General Albert Sidney Johnson, who had a ranch in what was to become Pasadena, died at Shiloh, which Californians of rebel ideas called Pittsburg Landing. General Joseph Lancaster Brent was "the last Confederate officer to lay down his sword" (of whom there were legion). General Brent did become the first president of the Los Angeles School Board.

BOOM TIMES AND LAND AGENTS

Military activities in Los Angeles during the Civil War came under the command of Captain Winfield Scott Hancock who was in charge of Drum Barracks in Wilmington near San Pedro Harbor (where a U.S. Camel Corps had existed!). In Los Angeles he saw to the organization of a militia of home guards to keep order and to see that government property was not destroyed (at least not too much of it) or stolen. Let the preacher preach, "We live on the edge of a great deep." War had brought a fresh prosperity to ranchers and farmers. Armies had to be fed and clothed. The beef and wool market was never better. The trading in horses and mules, before the age of the jeep and the tank, brisk. (Captain Hancock *almost* became President of the United States in 1880, as the Democratic nominee. He was beaten by Garfield by 7,000 popular votes.)

Captain Hancock kept fairly good order in Los Angeles County, and it is officially recorded that hotheads of both sides could list only one dead during his rule, and that was a result of a duel between gentlemen. There was no attempt to stop any rebel recruiting or the talking up of the Confederate side. Sophisticated propaganda techniques had to wait for the Spanish-American War. In the main, the men of property and business enjoyed the prosperity of wartime's hectic trading. Besides beef, leather, grain, horses and mules, every month more than $12,000 in gold was panned out of the San Gabriel Canyon. The only gloomy note, besides the rising lists of casualty figures, was the fact that from 1862 on there were years of no rain; the cattle began to grow thin as grass faded into browns and umbers, dust clouds formed and streams dried out. But there was to be enough wealth for some to buy the fancy carriages the Lichenberger Carriage Manufactory of Los Angeles was to turn out. No more need for the well-off to have to depend on importing its carriages, gigs, buckboards and fancy rigs from St. Louis and its farm wagons from Studebaker in Pennsylvania.

Almost none of the doers and movers among the successful businessmen went off to war. One could hire a substitute for $300 and the Union paid another $300 in bounty. So, as in the East, where J. D. Rockefeller and J. P. Morgan bought substitutes to go and die for them, many of the well-off in every state found it a splendid war. In the southern states, a man who owned six or more slaves, and had the bills of sale, was also usually free of military duty. A Californian who served in the Valley with Sheridan wrote, "You hear more and more of the Johnny Rebs and our own lads singing, 'It's a Rich Man's War and a Poor Man's Fight.' "

The returning war veterans found the usual indifference an ex-soldier finds. But there was a lot of open country and "a man could whistle to his dog and move off to homestead some place, or more likely—if he had enough brains to butter a cat—keep his eye open for a main chance in land speculation, merchandising or running a gambling rig" (from a letter east).

Many of the ex-soldiers in Los Angeles seem to have been Confederates, if one looks at the voting results of General Grant against Seymour for the Presidency in 1868: Seymour's 1,236 votes to Grant's 748. (In 1896 William Jennings Bryan carried Los Angeles against the Civil War ex-Major William McKinley.) But weevily army biscuits were forgotten and old wounds ached most at G.A.R. picnics. Los Angeles was busy swallowing more territory. And a growing city needs water. In Spanish and Mexican days water was delivered by carts that dripped their way from the old *zanja*, or canal, which tapped the river near Elysian Park. By gold-rush days the city had organized a department to run the operation of water supplies. In 1857 there had been handed out a franchise for the production of spring water: a steam engine powering a wheel to bring up the much needed water. But in 1862 a flood swept away engine and wheel, and a returning flood did the same in 1868. A brick reservoir was built in the Plaza and cast-iron water pipes laid down through Main and Spring streets. But floods mangled all this, so a private firm was given thirty-year rights to sell water to the town, paying Los Angeles $400 a month for the privilege. (In 1898 the city bought out the private water company for $2 million, and the city "set out to steal water from wherever it could from the rest of the state.")

The city had four hotels as the sixties moved toward the seventies, and simple folk found them extravagantly decadent; all were along Main

Street between the Plaza and Market Street. The old Bella Union was to become the St. Charles, the Pico House retained its name, the United States and the Lafayette took care of the overflow. All had ornate saloons smelling of frangipani, whiskey and hair oil—the last male sanctuary except for the barbershop.

Of 110 saloons, the most active was Buffum's, where the volunteer fire department of 1871 had its headquarters. The *L.A. News* covered the social event of Buffum's grand opening: "On Saturday evening, William Buffum's new saloon was thrown open to the public. We venture to say there is no more elegant and tastefully arranged place of the sort, on the coast. The mirrors, the engravings and paintings . . . the arrangement of the gas jets, the cozy little tables . . . the neat carpeting—in short, the whole interior finish is first class." A good place for the amenities of business and talk of disrespectful women.

Buffum's was the place for "a social game among card handlers, a splendid free lunch of cold cuts and pickled eggs, and lurking nearby in the Family Parlor painted ladies in crinoline and feathered bonnet, netted chignon, willing to unlace in rooms in the nearby Lafayette or Bella Union."

Good times or bad, the saloons and sporting houses did a thriving trade, while great droughts ruined the cattle business. In 1877 the sheep industry saw dry slopes with thousands of dead sheep. And when a sheep can't find food with its razor-sharp teeth that destroy grassland by eating out even the roots, then times are hard. One banker, J. A. Graves, with 5,000 dead sheep on his land, fed them to his hogs. When cadavers of sheep ran out, he fed them corn valued at nearly $2,000. But in the end, he only got $1,100 for his mutton-fed hogs. Blame it on irascible, capricious nature that didn't have the sense to rain.

Yet the city was tough and from oil lamps it had gone to gas; as the seventies ended there was talk of Mr. Edison's electric lighting. The Los Angeles Gas and Electric Company built a plant on Banning Street with a proud tank opposite the Plaza.

El Pueblo de los Angeles was passing, as the modern city began its climb to power in the late sixties and early seventies. Don Pio Pico had moved

The Bella Union Hotel, built in 1850, had the best bar in town and was the city's center for business gossip. (Ross collection)

with the times. He had bought and knocked down the old Carrillo house on the Plaza and erected the three-story Pico House, described by a reporter as "American Romanesque, with deep-set arched doors and windows, slightly ponderous and sturdy; the brick face was stuccoed and painted in imitation of light blue granite." The city was hardly ready yet for Frank Lloyd Wright. The roof was tin, the cornices heavy, and it had a cellar, a rare item in a Los Angeles house. There were mirrors and a grand staircase, birds in cages singing and a court with flowers and splashing fountains. Bell wires and speaking tubes allowed communication. There was "a luxurious bar with two entrances, Main Street or from the Plaza." One letter writer notes, "Uncle Wilbur broke a chandelier with his cane, knocked over a Chinese vase, but two barmen got him out of the Plaza entrance and one drove his team of bays home for him. The management of the Pico House merely noted the cost of the items destroyed and assured Aunt Alice in a note it must have been the oysters gone bad that Wilbur had downed at Buffum's."

Surviving guest registers of the Pico House carry the names of such guests as General Stoneman, Helen Hunt Jackson (who inflicted *Ramona* as a yearly pageant on southern California) and Helen Modjeska, the actress, who lost an earring down a water closet.

Actresses meant a theater, and in 1870 the Merced Theatre was built next to the Pico House. It contained an iron balcony on which bands played before curtain time. Inside, there was a drop curtain painted "with an Italian landscape" on the 35- by 25-foot stage. Red plush was plentiful, trimmed with gold fringing. Boxes overhung the stage and there were two dressing rooms, not coeducational. With the balcony, the theater could accommodate 400 theatergoers in its protuberant baroque embrace. A box cost from $5 to $10 for gala events, orchestra seats, $1.50, and the balcony, $1. There was a private passage to the Pico House and its bar. A legend says that General Grant tripped in this passage, but there is no authentic documented evidence to back this up. Stories of General Grant's drinking habits outnumber versions of Custer's Last Stand.

Twenty-four actors collected by Miss Kitty Blanchard (she did "mouth organ solos between acts") and Mr. McKee Rankin opened the new theater with *Fanchon, The Cricket*. They also performed *The Colleen Bawn* and *Rip Van Winkle*, and for the intellectuals, *Anthony and Cleopatra*. The California Minstrels and Johnny Allen's Burlesque Company followed. One senses the fugitive echoes of hedonism in tights.

Attendance fell off; some said the acoustics were bad and the stairs needed carpets. ("Los Angeles was always a poor theater town"—almost *any* out-of-town producer from that day on.)

Closing for a year, the Merced reopened with armchairs, new versions of Italian landscapes and a saloon of its own downstairs. This last item was a brilliant addition. Patrons did not any longer have to trek down a passage to the Pico House bar between acts and before and after the play. Whatever the reason, the theater had a period of success, with packed houses for *East Lynne, Uncle Tom's Cabin* ("real bloodhounds"), *Camille* and that ever popular favorite *Ten Nights in a Barroom,* "which did little to hurt business in the house bar."

The Merced downfall after 1875 was swift. It became Wood's Opera House, played lurid melodrama and served drinks and permitted smoking. Soon it was a variety house with Ladies' Night every Friday and early erotic kicking of legs on stage. Naughty stuff began to seep in between boxing and wrestling events.

Harris Newmark writes of the theater at this time as a western "song and dance resort being cut up into boxes where the actresses between the acts mingled with the crowd . . . patrons indulged in drinking and smoking and the bar . . . did thriving business."

In a letter by a Charles Terre we find out *what* went on in those boxes that Mr. Newmark was too shocked to report. "The most depraved scenes sometimes went on in the boxes, where women performed strange French acts on men, and the actresses, the waitress girls wore no drawers and were handled by the customers in the most depraved ways. There have been two knifings in these boxes, neither fatal. One woman while under the grip of drink, fell from a top box, but the matter was hushed up."

There was a cannon mounted on a platform in front of the theater which boomed to announce great or important events. It didn't help business. By 1876, Mr. J. H. Wood filed for bankruptcy. It became the Club Theatre. John S. Sullivan, "The Boston Strong Boy," was there in the eighties, and "silver dollars were thrown at the Stanley Sisters, a local pair," suggesting they were popular whores. The *Los Angeles Times* reported a ball given at the theater as "a prostitutes' carnival."

8 A Great Salesman, and the Silk Boom

They were remarkable men, those dedicated to money and power in the nineteenth century. The historian Matthew Josephson felt the times made them:

Shortly before or very shortly after 1840 were born nearly all the galaxy of uncommon men who were to be the overlords of the future so-

BOOM TIMES AND LAND AGENTS

ciety. They were born at a historical moment when by an easy effort one could as well look back at the mellow past as scan the eventful future. Their parents could remember the disturbed but very simple and light-hearted times of Mr. Jefferson, when pigs wandered unmolested at the steps of the Capitol; and it was only a comparatively few years since Mr. Jackson had "driven the money changers from the temple."

California was a perfect place for even earlier giants to prove themselves. A fresh country, undeveloped resources of rich promise, and the laws—what there were—were flexible enough not to interfere too much with one's progress or with land speculations.

Robert M. Widney was one of those powerful forces of vital drive that the nation produced. He had all the proper background of an early American legend, having been a poor farm boy born in western Ohio. Naturally he attended a log cabin school, and with little more education than that, at sixteen was a footloose mountain man, hunting and trapping in the Rockies. In 1847, he walked to northern California accompanying a wagon train.

In California, Widney applied for work as a woodchopper and bettered his education—he was a member of the class of '63 at Santa Clara's College of the Pacific. He was a doer right from the start, becoming a professor without pay, when college funds were low, until the school could afford to pay him a salary. He began also to teach mathematics and the much needed study of geology in a country suspected of having great mineral wealth. To fill up any time-space, this da Vinci of the rugged frontier also studied law and passed the bar examination in 1865.

Robert Widney was, however, more a man of physical action than the eastern "empire builders" (or "robber barons" if one disapproved; they were both). When he became a mining engineer in Austin, Nevada, he was known as one man who would draw a pistol if he had to and had flourished a gun once in open court when someone questioned his honor. In 1868 he arrived in southern California and set up a law office

A GREAT SALESMAN, AND THE SILK BOOM

in an adobe shack at Main and Arcadia streets to work as a land broker and do some law work, whichever came in first. The land boom was his golden ride to success. Rob Widney had the knowing skill of how to turn land into money, and along the way to get his share of the pie. His teams of horses and buckboards stood ready to carry the would-be buyers to the acreage, and Widney folders and maps, lithographed in splendid detail, were items that enhanced the overwhelmed buyer with an "idea you were buying a corner lot in Heaven and had the whiskey concession" (a letter).

It took less than a half-dozen months from the time Widney carried his trunk into his office for him to become a trusted agent, with deposits in the thousands of dollars from big land buyers giving him the right to pick and buy acreage in their names.

He married a college classmate named Mary Barnes and picked out a small house in which to settle down at the corner of Fourth and Main, the site where the great Farmers & Merchants Bank was to rise in modern times. He always had an eye for the future value of the right bit of land.

The printed word, Widney felt, was respected by a nation that had been educated in little country schoolhouses, so he bought a printing press and became the publisher, editor and writer of the monthly *Los Angeles Real Estate Advertiser,* a publication pushed free under every hotel door, given out in boardinghouses, shops or on street corners, wherever someone might be interested in land. And who wasn't in those boom times? Front and back pages might contain some news and the sensible advice to buy southern California land, but the inside pages were advertisements of large acreages for sale.

"The Santa Gertrudas Rancho noted as the richest of farm lands . . . the Stearns ranchos, where the farmer may select land for corn, for a vineyard, for semi-tropical fruits or for small grain. This paper gives a full and true statement of what has been done, what is doing, and of what can be done here by men of industry and capital."

It was common in those elated times for someone to sign a paper offering to buy a ninety-nine-acre farm for $1,900 and to resell the rights an hour or so later for $4,300.

BOOM TIMES AND LAND AGENTS

All this money to be made for just trading a land deed led, of course, to the rackets of selling land one didn't own or "stole by jumping the land of those who did own it." Land-jumping was a dangerous sport, a deadly game. And landholdings around Los Angeles were often scenes of shootings, killings and violence of all kinds, including the burning of barns and houses as "various parties made claims as to *who* owned *what* and *where.*" It was a God-sent business for lawyers, who "milked and bilked" as more than one letter east pointed out.

It must have been a polecat lawyer who had two men put in jail in Los Angeles, claiming they had threatened to kill him, then calmly seized their land, moved on to it and filed papers of ownership—and got away with it.

The rush to settle in and around Los Angeles was so great that one had to book passage a week ahead to get the steamer down from San Francisco. And even so there was space sold as "standing room" for the three-day sea-tossed journey south. Men without berths rolled up under the dining room tables, while the feeding went on overhead. Those who came by wagon, horseback, astride a jenny or a tom mule, made the outskirts of the city into vast camping grounds, recalling for many the Army bivouacs the settlers had known just a few years before.

They came from afar—farmers from Maine, southern F.F.V. aristocrats, ruined, they claimed, by "de warh." But mostly the wagon trains carried folk from Texas and Missouri.

In one year, from 1868 to 1869, cultivated land went from 20,000 acres to 35,000 acres. Voting and school registrations jumped 50 percent, "and whiskey swallowing, gambling and shootings, about one hundred percent. . . ."

There were strange booms in strange products based on claims being made that just about *anything* would do well in southern California. One just had to have "the divine liquefaction of the true faith," as one Los Angeles street-corner preacher, Bible Billy, had it.

The strangest boom to take Los Angeles and the susceptible was the silkworm culture that was to turn the south into "a silk production community equal to all the mills of China and France.

A GREAT SALESMAN, AND THE SILK BOOM

It was a Frenchman, Louis Provost, who entangled southern California in silken threads. On land near San Jose, he had been cultivating silkworms as a hobby. Provost wrote many letters to the newspapers endorsing the idea that California was just right to become the Middle Kingdom, the China of millions of yards of the best silk. The state legislature (as has been its habit up to today), always ready to give a hearing to anything that fattened its venal ear, passed a law with liberal bounties "to stimulate the culture of silk." Farmers shifted from grain, hay, oranges, grapes and tobacco to taking care of millions of silkworms chewing mulberry leaves on thousands of trays.

Louis Provost invested in a few thousand acres of Jurupa Rancho land and formed a company with pretty printed stock certificates announcing The California Silk Center Association, which insisted, in words of great promise, that it was going to produce a fabulous silk industry on the west coast.

The boom was on, a massive senseless race of buying and selling silk stocks, worm eggs, mulberry saplings.

By the spring of 1869, farmers who had worm eggs were selling them for $12 an ounce, and getting back from the state large subsidies for growing mulberry trees and cocoons. One Los Angeles farmer admitted to making $1,000 an acre from the sale of eggs, and that just in two months.

As always with booms, it resulted in unreasoning grand speculation with no one actually interested in producing silk cloth. To make silk, one must kill the moth before it tears open its cocoon; but to get the eggs, worth more than their weight in gold, one had to let the insect destroy the cocoon made of silk threads. So the state was paying heavy bounties for burst worthless cocoons that could not be spun into silk.

Farmers complaisantly paid to plant mulberry trees to feed the egg-laying silk-producing worms saw that this was better in this sanguinary world than any gold rush. And with fervid eloquence, the worm-egg speculators continued their praise of the silk culture.

The result was that trees replaced corn, trees took over land that should have been given over to vegetables and staple crops. The mulberry tree filled acres that should have shown oranges and lemons and grapevines.

The state's handout, the sale of eggs and trees, was producing wealth. It seemed foolish to think of building factories, laboriously unwinding the cocoons, spinning silk and then hunting a market.

In the summer of 1869 someone figured out that 100 million silkworm eggs were on the market. Too much, *too* many, and the price fell to $4 an ounce, *if* you could find a buyer. By this time the political boys had pretty much looted the state treasury, and in September 1869 a law revoked the subsidy to the egg and tree growers.

Egg prices went down and with no more state funds to pad the game, the speculation boom burst. It also killed Louis Provost "from overwork on his silk plantation in southern California" and most likely from the irascible damage of capricious speculation.

The *Los Angeles Daily Star* shed a few tears at his passing: "His place cannot be filled. A greater misfortune could not have happened in this lo- cality, nor to the State at large." At the same time millions of silkworms and mulberry trees were dying of neglect. Desolation hit thousands of acres, and hundreds of worm-egg farmers were ruined, while wily specu- lators who had dumped their holdings early counted their piles of gold eagles and double eagles.

Louis Provost's kingdom of silk, or at least his land, passed to a group of settlers who founded Riverside and began to plant orange shoots as quickly as they could pull up and burn the mulberry trees. (I own a heavy mulberry wood cane made from one of the trees, with the carved inscrip- tion "A.K. 1859.")

Not one yard of commercial silk was ever woven in California during the worm and egg boom. The only known bit of true California silk that was produced was an American flag intended to be flown over the Capi- tol dome in Washington. I have been unable to discover if that banner was actually flown there.

It was all a mood that was explained in our time by Hale Champion, once state director of finance in California and a financial vice president of Harvard University, in a *Los Angeles Times* interview:

A GREAT SALESMAN, AND THE SILK BOOM

In California the guidelines aren't laid out all over the place, and that has its advantages. A lot of people got a great sense of freedom. They moved out there and threw it all over. They were free and no one was going to look at them. They could do what they wanted. But the limits of freedom very quickly get reached, and it turns out to be the be-all and end-all and winds up with some people going off the bridge. The expectations for that kind of freedom were very large. Because people moved to California and threw off the normal restraints and inhibitions to which they had been subjected in their hometowns, you get a flowering of that eccentricity all over the place.

9 Los Angeles' Own "Wounded Knee"

The massacre of Sioux men, women and children at Wounded Knee by the Seventh Cavalry caused public uproar among some people and was a sensation in the press. But the mass killing and lynching of Chinese in Los Angeles in October 1871 did not ruffle the surface of American society, then or later.

LOS ANGELES' OWN "WOUNDED KNEE"

The Chinese story in California has been poorly recorded and mainly ignored by impartial historians. The Chinese were as much frontier pioneers as the types portrayed into myth on the screen by Gary Cooper and John Wayne.

A hundred thousand or more Chinese had been imported, mostly peasants from the Canton area, brought over by the Big Four building western railroads. At a dollar a day or even less, the Chinese dug, carried, handled explosives, set ties and rails. They rode the gandy (a tool to tamp down ballast), leveled mountains, worked river crossings and bored tunnels at their steady hardworking pace, their disc hats over the ritual pigtail.

However, they were more than muscle. The Chinese became shopkeepers, eating-house owners, very often laundrymen on a frontier where some Californians sent their dirty clothes to the Sandwich Islands (Hawaii) for a washing.

In both San Francisco and Los Angeles they became importers, merchants, professional gamblers, keepers of brothels and members of organizations of mutual interests that were to be exploited by the newspapers. As a minority, they were easy victims of violence.

The Chinese in Los Angeles lived inside a social system labeled as *tongs,* and there were makers of *tong wars.* The original tongs were close-knit fraternal orders, so that the Chinese could have their own rules of order, a form of private justice and some firm control over each other in domestic and business matters.

The Chinese on the west coast were a feisty lot, never the docile, silent, bowing "Chink" that journalists created and the country accepted. The Chinese had a splendid cuisine when they could afford it (both chow mein and chop suey were invented for white feeders in the United States and were unknown in China). They were zealous in their love of gambling, from fan-tan to the more solid poker-playing of the frontier (as Bret Harte knew when he wrote a once famous poem about the wily Chinese as a cutthroat poker player). Many were habitual smokers of opium, the importation of which led to gangster-style warfare among the tongs of

The Coronel Block, the building in the back, was the Chinatown of 1866. Here the terrible Chinese massacre took place. (Los Angeles County Museum of Natural History)

Los Angeles (as in many other American cities) for the control of its distribution.

The Chinese were always a sensual race, given in their homeland of the Middle Kingdom (the center of the world) to sexual refinements sometimes whispered about among the ranchers and clerks of the town.

It was the limited supply of Chinese women and the tongs' control over the flesh traffic that made trouble. There was a continual smuggling of Chinese slave girls into California up to the turn of the century, for the lowly cribs and for the sporting houses as well as for those wealthy Chinese who could afford concubines.

In early October 1871 a tong war seemed in the making over a beautiful Chinese girl desired both by the Hong Chows and the Nin Yungs. The Hong Chows, after a judgment by tong leaders, seemed to be the winners in the wrangling, and she was married—after the tong's court of appeal—to a Hong Chow in good standing. The formal Oriental wedding was a splendid one.

The Nin Yungs, however—after the wedding feast—did not take any comfort in the peace, and there was a sharp increase in the buying of pistols and cartridges, shotguns and some rifles. White shopkeepers sold weapons openly for cash to any minority "except Indians."

On October 23rd three shots were taken at the headman of the Hong Chow tong in the Calle de los Negros district. It was an omen made of lead, and both tongs began to prepare for a war. The next afternoon hatchetmen were out in the alleys, among adobe and plank buildings, their large sleeves concealing the short-handled razor-sharp steel axe they used in their ritual warfare. But mostly the mob of Chinese that gathered with talk of tong trouble were armed with Colt 45s and Smith & Wesson six-shooters.

The fighters of the two tongs met in shouting street charges and shooting began. So far, it had been a battle between Chinese, and as with the later gangster and Mafia affairs of the twentieth century, respectable citizens shrugged it off as an event in which "they only kill each other."

There entered, however, a new element to the mixture in the form of a mounted policeman. Spotting one Chinese, who seemed to be exhorting the mob to more violence, the officer leaped from his horse to collar the agitator. However, the Chinese, using the mob for cover, eluded him and made for the safety of the Coronel Block, a structure that housed Chinese and some of their enterprises. It stood at Los Angeles and Arcadia streets. The Coronel, once the town house of Don Ygnacio Coronel, was made of adobe, roofed with tile and was no longer one of the splendid houses of the city.

The eager officer had no sooner mounted the porch and entered the building when there was heard a shot and he came weaving out of the entrance, a bullet in one wet, red shoulder. Grasping an awning for support, he reached for his police whistle and blew. He was still desperately blowing when two Chinese, pigtails flying, came out and let him have the contents of their revolvers close up before retiring quickly into the interior of the building. The whistle had brought out several whites on the run, emerging from saloons and stores, groggeries and gambling dives.

One such person—most respectable—was Robert Thompson, a rancher, and he never traveled without belting on his pistol holster. He drew his revolver and lunged for the doorway of the Coronel Block, even as several onlookers warned him "the Chinks are shootin'." Thompson fired once blindly through the doorway and followed up his shot by moving forward to see what effect his shooting had inside. He was at once fired on in turn from the interior, staggered back and fell, having taken, as one news item put it, "a mortal wound."

The shock to the converging mob was great. Two white citizens of Los Angeles were now dead at Chinese hands. The Chinese, not fazed or cowed—or perhaps not fully aware of the situation—decided to fight. (We have almost no information from the Chinese viewpoint.) A half-dozen armed Chinese emerged onto the porch of the building and began firing at a curious crowd collecting to watch the ruckus.

The crowd scattered under the Chinese fire but returned to the scene as soon as it could find weapons.

Mob action at the moment became a satisfying catastrophic experience—a collective, mindless action oiled on hatred and raw whiskey.

It was clearly a racial mob; as a member of it later wrote in a letter,

"American blood had been shed. There was, too, that sense of shock that Chinese had dared fire on whites, and kill with recklessness outside their own color set. We all moved in shouting in anger and as some noticed, in delight at all the excitement, we moved, a mass, from the head of Los Angeles Street up the Calle de los Negros, and one part separated to go up Sanchez Street hemming in the Coronel Block on both flanks." At the rear of the building, facing the old Plaza, there was soon another armed group. As dusk came, the building was under siege, surrounded on all sides by a frenzied mob which, as torches appeared, had been joined by Mexicans making a united group against the Chinese, outlanders who had been labeled "cheap labor."

So here (this letter noted) was a chance for getting back at the hardworking Chinese, growing in dangerous numbers in the laboring market and creating a wealthy merchant class.

"Cries rose of, 'Hang them! Hang them!' Soon led to howls of 'Burn them out!' shouting foul oaths" (but in the less permissive prose of that day, when damn was usually printed d _ _ _ _, the oaths were not recorded).

Sheriff James F. Burns came up on a run and saw he had to dampen down the temper of the mob before serious killing took over. Someone rolled up a barrel for him and he mounted it, held up his arms for quiet. In a firm voice he ordered the mob to disperse; this was a matter for the law, and the rioters could be assured that he would keep the house under close observation until dawn, then would proceed to arrest all the Chinese within it. He also, in sonorous solemnity, called for volunteers to be sworn in as deputies. Gesturing earnestly, he suddenly felt the head of the barrel giving way beneath his boots. He plummeted down inside the cask in a comedy drop that brought out laughter and destroyed his earnest efforts to sway the crowd. Pulled out from between the staves, he called for volunteers to patrol all around the house so as to prevent any Chinese from slipping out. (Also as protection to keep the raging mob from lynching the Chinese.)

The mob began to turn on the sheriff as a spoilsport and cries were heard.

LOS ANGELES' OWN "WOUNDED KNEE"

"Godd____ the sheriff!"

"Shoot him!"

"Hang him!"

Sheriff Burns, aware that the mob leaders were bringing the rioters to a fast boil, turned over the action to the city marshal and rushed off to see what solid armed backing he could get from more respectable citizens.

The mob had grown to about 400 (some later estimates said 300, some said 500). They presented a sea of shouting faces and lifted weapons. The doors of the Coronel Block were suddenly opened and (it was assumed later) the Chinese had decided to parley terms of surrender. A couple of hundred guns were at once aimed at the open doorway. Forty slugs were later counted in the doors and walls. The Chinese fell, dying, back into the interior. Another Chinese tried to make a break but was met with a new fusillade that shattered him. He was replaced by a tong member with a hatchet held high and ready.

The crowd closed in for the kill, cornered him and went at him with pistol butts and canes, boots and rifle stocks.

"Hang him!" yelled those unable to strike a personal blow because of the press of eager bodies. However, by some miracle of shoving and shouldering, Emil Harris, a city detective, managed to get hold of the battered hatchetman and proceeded to march him down Main Street toward the brick jail on Spring Street.

But at Spring and Temple the mob closed in, overpowered Harris, pinning his arms to his body, and took over the now badly battered Chinese. They roughhoused him up Temple Street, shoving, kicking and beating him to the Tomlinson Corral, the scene of some previous lynchings. Here they found rope and willing hands and hung the Chinese on the gate beam. But the rope was old and frayed and the struggling body broke it. A better rope was knotted up and soon the struggling body, hung like overripe fruit, was still at last. The rioters, delighted at their performance, cheered themselves until throats grew rasped.

At the Coronel Block, the major part of the mob had come around to a plan for smoking out the remaining Chinese.

The cry went up, "Burn the building!"

One of the sheriff's men, boldly facing the mob, announced he'd shoot the first man who tried to burn the building. It took a brave man to face them down, but he did, at least for a few minutes (the boldest voices of rioters are often those that draw back from any suggestion of danger to themselves). Someone discovered a city water hydrant and some fire hose was brought up and uncoiled; it was decided to "try and wash 'em out."

But the stream of water didn't affect the adobe walls, no matter how hard it gushed. A ladder was dragged to the corner of Arcadia and Sanchez streets, and about a dozen men got up on the *brea* (tar) and tile roof, and with axes began to hack their way into the interior. Once a hole was chopped out, a volley of many six-shooters was fired down at the Chinese massed in the interior. This action drove one of the besieged men to try and escape, to bolt up the street. Being fired upon, he tried to get back inside but died on the porch where he was soon joined by another Chinese trying to make a hopeless run for it. He, too, was killed.

Meanwhile, the law was slowly gathering strength. Robert M. Widney had collected a force of ten men to assist the sheriff. They moved as a unit toward the mob but were just in time to see them break into the building.

The sheriff moved forward, but Widney discovered he had no weapon, and he ran off to see if he could borrow a shooting iron. It added an ironic, unreal note to the dreadful events, to find a posse leader with no pistol.

Inside the building mob members were battering down all doors, dragging out the Chinese by their pigtails or limbs along the ground. Many of the mob stopped to do extensive looting, a kind of reward for their efforts. Silks, hangings, pots, mysterious bundles, all were carried off. Rice was scattered about; potent drink in strange bottles was gulped down.

The sheriff and his men beat their way to one victim and saved him, and two other wounded Chinese were carried off to the safety of the jail.

But it was clear the mob was too large and too strong to be stopped. A group of Chinese was dragged to Commercial Street by rioters to the sides of covered wagons (one report called them "sagebrush schoo-

LOS ANGELES' OWN "WOUNDED KNEE"

ners"). Four Chinese were hanged from the tall wagon bows. Then, to make sure, the bodies were stabbed and shot at.

Other sections of the mob were gleefully dragging victims off to Temple and Van Buena streets, toward the execution grounds of the Tomlinson Corral gate. Four more Chinese were brutally lynched here. Robert Widney, still without a weapon, tried to stop this, but he was pushed aside.

One mob member put it to him directly, "A damn lot of white men 'round *here* we oughta string up too."

Widney left and on Spring Street he found more Chinese being hauled to execution. His brother Willie showed up at this point and slipped him a Colt Navy revolver.

Putting the weapon to the chest of a man holding on to a Chinese, he said, "Get away, or I'll kill you."

Assistance came up to help move several other battered, but still living, victims to the protection of the jail.

The sheriff, organizing a band of law-minded citizens, led them up Los Angeles Street to the Coronel Block. Here he called for two dozen volunteers to act as his deputies to guard the house, now gutted, smoldering and empty. The mob, seeing the determined volunteers, muttered curses but the starch of the excitement was out of them. The rioting and lynching had run four full hours. The mob dispersed, mostly to the grog shops, honky-tonks and saloons on Commercial and Main streets to celebrate the massacre.

It had been a deadly and brutal few hours. Five corpses hung like carrion from the Tomlinson Corral gate. And suspended from the awning of a wagon shop and saloon, swung six dead Chinese. Four Orientals had died on the wagon bows of freight wagons, and sprawled in death's careless pattern around the Coronel Block were four more dead. Nineteen men (and boys) had been lynched in the carnage of a white mob's lawless violence—brought on by one guilty Chinese.

In some ways the Los Angeles massacre differed from that of the Sioux at Wounded Knee; the number of the murdered was much smaller, there was no freezing weather to finish off the wounded and the weak, and there is no record of any of the Chinese dead being women, although two boys were victims.

The Los Angeles newspapers that had often led in the outcry for direct violent action now put on printer's ink sackcloth.

"That the murderers of Mr. Thompson . . . [the *News*] . . . deserved swift and summary punishment, none will deny; but where are we to look for justification of the wholesale slaughter . . . and the general and systematic robbery of the Chinese quarters that was carried on while the denizens were being butchered?"

The effects of grand-jury action in November resulted in the bringing out of a couple dozen indictments, and some men pointed out as ringleaders were held in jail for the crime of inciting to riot. Only seven rioters were convicted in a series of noisy, hoot-and-holler trials that resulted—a stormy time being had by lawyers, judges, juries and the accused. The indictments did result in an exodus of a part of the mob, those who felt that it was healthier to "strike out for parts unknown."

Things calmed down; the massacre did not stop the growth of the city's Chinese population. Wrecked buildings were repaired; of those who had fled, many came back. New Chinese appeared. Family life went on, business recovered. And the Los Angeles Chinatown, the Old Chinatown, grew, not to be molested again until the 1930s when it was replaced by the huge ornate railroad station.

10 The Town and the Great Rain

By the middle of the nineteenth century, up to the Civil War, it was anyone's guess which way El Pueblo de los Angeles would turn. But the land developers, ranchers and merchants were guessing it would never stop growing. Building was going on; rubble, bricks, barrels of tarlike substance from the La Brea pits for roof topping, earth in mounds, raw sawed timbers lay about. Riding horses, wagon horses and dray mules added their own confusion and dropped fresh litter. There was as yet not a fully expert rubbish collection, and dead dogs, old boots, bottles, kitchen leavings, overflow privies, slaughtering pens and tanneries made parts of the city strong smelling.

The nineteenth century did not have the same sensitivities to the stench of progress as we do, and yet they too commented in letters to the press at the fearful odors. At such times a chain gang of shaggy prisoners might come from the jailhouse with rakes and shovels, barrels and carts, to try and set back a bit the tide of refuse.

Business and merchandising added crates, boxes, kegs and bundles to the earth sidewalks curbed by planks. Under awnings, loafers and whittlers "set in chairs," while clerks inventoried new shipments of dry goods and notions and checked lists of hardware and china. Commercial, Main and Spring streets, all were conscious of money to be made in trade, in buying, selling, while on the sidewalks, the tobacco chewers might lean forward in their chairs and spit amber into boxes of sawdust or brass gaboons (also called spittoons), a "cock fight would be set up or someone promoting a dog fight, or throwing a dead rat at a passing woman." There was the bedlam of street peddlers offering drinks, fruit, buttons or spot remover, and snake-oil and medicine showmen at their pitches, bootblacks working on dusty or muddy boots. All of it scenes out of Hogarth's engravings transported to southern California.

The town was a strange mixture of those who were up and doing, the promoters, the yea-sayers, and those others who had been defeated by drought, bad crops, debt, bad luck, illness, foolish investments, merely existing in broken boots showing obscene toes. There were also those who watched and observed: the Mexicans—"*Un sueño loco. Ay Dios, Dios*"—under their wide hats; the Chinese, pigtailed, carrying burdens, saying little when away from their shops and homes.

Noisy would be a ride past a band of *vaqueros* in from some rancho with a herd; the shipping of beef in any large quantity still waited for the later cattle cars, and the reefers and icers. "Often herds of wild ranch longhorns would fill the street, building to building with dangerous cattle, stirred along on the run by their herders snapping whips and enjoying the

THE TOWN AND THE GREAT RAIN

confusion they caused to more placid citizens. The townspeople would have to leap for safety and wait out the passing of a herd on its way to its destination. . . ."

While insect life haunted the clapboard, false-front boardinghouses, the streets were besieged by nearly 500 dogs of an evil mongrel appearance, more than half strays without owners.

As one letter writer described the plague of roaming mongrels, "They sleep on the sidewalks, trot through the streets, run between your legs, push children down, trip horses, throw riders and fill the whole city with fleas." Often the horsemen—once the mayor himself—drew their pistols and ended the careers of street curs on the spot. At night the hungry animals, homeless, brutalized by kicks, firecrackers or tin cans tied to their tails, howled in chorus, making a nightly din that sent pistol and rifle shots in their direction. When the howling reached a certain crescendo of sound, meat scraps baited with strychnine or arsenic of lead were placed about, and in the morning the jail work gang picked up the stiff corpses of the night's poisoned hounds.

Spectacular auto and plane accidents did not, of course, yet exist, but runaway teams of horses were daily dramas of hysterical action, danger and excitement. The teams of the Overland Stage made a mad dash through Spring Street when frightened, dumping the driver and spilling passengers. Berserk brewery horses would smash their drays to kindling and send beer kegs rolling down Los Angeles Street to the delight of the penniless thirsty. The Los Angeles Daily Star got bored with runaway horse news. "The usual daily runaway occurred yesterday. There will probably be another today, so look out for it." And there usually was.

Most of the native-born citizens enjoyed their town and would have agreed with the late T. S. Eliot: "On the whole, it would appear to be for the best that the great majority of human beings should go on living in the place in which they were born."

Outside the town there was even less of a great-city-to-be, a city that would by the middle of the twentieth century swallow all the little communities about to be laid out and sweep nearly the whole Los Angeles Valley and county into its maw.

Commercial Street in 1873 belies its name, but it was a main business center. Two clocks show different time; they are most likely painted signs. The sports on the right are driving the popular buckboard. (Security Pacific First National Bank)

BOOM TIMES AND LAND AGENTS

At the middle of the nineteenth century, however, the valley was mostly wild land from town to sea, toward the port of San Pedro and the bays of Santa Monica.

To travel out of Los Angeles by road and coach was difficult. The only fairly dependable connection was by water. Steamer Day meant that the side-wheeler *Orizaba* had brought down seasick passengers through three days of rough rolling on the Pacific from San Francisco to San Pedro, the ship to unload and make up cargo, hides, ore, the first oranges and other local products, for the return trip.

Only the bold took the alternative route north on wheels, the jolting dusty Coast Line Stage. It left once a day from Los Angeles, passing through Santa Barbara and San Buenaventura, a trip that lasted four backbreaking days in a rattling badly sprung coach on bad roads, the crossing of bridgeless rivers and the spines of mountains, to which often could be added a holdup, the looting of baggage and persons by some highwayman. And if luck was out, an overturned coach or a washout by a cloudburst, which left Los Angeles passengers, if fortunate, merely marooned in some station cabin with wet-wood smoke and deadly fireplace cooking out of a greasy spider skillet.

The Los Angeles stage could also take one south to San Diego, and as for trips eastward, they struggled as far as the Mormon village at the foot of Cajon Pass, San Bernardino, a place destined to become a noted railway town for the Santa Fe and already referred to as San Berdo. From there east was like Stanley in Africa, feeling one's way in dangerous places by the "Mud Wagon," a four-horse rig that once a week carried fools and adventurers on to Arizona Territory where, in season, one was sure to find beyond the Colorado, the Apache out on a war party, wanting to make coups on white men and take scalps if they could; Geronimo was soon to come of age. (It was pronounced "Horonimo" during his lifetime.)

It was these slender and feeble threads of transportation that connected Los Angeles with the outer world, and these could be snapped by

THE TOWN AND THE GREAT RAIN

nature—by a storm at sea, or as happened in December 1867 by a mighty prolonged rainstorm that became a flood and took away roads and trails. The continual downpour seemed made for a new Noah. The telegraph line went down, and no one could find or follow roads that no longer existed, roads that were under many feet of silt. Bridges dissolved as if made of brown sugar.

All business was halted, and transportation of any kind was out of the question. In poncho and storm gear, citizens watched the waters rise; roofs leaked, and ancient adobe walls jellied into mud. Still it rained. The dam, people asked, the dam, *will* it hold? The local waterworks had taken pride in its earthen, log and stone dam. But too much angry water was piling up behind it.

The dam burst and the streets became rushing streams. Growing crops ceased to exist. Drinking water could only come from carts after that. Acres that hopeful farmers had planted, thousands of acres, became inland seas. Still it rained. The San Gabriel River changed its course, boiling over brown land, trees in its whirlpools, and it washed out a good section of El Monte in the move.

For a month there was no contact with the outside world. Several thousand Robinson Crusoes viewed their isolated, sodden world in which mold was spreading, walls were turning to slime and foundations were collapsing. It was not until the middle of January that the leaden skies slackened their downpour and there was hope that the worst was over. On the sixteenth of the month, the stagecoach company pushed through a mail delivery, using not a coach but pack mules. Three days later the rains stopped for good, and in every place above water there was a bright apple-green beard of vegetable growth over the land. The sun came up boldly and with all the dripping and runoffs of muddy water, there was hope of drying out. The roads were hunted out and work crews went out with carts and rubble, shovels and rakes to bring back some kind of surface so wheels could move again.

It had been a bitter lesson, a fear that came to many as they realized just how isolated they were and how much they depended on the slender line of coaches, the freighters' wagons, four- to six-team horses, the plodding of the mule packtrains.

As usual (up till today) the natives insisted that the protracted rains, the continuing storm, was "unusual weather," and there was room still for lots of people to settle.

The draw to southern California seemed natural to the farmers and ranchers of northern California. Life was grim along the Sacramento, in the valleys of the Napa and San Joaquin. Places from which to move away, for in the north the floods had been even worse, and there the sun did not shine as brightly or as often.

By October 1867 the first northern wagons were in Los Angeles with other wheels following in their wagon tracks, an exodus reaching the Promised Land. Settlers swarmed all over the riverbeds, the valleys, offering to buy land on the great ranchos, the San Antonia and the Santa Gertrudas. Not many ranchers, even if ruined by the great rain, subdivided at first.

The subdividing began when the biggest landowner of all—and one in debt—Don Abel Stearns began to cut up his vast holdings. He had come out to the coast in 1828, "a Yankee merchant" said the records, but obviously of Jewish descent. He had married into a proud Spanish family ("Was there ever an unproud Spanish family?"—O. Henry) and until the great storm, Stearns had been building himself into the position of "the leading landowner in southern California."

Soon he was joining others with vast holdings to create the Los Angeles & San Bernardino Land Association, to cut up such once great ranchos as Jurupa, La Sierra, Bolsa Chica, Las Bolsas, La Habra, Los Coyotes and others. In all, there were nearly 180,000 acres of land to be surveyed. By July it was on the market: "Take your pick, five dollars to thirteen dollars an acre."

A tremendous pressure-selling campaign was started, big even for those pre-Madison Avenue days. Travel writers, authors and lecturers were hired to endorse and to create prose saying wonderful things about the Stearns' land sales. Folders, maps, sales letters and brochures were sent all over the West. Plans of plats for proposed town sites and tracts were passed out to all south-going wagon trains. Once the prospects were in Los Angeles, herds of land salesmen waited with good horses, carriages, hacks, gigs and buckboards for a quick drive to view "the last special acres of rich bottomland.

By the end of 1869, 20,000 acres had been sold and were under cultivation. Abel Stearns, who had come out of the great rain a ruined man, died in 1871 with everything paid off and a good balance socked away for his heirs. The Land Association he had helped to form and guide made more than $2 million "on land they couldn't give away at five cents an acre before the people crowded in" (a letter).

Abel was no salesman; he had acquired Robert M. Widney, then aged thirty, as the southern agent for the Land Association. "He couldn't have found a better man—who could have peddled coal to the devil. He was the dean of all land sellers."

Robert Widney was one of those men that the historian R. E. Riegel set down as the type of westerner who "expected to become wealthy and famous; each city expected to become the metropolis of the West; and each state expected to become the industrial and artistic center of the nation. Some of them later reappeared with increased force and potency, but others were gone forever."

Sometimes the expectations turned sour—as in the Great Wool Year.

11　A Panic in Wool

The disaster in silkworm-egg speculation taught no one a lesson.
Few would have understood William James' symbol of "The
Bitch Goddess Success." They wooed her ardently, and if not
with a silk crop, the next turn was wool. In 1871 the amount of wool clip-
ped, that came to the American market, was the lowest since the Civil
War. In an expanding, sprawling nation moving west and with new im-

migrants homesteading in their soddies, there was demand for woolen cloth from the eastern seaboard to the western ocean.

Los Angeles County, which in 1868 had produced 620,000 pounds of the smelly, tacky stuff, was by 1871 weighing in at 1.5 million pounds. Speculators rushed in to make a good thing of rising prices and Los Angeles dealers were offering 20 cents a pound. Merchants and middlemen did not wait for any shearing season to denude the sheep, but began to buy up wool futures with the fleece still on the animals' backs. Wool going north to San Francisco was warehoused by dealers there who waited for the eastern millowners to come begging for bales of wool at any price. "Supply and demand" was whispered with pleasure by speculators as they gathered in the Palace Hotel bar—its floor set with silver dollars—to enjoy their Pico Punch. It was extortion cried the millowners as the textile factory wheels and looms began to slow down in New England. Harassment, offers and rejections went on.

Anything woolly could sell. Short staple stuff from southern California, full of dust, burrs and gook, was selling off the Golden Gate for 45 cents a pound. Speculators in Los Angeles began to offer as high as 49 cents a pound as the grazers held back their shearings at even that price. The sky's the limit in wool prices was their philosophy.

The mills and eastern buyers moved warily, *not* rushing in to buy at the inflated California prices. They had a shrewd sense of self-preservation. The dealers had overlooked the Australian wool potential. And then suddenly it was *there,* ships with large consignments of Aussie wool piling up on the San Francisco docks, to be bought up quickly by the mills, and good riddance to all those greedy bastards stuck with huge holdings in California wool.

Wires went out to Los Angeles middlemen: BUY NO MORE WOOL AT ANY PRICE. By the end of April there was no market at all for the wool in Los Angeles warehouses (or still on the sheep), much of it costing 50 cents a pound. Half a million dollars had been paid out to pay for the spring shearings. Depression, then panic, came to wholesalers and wool growers.

One of the first orange orchards—about 100 acres—located in what is now the heart of Los Angeles, between 4th and 7th streets.

California oranges for an English Christmas in 1874. This is a good picture of the early steamships, some of which still carried sail.

By September the stored wool was offered at 12½ cents a pound, and in the debacle that followed, there were firms that lost more than $50,000. All the wool men took a beating, from sheep raiser to dealer. The strange speculation did lead to a better washing and cleaning of wool, and the early Mexican breeds were improved by imported French Merino rams. However, both sheep raisers and wool merchants walked a little more carefully from then on. They hedged their bets on wool by turning to more diversified crops. Corn and barley paid off better; they needed little water. Barley could yield a few hundred bushels an acre and was good for two crops a year. Wheat had a rust problem and the sea mists didn't help it much either.

It was a time of planting grapevines which produced not the rare vintages of France, but drinkable stuff, and also a kind of brandy "to make Lazarus git up and do the cakewalk."

Good or bad vintage, by 1870 Los Angeles County was producing one-sixth of America's wine. It took three years for a vine to begin to produce mature grapes and four years before the acres of vines could show a profit. The grower had a big investment, for he usually processed his own wine, and even the primitive winepresses, the building of storage cellars and the cooperage cost of casks made the wine industry something only a man with cash on the barrelhead or credit at the new Los Angeles bank, soon to be formed, could make a go of.

Oranges paid well, but it took seven years for a tree to begin producing prime fruit. And one had to have the right hardly sour rootstock, whose fruit was not worthwhile, to graft on to the sweet orange wood. Many a would-be orange farmer was the victim of some sharper or drifter selling him willow saplings for "certified orange wood stock."

Still, a twelve-year tree would offer up a thousand oranges a crop to the owners and pickers. At 3 cents an orange in San Francisco that was several dollars in somebody's jeans (not all were shipped of course). A farmer with a bearing orchard put it this way, "why it's just like finding money in the street." Hardly that, figuring the cost of land, twelve years of nursing the trees, trimming and later the costs of fertilizer and spraying, all added to the overhead of boxing and paying the pickers. In four years, the number of orange trees blossoming in Los Angeles County went from 9,000 to 34,000.

The last of the cattlemen and sheepmen went down to defeat when their "no fence law" was thrown out, and fencing ended the free drift of half-wild cattle eating whatever crop was in their path. A farmer shot a rancher's horse from under him, as a warning to keep steers out of the growing fields. A community leader, when a strong fencing act was passed, looked toward heaven and was quoted as saying, "It is a contest between advancing civilization or obsolete barbarism."

The joke about the Irishman and the Jew was taken seriously in Los Angeles, for John Downey and Isaiah Wolf Hellman brought professional banking into Los Angeles, pointing out that without banks the city would have had no growth.

Downey was born in Ireland in 1827, and by age fourteen, in the hull of a reeking steerage ship, he headed away from the "Auld Sod" he never regretted leaving. He was doing well in a Cincinnati drug business in an age of cure-all medications. Alcoholic female drinks (containing at least two martinis in every bottle) were popular. But Downey felt he'd like to try his luck in the California gold rush of '49. He found little gold and decided to head for Los Angeles and go back to running a drugstore. He was a man with a penetrating acumen: "Never waste time with a loser."

He opened his shop on Los Angeles Street in an adobe shack and soon became a rich man, gathering the sick and ailing and those who felt doses of bitter medicine meant health, customers coming from as far away as Texas and Sonora Mexico to show him their tongues or explain their aches.

He was also—more importantly—a moneylender. Said one victim: "A mick Shylock, and calling himself a Roman Catholic was all right, but he liked the sound of coins falling on his counters better than a Mass."

He foreclosed without mercy on notes and mortgages and got ownership of some huge ranchos. He was like Arthur Miller's salesman. He didn't want to be just *liked,* he wanted to be *well liked,* so he was active in civic progress and was always ready with a donation in return for newspaper space. Politics was a step up, and he helped mold the state's Democratic Party. At thirty-two he was governor of the state of California. As one saloon wit put it: "If he got all the votes of the people he pressed blood-and-interest out of on their notes, it must have been a landslide."

However, he was against monopoly (at least not of his own making) and he was a good governor, vetoing a bill giving special interests strangling controls of the San Francisco waterfront. The Civil War drove him from public office as, for some strange reason, Downey was full of love and sympathy for the Confederacy.

In 1865—out of office—he began to subdivide his vast landholdings. On the corner of Fourth and Main he built a "brick mansion, the first residence in Los Angeles with a private ballroom . . . ." He and his wife, Maria Guirado, became the town's semiofficial host and hostess to the best people, local and visitors. Many news items spoke of them as being "the center of the town's social scene."

Downey—a man of imaginative precocity—was keen enough to sense the need for a bank in Los Angeles. Land sales, crop movements, buying and selling in futures of grain crops and wool, all could use local credit and banking procedure. So with a San Francisco moneyman, J. A. Hayward, as partner, the first bank in town opened its doors in February 1869, with a capital of $100,000, in a small adobe building on Main Street (where the later Federal Building now rises, an invasion of national power that many were to think brushed aside city and state rights).

The brave new bank sign stated: THIS BANK STANDS TO DEAL IN GOLD DUST, BULLION, LEGAL TENDER AND GOVERNMENT VOUCHERS.

Downey's interests also involved him in the Los Angeles City Water Company whose purpose was to pipe water through city mains rather than depend on water carts and unreliable shallow wells. With Phineas Banning, he dreamed of a scheme for Los Angeles to have a railroad of its own, just a teeny one, *The Los Angeles & San Pedro R.R.,* to run twenty miles or so from the port to the town.

Besides water mains, Downey and his partners began to really bore down deep into the earth, producing artesian wells with their tremendous flows that irrigated farmers' fields and orchards, at a price.

With city lots rising in value, with business building going on so bravely, some structures with three full stories, like the Temple Block, there was need for more banks. Just half a year after Downey opened his bank, Isaiah W. Hellman, just twenty-five years old, opened another bank in a new building near the Bella Union Hotel. Words like "Financial Wizard" were passed around about Hellman, a German Jew who had come over from Bavaria in 1859 and would later try his luck as a shop-keeper. But banking drew him, for he had heard the story of the fabulous Rothschilds at his mother's knee. To involve local people, he formed an arrangement with William Workman, who was one of the first to dare take a wagon train across the desert. Workman preferred to stay on his Puente Rancho, and so he had his investments in the new bank handled by his son-in-law, F. P. F. Temple.

Francis Temple was a bit of a personality, not a mere son-in-law. He was just nineteen when he sailed from Massachusetts to California around the Horn. His older brother, John, had "opened the first store in Los Angeles," which meant of course the first shop by an "American." Francis married Workman's fifteen-year-old daughter, Antonia Margarita, in 1854, and again the wording of the event in some texts is rather taste-less: "the first couple with American names to be married in Los Ange-les." As the Mexican Republic ruled the town at the time of the wedding, to make the marriage legal, Temple entered the faith and was baptized a Catholic. He took the name Francis, and from documents we know that his original name was Phiny Fiske Temple. He was only five-foot-four, and the Mexican-Americans called him "Templito."

As a banker, Temple soon proved himself a failure. He lent money to almost anyone who needed it. In disgust, Hellman bought out his inter-ests in 1871, and said: "Mr. Temple's only qualification in a borrower was that he must be poor. I saw doing a banking business on *that* basis would soon leave *me* poor also, so I dissolved the partnership.''

Hellman then merged his banking interests with John Downey to form the Farmers & Merchants Bank. Temple felt a little put out—as a discard—and perhaps liking the title *Banker,* he went into partnership with his father-in-law, William Workman, and in November of 1871 in a new three-story edifice at Main and Spring, the Temple Block, there was a grand opening of the Temple & Workman Bank. John Downey came over to offer up a toast in California champagne, ''To Mr. Temple, and the prosperity of his new enterprise.''

With all this banking, it was felt that the city needed a little more in the way of property protection, and the same year the new bank opened, the Los Angeles Fire Company Number One was founded by some of the leading town dudes and sporting gentry, done up in uniforms from San Francisco. Their horses were furnished free by livery stable teams. The first team reaching the fire company's Amoskeag Steamer, a steam-powered pump, had the honor of dragging it to a blaze. The signal for ''horses wanted'' was the firing of a revolver in the air, and the gathering of nags followed—something out of Ben Hur's chariot race.

Lots that had sold for $1,000 were getting $3,000 a couple of years later. And it was often hard to get lumber to build on them. A brick kiln found it was worth more money to sell its firewood as lumber to builders than to bake bricks with it. As new buildings and new businesses arose, the town was developing a traffic problem.

The *Los Angeles Daily News* was frank about it all: ''It is now a settled fact that we are to have a large town,'' and a little later added, ''The old lethargic spirit, which has so long held us in its embrace, is breaking up and rapidly disappearing. The new era has dawned.''

As the historian Josephson stated, ''The development of the Great West during the '70's and '80's continued unabated. Its outward effect was one of extraordinary material progress, whose wonders were perpetually recited by the pioneers; while obstacles or deficiencies in the total plan were dismissed with that brimming optimism . . . particularly prom-

A PANIC IN WOOL

inent in the Westerner. . . . The Westerner had come from the East partly because he chafed under the restrictions of a well-organized society and partly because he had faith that, with an equal chance in a new country, he would be able to amass the wealth he had failed to win in the East.''

12 The Great Bandido

When I was a boy, reprints of the early dime novels were still being traded among us. When the villains in them weren't bloodthirsty Indians of predictable behavior, or sly Oriental "yellow devils" planning their evil deeds in the scent of joss sticks and opium, they were Mexicans (never called Mexican-Americans), usually pictured wrapped in sarapes and dedicated to the cowardly use of the

THE GREAT BANDIDO

knife and dagger. Frequently described as oily or greasy, they were referred to, as a group, as *Greasers*. (*They* called the whites *Gringos*.)

In actual fact southern California had a large, placid, family-loving Mexican-American population, some of them robbed of their land grants, their best ranches lost in forced or rigged "tax sales." These once proud *caballeros* were referred to as "of Spanish descent," the young women as *señoritas*. The majority of the Mexican-Americans, however, were poor, many on a poverty level, and were never spoken of as anything but of Mexican origin, never as Spanish. In reality, both groups were also of Indian descent to a more or less degree, with a touch of black tinting here and there. (As were many of the native sons classified, in optimism, as white.)

There were, of course, Mexican-American badmen. And every American road gang of highwaymen or stock rustlers usually had an individual known as "Mex." Some became part of western legend and myth as *bandidos,* western Robin Hoods, often falsely respected "as righting the wrongs done to our people by the Americans." Truth was, a bandit, an outlaw, was usually shiftless, a moron hastening toward a violent death, while he often practiced every cruelty and vile act he could in a desperate and meaningless life.

The most famous of all Mexican-American outlaws who became legends in California were Joaquin Murietta and Tiburico Vasquez. The southern California counties played out in full the final drama of the bandido Tiburico Vasquez, written of as "the Scourge of California." He, with a fellow caballero, Cleovaro Chavez, began to make crime history around Los Angeles in February 1874 at Coyote Holes Station (a U.S. map survey team changed it from its original name of Coyote Assholes). A miserable enough structure, the station stood at Walker Pass where it merged with the Los Angeles bullion trail that brought silver ore from the Cerro Gordo mines into the city for shipment north to the refineries. Here, on the morning of February 25th, the two badmen, Vasquez and Chavez, began their attack, firing their rifles into the walls of the shack. Vasquez yelled, "Everybody come out, or I burn the place down!"

Billy Raymond, the station keeper, was not present, having gone to the privy, but his wife and a half-dozen mule hands and horse drivers made for the door at his order. Vasquez announced himself by name as the famous bandido from up north (he had a pathological urge to always identify himself) and then is reported to have added, "Tell everyone to come out. It is the position only that I want. I am going to rob the stage when it arrives."

Someone with a bad ear certainly edited the bandit's speech into this clumsy but polite prose. Whatever the actual words, six men and Mrs. Raymond came outside, their hands in the air, and Vasquez's "burly lieutenant, the bloodthirsty Chavez" covered them with his Henry rifle. Vasquez collected their weapons and whatever they had in money and jewelry. Several other men appeared from the station stable where they had been bunking, and they too were ordered to turn over their valuables. A drinking party had been going on in the stable, and there were several drunks not fully aware of their danger. One of them pulled out his revolver and fired off a wavering shot at the bandit chief. It missed, and in return the drunk got a rifle slug in a thigh. Vasquez proudly said he could just as well have killed. "So next time I order, you obey."

The whole group, minus the wounded drunk, was sent off to lie low in the sagebrush behind the station and warned to remain still. The bandits took over the station and set themselves down to wait for the stagecoach.

It was two hours before a cloud of ochre dust showed that the stage heading up-country was about to enter Coyote Holes Station. Four rather tired horses pulled the Concord coach, having come a hard haul from the mountain mining camp at Havilah. It was no ordinary trip; by the driver's side sat Mortimer W. Belshaw, kingpin of the Cerro Gordo mine holdings, now returning to Owens Valley from a business trip to San Francisco.

Vasquez cried: "Stop! Hands up!"

The driver braked the coach to a full stop and the passengers were ordered out. There were two passengers inside who came out without protest. One gave up $5 in coins and $10,000 in mining stock but held on to a pair of new gloves. He pleaded that in this foul weather he needed

THE GREAT BANDIDO

them to keep his hands warm. Vasquez shrugged, smiled, held up $2 of the passenger's money. "I'll buy them . . . give you two dollars for them."

Mortimer Belshaw, the mining king of Inyo County, was slim pickings for the outlaws. Twenty dollars in gold and only a silver watch, but the bandit chief did carry off Belshaw's new, polished cowhide boots.

The real hope for booty was the Wells Fargo box. However, when forced open it contained not coins or bills but only a set of heavy calf-bound lawbooks in transit from one legal eagle to another. Vasquez, a bit flummoxed by this, cursed the law even more than was his usual habit.

But then, clear as music, came the jingle of mule bells of the freight teams heading north to the Cerro Gordo mines. The mule skinners found themselves greeted at the station, not by meat, beans and drink, but by the two bandits who stripped them of what small valuables they had. Leaving the sixteen victims with a warning not to follow, Vasquez mounted his horse (in one jubilant version, "leaped on to his palomino steed") and rode off with his fellow bandit.

One passenger began to gather up his mining stock discarded all over the landscape, while Belshaw, now safe and throwing his weight around, commanded that four of the freight mules be harnessed to the stage to replace the worn-out horses, and soon he was off to spread the alarm that Vasquez was in the region and harassing rich men.

Vasquez contained in himself a wary confidence, a feeling of some greater mission. He saw himself progressing from a bandit to a Mexican-American underground fighter. Tiburico Vasquez the folk hero, the political rebel—or so he was to claim later. In the brush of the Solodad hills (his brother Chico was a Solodad citizen, and he had friends who lived along Tejon Pass and Lake Elizabeth) he hoped to rally around himself a dedicated band of camaradas, machos, loyal followers for a Mexican-American revolution against Los Angeles, San Diego and towns in between. It was to be a limited revolution against the American interlopers—to sweep down on them in the spring and raise the old Mexican cries of "California for the Mexicans!"

This coup d'état would need arms, horses and supplies, and for all that he needed U.S.A. dollars. Two attempts to raise a big war kitty had failed. Thirty thousand dollars of a payroll designated for the cattle king Henry Miller was supposed to be at Firebaugh's Ferry in the hands of the stationmaster, but no such sum turned up in a quick bandit raid. Next, the plan was to stop the southbound Southern Pacific pay train above Gilroy. Again, all went haywire when, against all rules, the train, which usually ran late, came through early before the gang could properly remove a steel rail to halt it. Destiny seemed to have an insensitivity to a folk hero's plans.

As rumors filtered through that Vasquez was planning something startling, Sheriff William R. Rowland of Los Angeles County alerted his lawmen.

He had tried to flush Vasquez out of the hills and found it futile, so he now prepared extra arms and horses and waited for the band's next move.

The bandido turned revolutionary had failed to raise the funds needed to supply a rebel band; in fact, he had not even been able to raise any really impressive group of followers for El Movimiento.

On April 16th he led three fresh recruits and Chavez down from the hills for a look around at a ranch near El Monte owned by an Italian named Alessandro Repetto. Calling themselves sheepshearers, they were admitted into the ranch house and at once pulled out their pistols and announced they wanted money and wanted it right away. *Pronto!*

The Italian offered up all he had, $80, which they took, but told him he lied. Vasquez said, "I am informed you sold nearly ten thousand dollars' worth of sheep lately . . . you must have plenty money buried about the place somewheres."

The Italian said he had spent most of *that* money to buy land and had the figures and papers to prove it. The accounts the bandit examined showed that to be true (disproving some claims that Vasquez was illiterate and could not read or write). However, the accountings recorded that the rancher had a nice fat balance credited to him at the Temple & Workman Bank of Los Angeles.

Tiburico Vasquez, the most famous of all the Los Angeles bandits, became a folk hero who was chased all over what is now the modern city. This photo was sold to thousands of admirers.

Sheriff William A. Rowland, a hero who captured bandits and led posses. (Ross collection)

Vasquez suggested that Repetto could "lend" him $800 and he would be repaid in thirty days with interest. The rancher didn't seem to be impressed by the idea of a loan. Vasquez, with the pucker of a wine taster, announced *if* no loan, then Alessandro Repetto would hang from one of those fine olive trees on the ranch.

To show the rancher they meant business, Repetto was tied to one of his olive trees and two loaded pistols were pressed to his head, one in each ear. That did away with any reluctance to advance the loan, the rancher seeing that the imbecile game was serious. He wrote out the check and handed it to a young nephew observing all this, who was to hasten on horseback the six miles to the Los Angeles bank, cash the check and come back to save his uncle's hide. Vasquez added that if the boy wanted to keep his uncle whole and alive, he would just cash the check and *not* say a word about events that morning at the ranch. The boy riding off, Vasquez, who took pride in his cooking, set about preparing breakfast for his band.

On reaching the bank the boy was so nervous while facing a teller that the president of the bank, P. F. Temple, took over the questioning of the rancher's nephew. After a few stuttering replies, the boy broke into tears and confessed the entire nightmare situation at the ranch.

Sheriff Billy Rowland was sent for, heard the story and moved quickly. He made up three groups of lawmen, one to raise a posse in El Monte and move in from the rear; the second to ride for the Los Angeles River Pass and bottle that up in case the bandits picked that route in their retreat and Rowland himself headed seven hard-riding men. They went off in a dust cloud, heading down Aliso Street for the Italian's ranch.

The nephew pleaded with the banker for the cash, insisting the bandits would kill his uncle as soon as any of the sheriff's groups were sighted. The banker gave the boy a bag containing $500 in gold and off rode the nephew, taking turns only he knew in the hills beyond the river. Soon he had passed Rowland's group and reached the ranch before them.

He put the bag of gold on the table and said nothing. The bandits, mighty pleased, began to divide the gold coins at once. A sentinel posted at the window cried out that a lot of riders carrying rifles had just topped a far rise. Grabbing the gold, the bandits mounted and rode off jubilantly. Rowland's party sighted them and gave chase, but their horses were winded, while the bandits' mounts were rested, and soon the sheriff's men were outdistanced. The bandits rode in the direction of Pasadena to colony holdings near Arroyo Seco. By nightfall, Sheriff Billy Rowland had lost them. The bandits on their comic-opera raid, backed by firepower and luck, had gotten clear away.

The newspapers felt outraged and sounded the call for action: "Vasquez and his gang must be exterminated at whatever cost. We cannot tolerate a banditti dominating this section of the country with perfect impunity. . . . Let our people raise means and equip a party of intrepid men to run down the gang. . . ."

Government, state government, now aided in the chase of the bandido Vasquez. Money in large sums was offered to help hunt down the outlaw. On May 8th, the governor of California put a cash value on the bandido's head, still free, free out there under an interminable expanse of bluesky.

EIGHT THOUSAND DOLLARS ALIVE!
SIX THOUSAND DOLLARS DEAD!

It was a temptation, and there were muchachos who could be tempted to betray a camarada. One of these went in secret and told Sheriff Billy Rowland that for a share of that big reward money he could lead the law to where the bandit chief was holed up. Rowland himself couldn't go after Vasquez, for the bandido's friends were watching every action of the sheriff, ready to report to Vasquez if he made a move.

It was decided that the sheriff would play possum and stay in town and that Under Sheriff Albert Johnson and City Detective Emil Harris would move out with a seven-man posse at one thirty in the morning. Emerging from the corral at Spring and Seventh streets, they rode off quickly, accompanied by their own war correspondent, George Beers of the *San Francisco Chronicle*. It seems that Los Angeles was already at this early date well aware of good publicity coverage for any of its events.

The hideout Vasquez had picked for himself, and where he had been at his ease for a month, belonged to a Smyrna immigrant who had come west in 1865, as an expert camel driver, a trade he had learned as a boy. Camels had been tried as western carriers by the United States Army, and they were in use during the construction of the Butterfield Stagecoach road.

The camel driver's ranch was near Nichols Canyon. He was known as Greek George, with a last name translated from some Smyrna original as Allen. The ranch was fairly well isolated, two miles past Cahuenga Pass on the south slopes of decomposed granite that made up the Santa Monica Mountains. (Today the site is the busy intersection of Santa Monica Boulevard and King's Road in Hollywood.) The bandit had grown careless. At noon on May 14th he was sitting in Greek George's kitchen, his guns in another room. His palomino horse was tied off nearby to a willow tree. Greek George was in Los Angeles watching Sheriff Rowland for any move against Vasquez. Present at the ranch were only Vasquez and a follower, *not* his right-hand man, Chavez, who was off some place bushwhacking. Also in the house were George's wife and their infant.

The Johnson posse crowded itself into a farm wagon and got two Americans to drive it up to Greek George's ranch, Mexicano, where the informer had sworn they'd find the bandit. A hundred yards from the ranch, the posse leaped out and were seen by George's wife. She gave a shrill alarm and tried to close the kitchen door. Emil Harris wedged the door open with the barrel of his rifle just before she could get the bar in place. He slammed his way into the kitchen in time to see Vasquez dive out of a window.

Harris shouted, "There he goes!" and fired through the window at the fleeing bandit. Another lawman, Frank Harley, outside the building lifted his shotgun and got a load off at Vasquez who dropped prone on the earth. But he sprang up at once and started to dash for his horse. Just then, around a corner, came the newspaperman, George Beers, with a rifle at the ready. Point-blank, he got off a snap shot, hitting the bandit in a shoulder. Later it was said it was dirty pool for a reporter to take sides like this and be a part of the capture. Yes, or no, Vasquez, facing the armed reporter, put up his hands.

"Don't shoot. You've got me."

He was bleeding from not very serious wounds in his arms and one leg. The posse moved forward warily and with weapons ready. For once the bandit did not admit his identity.

"You boys have got me. My name is Alejandro Martinez."

Under Sheriff Johnson shook his head. "Nope. Seen your photograph for years. I know you're Tiburico Vasquez."

"Been a damn fool. Shouldn't have tried to get away."

As they dressed his wounds, he added, "I'm a goner." (Beers reported it as "I'm gone up.") The reporter assured the bandit his wounds were neither fatal nor serious. This seemed to cheer Vasquez up, and he became again his own unique image of himself, almost unctuous.

"Take care of me. Fix up my wounds." He winked at the posse. "You boys get eight thousand dollars, eh! So if you let me die, you only get six." He was smiling as he added, "You'll make two thousand dollars just for being kind."

It was clear from this statement that (like so many other later Hollywood figures) Vasquez read his publicity with some interest and pride.

THE CHASE CONTINUED

In the adobe city hall on Spring Street, back in Los Angeles, the long afternoon had droned away; the clerk was reading some dull text when the meeting became aware that outside on the street a few hundred citizens were gathering, passing to each other some exciting news. It boiled down to: "They got Vasquez! Vasquez is captured!"

Officeholders, clerks, councilmen, loafers, political freeloaders, all ran into the street. Sure enough, in the jailyard, in a wagon, lay the bandaged figure of "the terror of California." He seemed rather a small man and not at all the ferocious-looking bandit of legend. In fact, he was rather mild-looking, with a bit of a moustache, a neat chunk of beard. It seemed to many a sellout of a dream to accept this man as "the desperate brigand who had ruled the highways for years."

In a cell, the bandit was introduced to Sheriff Billy Rowland and a bottle of prime whiskey was produced; glasses were filled and Vasquez showed charming manners. Lifting his glass of the potent bourbon, he offered a toast with true elegance.

"To the President of the United States!"

The bandit was well on his way to becoming a folk hero, as those privileged to visit his cell observed how brave he was—not a flinch or a moan when the county doctor, a notoriously clumsy man, probed the wounds. The physician also commented on the bandit's courage and told the sheriff, "Why, he's still game for a long day's ride." The sheriff reserved any reply he had on *that* idea.

Film stars of a later era would have understood the bandit's endorsing a product as part of being a celebrity, for an evening newspaper carried a large advertisement:

> **VASQUEZ SAYS THAT MENDELL MEYER HAS THE FINEST AND MOST COMPLETE STOCK OF DRY GOODS AND CLOTHING.**

What, and *if,* Vasquez was paid for this plug, we don't know.

The bandit held daily court in his cell. In the next few days it was one of the daily pleasures of the town to go to visit the cheerful and charming prisoner. Some ladies brought flowers, and one a health-giving pot of broth. A photographer carried his bulky wet-glass-plate camera into the cell for the bandit to pose for an official picture. Copies suitable for framing could be had for 25 cents each at the Cottage Photography Gallery on Main Street, just across from the Pico House.

Some of the celebrity shine rubbed off on others, among them the Italian rancher, Alessandro Repetto, who had made the forced "loan" to the bandit.

Said Repetto to the prisoner: "Signor, as far as I am concerned, you can settle that little account with God Almighty. I have no hard feelings against you."

Vasquez, grandstanding a bit, replied he hoped to repay the loan.

The Italian said, "No, no, I don't expect to be repaid . . . but . . . if you ever resume operations, do not come for another visit to my house."

"I will take the earliest moment to pay you, Señor Repetto. I am a cavalier with the heart of a cavalier."

(This entire conversation has the sound of a journalist with a lead ear, but other accounts seem to indicate that the content, if not the wording, was close to what took place between two men showing off. The bandit had a certain *dignidad y unidad*—dignity and composure.)

The Los Angeles Merced Theatre announced a burlesque entitled *The Life of Vasquez.* The bandit himself coached the actor who was to play him in the show, and loaned him some of his costumes for a truer lifelike portrait. Vasquez went as far as to offer to "myself play the leading character, that is if Sheriff Rowland would agree." The sheriff decided on bars, not footlights.

The Life of Vasquez, without the original playing the bandit chief, was a howling success, a "real knee-slapper." No script has survived and, as with some of the lost plays of Shakespeare, we only surmise its contents.

Nine days after he was captured—in the late afternoon of May 23rd— Vasquez was taken from the jail, put into a closed hack and rushed to the railroad station by three lawmen, the sheriff in attendance, all done to foil any rescue attempt by Chavez and any of the band still running loose.

THE CHASE CONTINUED

From the depot, Vasquez was taken to the side-wheeler *Senator* and shipped north to stand trial for some murders he had committed in Tres Pines. On February 23, 1875, at San Jose the verdict was guilty and Vasquez was sentenced to death. To be hanged, it was hoped, in a dignified ceremony, a cavalier to the end.

Chavez had made some bold talk about what would happen if his chief was executed. He sent written notice to the authorities. *"I have returned with the aim of disclosing the falseness of the evidence sworn against him, and if Vasquez should be hanged, to quickly mete out a recompense. . . . the just and the unjust alike will be reached by my revenge. . . ."*

Who wrote this out (or invented it for Chavez) we don't know. Chavez himself was illiterate.

Chavez never amounted to much as a bandido leader after Vasquez, noose around his neck, dropped through the trap of the gallows on March 19th. Legend recounts his last words were *"Hasta el infierno"* ("till we meet in hell"). Chavez, trying to show he meant to revenge his leader's passing, five days later attacked Little Lake Station on the silver bullion road. In another raid to get barley feed for his horses at Granite Springs, he rode off, announcing:

"Adios, you catch me maybe."

Chavez went on robbing and moving around, and from his late master he also took to the habit of announcing himself to his victims. To one rancher who pleaded that his animals were all he had, the bandit answered, "Si, señor, they are your horses. I am Chavez. I do not take from a poor man. Rich man—*caraho!*"

In November, with a reward of $2,000 on his fat body, two bounty hunters cornered Chavez while he was unarmed, killing him with seventeen buckshots fired into his paunch. His band was captured in San Diego County and hanged, as one record states, "to the nearest cottonwood trees . . . ," showing "the rest of California how to treat bandidos. . . ."

14   The L.A. & S.P. R.R.

Phineas Banning was the genius of southern California transportation. There are many references to his jollity, booming voice and hearty laughter. There was also a fury in the man. He had a rawhide and flint side. When his brother-in-law was murdered, he appeared in court, pulled out a pistol and tried to gun down the killer. Only a football rush by people in the courtroom prevented another murder. Stopped that day from public assassination, he organized a vigilance group (read: lynch mob) that snatched up the killer from the law and hanged him from a gate crossbeam. Before condemning Banning we must see him for what he was: a man living the life of his times, and yet an able organizer who would today be able to run General Motors or U.S. Steel.

In preparing short biographies, free of the "official" lives, I have been struck by the recurring pattern in so many of the lives of the doers and makers of California, and particularly of Los Angeles. Phineas (it is too bad the naming of children today has lost its daring) came west from Delaware at the age of twenty in the year 1851. Already able and smart, he established a transportation and freighting line between Los Angeles and its nearest harbor, San Pedro, a score of miles away.

For Los Angeles, with hopes of becoming a great Pacific port, was twenty-one miles from the sea. Its river for most of the year was a dried-out ditch with a few puddles. So Banning became the artery that kept the town alive to traffic to and from the sea. By 1854 the Banning services consisted of forty wagons, fifteen stagecoaches and 500 mules to service them. By the time Banning was twenty-five, he was the freight-carrier king of the region. He opened regular wagon freighting to Salt Lake and sent his wagons to Fort Yuma, Arizona, virgin territory for California. His foulmouthed mule skinners moved his wheels a hundred miles north to Fort Tejon.

Big, healthy, animal enough to lead a killing mob, expansive and a remarkable administrator, he delighted in making money—and would not excuse his excesses, as J. D. Rockefeller did, by claiming "God gave me my money." Also, unlike so many men who piled up wealth and watched it, sheltered it, Banning enjoyed spending, enjoyed whatever it was money could buy. To have his own outlet to the sea, he set up next to San Pedro, a place he called Wilmington (named after the capital of his home state). Here he erected his two-story mansion (now a historic item) and entertained as would a king at lavish dinners—with table settings of Sevres—often seating a hundred guests. He was no retiring host but led in the telling of jokes, in the laughter, the mocking or teasing of

Phineas Banning, one of the first great men of money of Los Angeles.

the guests, enjoying jests against himself. The revels of a Tudor king are suggested without—as far as the records show—the sexual freedom.

It was part of Banning's way of doing business. Feed 'em, charm 'em, treat 'em square, and you'll get their haulage business. During the Civil War the officers of Fort Drum in Wilmington had eaten so much of his food and drunk up so many cases of his wine and whiskey, it seemed only proper that the freighting of Army supplies should go to the Banning lines. Ambrose Bierce was to write of practical politics, "The conduct of public affairs for private gains." For all the napkins of crisp linen, the solid silver service, crystal wine goblets, Banning prided himself on being, as one letter said, "just folk and a rough diamond."

Banning liked honors and during the war when appointed brigadier general of a California Militia brigade (that never existed and was never seriously considered even on paper), he appointed a full staff of officers, all in grand uniforms, and insisted, in those serious and difficult times for the Union, on being called "General Banning." (Vanity in big men who get things done, as Churchill was to discover, is acceptable.)

Banning saw that owners of horses and mules would always try to act as his rivals in control of harbor shipping and the traffic from the town to the port. It occurred to him that gaining control of a rail line, an exclusive right-of-way over the route, would be a judicious move, so in 1865 he had himself elected to the State Senate, and no one was surprised when he pushed through a bill for the building of a railroad from Los Angeles to San Pedro. There was, however, strong opposition to having the tax-payers of the county lay out a subsidy for the building of the railroad line.

Putting on pressure, giving bigger dinners, talking money to the right people, Banning, by 1868, had a charter for something called the Los Angeles & San Pedro R.R. And the city had come around to asking the voters to approve bonds in the amount of $225,000 to buy into the S.P. & L.A. R.R.'s $500,000 capital issue.

It was a hot and heavy "yes" vote-seeking campaign. Banning used everything—banners, booklets, circulars, speechmakers—to het up the newspapers into backing him (he was a heavy advertiser), and he was a force of enterprise and progress to the town. The whole project, it was pointed out, was that *this* small rail line would be the first link in the chain to connect them with the giant Southern Pacific when it moved south, and it would, as the *News* said in its best type, be a move "to force the Southern Pacific Line Railroad through the Los Angeles Valley . . . give rapid growth, not only to Los Angeles, but to all Southern California."

Even so, it was only by thirty-nine votes (some of them dubious) that "Phineas Banning nicked the taxpayers for his railroad." It should be pointed out in all fairness that the project was needed and worthwhile, even if the dream of a transcontinental tie-up would not be as simple or as honorably furnished by the Southern Pacific as they thought.

In September 1878 a railroad gang set picks to the earth by Banning's own wharf on the Pacific (near what is now Avalon Boulevard). More than a year later, on October 26th, the L.A. & S.P. R.R. formally opened, carrying 1,500 men, women and children to the sea and back to attend the grand ball at the Los Angeles Depot. The Drum Barracks Military Band set themselves into a dance tune and 2,000 people danced and moved about, many until dawn.

Banning, once down to a timetable, set a tight schedule of two trains a day, $5 a ton for freight and $2.50 a head for each passenger. Both categories continued to travel to near capacity. Of course there is, and were, more rewards in building a rail line than in getting it running. The big money was in real estate near both railheads and at vital points between. Land values around the depot rose like skyrockets. The depot on a busy day was a sight to satisfy anyone holding land rights or rail stock and watching the town grow.

As the gambler said when told he was sitting in on a crooked game, "I know, but it's the only game in town," so to Los Angeles, it might be a small silly line, but it was the only railroad in southern California. A sample, the boosters said, of what they were sure would someday connect, "make junction," in railway talk, with the Southern Pacific. *If* it could be lured to pass through town. It was noticed that the turkey buzzards in the sycamores had moved away.

A newspaper editor admitted "we never fully made up our minds to be anything more than a country town, until work was commenced on the San Pedro & Los Angeles Railroad."

Brave words, but as one letter writer noted, "I don't share all this jolly thinking its going to be so easy to come to any fair deal with those sons-ofbitches Stanford, Crooker [sic] Hopkins and Huntington. They'd skin a grasshopper and sell its hide for leather."

But the Los Angeles boosters felt no fears, or at least expressed none in public.

The mystique of the frontier expressed by men like Banning, Widney and Downey was studied by the historian Frederick Jackson Turner in his essay *The Significance of the Frontier in American History* (1893): "The frontier is the line of most rapid and effective Americanization. . . . In short, at the frontier the environment is at first too strong for the man. He must accept the conditions which it furnishes, or perish. Little by little he transforms the wilderness, but the outcome is not the old Europe. . . . The fact is, that here is a new product that is American. . . ."

It served to explain, perhaps for some too simply, the things done that those who came later might be critical of. But it is good to hear:

the frontier is productive of individualism. Complex society is precipitated by the wilderness into a kind of primitive organization based on the family. The tendency is anti-social. It produces antipathy to control, and particularly to any direct control. The tax gatherer is viewed as the representative of oppression. . . . The result is that to the frontier the American intellect owes its striking characteristics. That coarseness and strength combined with acuteness and inquisitiveness; that practical, inventive turn of mind, quick to find expedients, that masterful grasp of material things, lacking in the artistic but powerful to effect great ends; that restless, nervous energy; that dominant individualism, working for good and for evil, and withal that bouyancy and exuberance which comes with freedom.

No one has better explained the strong men of "coarseness and strength," who built Los Angeles from a casual pueblo to a thrusting insatiable city. Some lived long enough to read Turner's essay.

BOOK III

POLITICS
AND
POLECATS

15 Send Us a Big Railroad

Los Angeles still needed a major railroad to connect it with the rest of the nation. Not enough were a weekly or biweekly ship, a couple of stagecoach lines on dreadful roads. "We're more than up shit creek with no paddle, we ain't even got a canoe" (a comment on local transportation overheard by a salesman at the Bella Union and reported home to an uncle in Boston).

POLITICS AND POLECATS

Los Angeles was pleased to hear in 1871 of the Railroad bill being framed by Congress. It was one of those progressive measures crossed with pork-barreling to fatten contractors, the railroads and right-of-way owners. And woe to the town that didn't have lobbyists and friends around Capitol Hill (read *The Gilded Age*). Such a town could end up miles from a railroad line (and often did) and die slowly, while some mud-puddle village would have the tracks, a new depot, a freight yard, cattle pens, and grow quicker than you could say the Southern Pacific.

The bill up for passing had one section that stipulated that the Southern Pacific track building south from San Francisco would pass through Los Angeles and *not,* as some special interests wanted, take the shortcut through Cajon Pass, east of Los Angeles by thirty miles. That would have made San Bernardino the major southern California city, and with the Texas Pacific tracking north from San Diego to connect, Los Angeles would have been frozen out and never heard the sound of train whistles from the big Baldwin locomotives.

As with all favor seekers among the fat cats in Washington ("all politicians are guilty until proven innocent"—Mark Twain), Los Angeles had a man on the ground to see that the Railroad bill of 1871 had inserted into it just five simple words, "by way of Los Angeles." The heavy courtship of the chairman of the Senate committee was left to Los Angeles' Benjamin D. Wilson, better known in California as "Don Benito." The local press hailed him as "a prosperous ranchero and fruit raiser, an influential and respected citizen . . . an old mountaineer and a gentleman in every sense of the word. . . ."

He was born in Tennessee in 1811 and was, "as a young man, a hunter and trapper in New Mexico," which meant a drifter looking for a querulous encounter with the main chance. He joined up with William Workman's wagon train to reach California in 1841. There he acquired Jurupa Rancho acres, and as one account of him has it, he led a good life "raising cattle, hunting grizzly bears, and leading expeditions against renegade Indians." A "renegade" Indian was any red man who didn't give up his weapons and retire to starve on a reservation, with the politically appointed Indian agent getting rich withholding supplies from his wards (the Indian reservation scandals of the Grant administration are still a remembered disgrace).

So overlooking a little Indian massacring, Don Benito "endeared himself to the native Californians." In the war with Mexico, when the Americans planned to seize California for the United States, Don Benito was captured at the battle of Chino. But with the end of the war, he became a spokesman for the Mexican-Americans and did it fairly. Whatever Don Benito advised was accepted by the *los Americano olvidados* as the right course to follow.

When in 1868 the railroad route problem first began to simmer, he came away from the ranch to be elected as state senator on a platform of "seeking a transcontinental railroad for Los Angeles." He supported the "Five Per Cent Act," which made California counties cough up a subsidy to the railroads of 5 percent of their assessed value to sweeten the attraction for the railroads to build rail lines through the counties. Eight counties, including Los Angeles, decided they might go along with the deal.

So when the Railroad Act of 1871 was up before Congress, Don Benito was in Washington, at his own cost, wheeling and dealing with vigor to get the words "by way of Los Angeles" written into it and solidly.

On March 3rd in the offices of the *Star* the telegraph keys clicked off a message from Don Benito in Washington:

THE SOUTHERN PACIFIC RAILROAD BILL HAS PASSED.

The *Star* got out extras, and tar barrels and privies and fences were burned in vast bonfires of celebration. Citizens marched in torchlight parades, and everybody who could make it rushed downtown to stand around and cheer. There was often someone at a street corner making a speech about Los Angeles' Coming of Age. The balcony of the Bella Union held a bevy of important speakers who polished up the theme of progress, growth and increased prosperity.

However, Los Angeles was dealing with the notorious Southern Pacific (read Frank Norris' *The Octopus*), run by the Big Four, £eland $tanford (as Ambroṡe Bierce spelled it) and three partners. The Big Four were (according as to how your bias viewed them) four of the greatest empire builders of the expanding West, men who made California a major state, gave employment to thousands. *Or* four of the biggest thieves, looters of the national treasury, unsavory exploiters of public property, bribers of judges, congressmen and senators. You could take your choice and prove *both* estimates were close to the truth.

The Southern Pacific surveyor crews had already come to Los Angeles and laid out rail lines on maps to show just where all this would connect with the Southern Pacific coming south from San Francisco—on paper anyway.

The Southern Pacific by the spring of 1872 had its tracks in place as far as the San Joaquin Valley, and there by-passed the principal town, Visalia, by seven miles to punish it for not approving the subsidy.

Los Angeles took the lesson of Visalia (and where's the Visalia of yesterday?) to heart. Voices were heard to caution, to walk carefully when dealing with the Big Four.

The news was passed to Don Benito: "Nearly every merchant and lawyer in Los Angeles city I think could be induced to favor a subsidy." Even if Stanford was obligated by law to put rails through Los Angeles, "his power and influence at Washington could secure for him a change of charter . . . in case he needed it."

It was a time of calling the important citizens of Los Angeles together— 400 at the courthouse in May, a group headed by John Downey, Harris Newmark, Robert Widney, F. P. F. Temple, Phineas Banning and Don Benito. These men were not just representing the interests of Los Angeles, they *were* Los Angeles.

It was agreed to give the Southern Pacific the requested 5 percent of the county's valuation and to sweeten the pot by making up part of the sum with capital stock held in Banning's San Pedro Railroad. ("Big fish eat little fish," someone commented in a letter.)

A Committee of Thirty was appointed to carry the sacrificial offering north to the den of the Southern Pacific. Downey and Newmark in person presented the committee's decision to Stanford and Huntington. These Two of the Four demanded a *full* controlling share of the San

Pedro R.R., *not* just a chunk. Downey admitted that "the conditions are pretty hard." But Don Benito joined in the talks and after a month of wrangling, finger-pointing and back-slapping, there was an agreement. Los Angeles was moving with humility and forbearance.

Yes, the Southern Pacific would run its main trunk line through Los Angeles for a donation of $602,000 in rail stock and bonds. In fifteen months it promised to have rails laid twenty-five miles north to the San Fernando mission and twenty-five miles of finished right-of-way east to San Bernardino.

So far, so good, but there were those who felt the payment was a swindle, a bribe, blackmail. And some even were crying "stealing public funds!"

The Southern Pacific was represented by its special agent, Colonel William B. Hyde ("Colonels on the frontier were as common as whale shit at sea," attributed to General Sherman, who also said, "If I owned Hell and Texas, I'd rent out Texas and live in Hell"). Colonel Hyde came down to Los Angeles, loud, blustering, swinging his arms and making threats. There were fears the railroad would indeed pass them by if the loot was not forthcoming. "What guarantee have we that the Stanford Company may not finally discover . . . that the trunk will have to be built after all on the other side of the coast range to San Bernardino?"

Colonel Hyde, not playing the good guy, Dr. Jekyll, said that the Big Four were sorry they had ever seriously talked of the offer, and he was packing his portmanteau to catch the next steamer north. "The whole thing was hazardous to our own interests, and the shorter route of Cajon was best for us."

John Downey got angry at this bald, obvious pressure play.

"I would rather die than vote them a dollar under a threat."

However, the Big Four had a man on their side, H. K. S. O'Melveny, president of the City Council. (Harvey to his friends.) He let it be known, with a wink, "We . . . sometimes do unpleasant things from necessity."

O'Melveny, elected county judge, was spoken of as "a little given to bearing down on the lawyers" to bring his power to the attention of the

*After a great deal of skullduggery by Leland Stanford and the Southern Pacific,
Los Angeles was finally connected by land to San Francisco and the East. The
7,000-foot tunnel to Los Angeles was completed in 1876. (Ross collection)*

California! Dining car passengers viewing the new landscape while traveling in luxury. Air travel today is steerage compared to it. (Ross collection)

Overripe publicity came early to California, as seen in the railroad poster meant to lure newcomers to a land "without cyclones or blizzards."

SEND US A BIG RAILROAD

jury. About the Southern Pacific agreement he made no bones, "Pay 'em if you have to, get 'em any way you can." His pressure for the measure got the offer passed by the committee and moved to the county board of supervisors who were told to get rolling. Harvey told *them* they "had the destiny of this county in your hands."

Petitions for and against made the rounds, and it was decided to put the matter to a vote of the people. Let the public decide, the supervisors felt.

The Big Four acted as if they'd rather pass it all up and sent a telegram.

> IT IS A GOOD THING FOR THE COUNTY AND I HOPE IT IS FOR THE RAILROAD; BUT IT IS A BIG UNDERTAKING TO BUILD THAT AMOUNT OF ROAD AND WITHIN THE TIME SPECIFIED.
>
> LELAND STANFORD.

The city's newspapers were for Harvey O'Melveny and the Southern Pacific. Colonel Peel of the anti-payers warned paying did not mean prosperity. He recalled fifty towns "that gave large subsidies to have a railroad run through them, and that were literally gutted by the road."

It would take me a whole volume to detail, even in outline, the battle between Los Angeles and the Southern Pacific, which was waspish, vicious and loud. Colonel Hyde was back and loudly proclaimed the vote by the citizens on the deal was unlawful. And he had papers from the State's Attorney General on some legal technicalities proving it unlawful. But the election was called for anyway, and Colonel Hyde threatened to get orders invalidating the result (*if* it went against the railroad, that is). A new subsidy scheme was presented by the anti-Southern Pacific party.

Robert M. Widney was now a judge, and when Colonel Hyde put it to him that the railroad was abandoning the fight, Widney came out roaring for the Southern Pacific: "If the voters once understood the real facts, they'd vote the subsidy. . . ."

To help the railroad Widney produced a fourteen-page booklet. "What Subsidy Should I Vote For, or Shall I Vote Against Both?"

The *Star* printed it and every voter in the county got a copy. It proceeded to become a louder campaign—parades, torchlight.

Colonel Hyde bought the last round of drinks after the voting and left for the north with the winning voted-in contract in his luggage.

On paper the city had a transcontinental connection in its near future, had beaten San Bernardino's Cajon Pass route and San Diego's try to grab important track.

The *Star* remained wary: "We sincerely hope that nothing may ever occur which will cause us to regret the almost boundless confidence we have this day reposed in the great Southern Pacific Railroad Company."

In the nation the high-handed ways of the railroad kings did stir the anger of some decent people. Senator George Hoar could rise in Congress to speak out:

"When the greatest railroad of the world, binding together the continent and uniting the two great seas which wash our shores, was finished, I have seen our national triumph and exaltation turned to bitterness and shame by the unanimous reports of three committees of Congress that every step of that mighty enterprise had been taken in fraud."

But that didn't change anything. Corruption dominated most of Congress.

Huntington was a major briber to get laws he wanted. "It costs money to fix things," he wrote. "I believe with $200,000 we can pass our bill." He hated to waste money. "I fear this damnation Congress will kill me. It costs so much money to fix things. . . . We should be very careful to get a U.S. Senator from California that will be disposed to use us fairly. . . ." He was frank. "If a man has the power and won't do right unless he is bribed . . . it is a man's duty to go up and bribe. . . ." Of a congressman named Carr he wrote: Would he "agree to control his friends for a fixed sum . . . ?"

Los Angeles was dealing with the Devil.

16   Panic at the Banks

In the East in 1873 there was a great panic that historians are still trying to fully explain. In the West it was hoped the thing would not spread to the Pacific Coast. After all, a man could still feed his family with a rifle in most places beyond the Rockies and take fish on a trotline, or even grow himself a mess of greens and pick fruit. But the general depression was bigger than a mere setback, a condition beyond the ken of

POLITICS AND POLECATS

the ordinary American just aware of talk that it was the nabobs and promoters and the makers of big talk who in some way made a panic.
Nothing changed on the level of a need for working and eating and facing up to mean or hard times.

Los Angeles by 1875 knew the infection had come west, taking two
years to do it, when the telegraph keys tapped out the news that there
had been a run on the Bank of California and its president, William Ralston, one of the makers of San Francisco, locked the bank's doors and
announced the suspension of payment of money to depositors.

William Ralston's body was found the next day floating in the bay.

Businesses were failing all along the Pacific Coast, despair, suicide and
embezzlement in their train. Bankers in Los Angeles smiled, patted their
increasing girth and kept insisting that *their* institutions were solid as
bedrock. Announced Henry Ledyard, cashier of the Temple & Workman
Bank, run by Francis Temple for William Workman, "The Los Angeles
banks . . . are *all* sound." The Farmers & Merchants Bank proudly announced, "Our bank was never in a better condition, we have now in
our vaults twice as much coin as is needed in the transaction of our business." The F. & M., headed by John Downey and Isaiah Hellman, who
was away in Europe with his family at the health spas, was a bank in
which people had confidence.

Francis Temple was not cut out to be a banker. He left most of the details to his cashier, Ledyard, a Canadian, who also was secretary to
Temple's Cerro Gordo Water Company. When things were going well
with a bank, and the cigars were good Havana, a bit of slack here and
there did not matter. But now that the local bankers were protesting a bit
too much their soundness, the nervous depositors began to see in great
horror the truth that the public never admits to itself: that when they put
their good money into a bank, the money *does not remain in the bank
vaults* but is disposed of in various, usually legal, ways.

So began a local panic. By noon of August 27, long lines of shoving,
frightened people were trying to pull out their savings and business accounts from the two banks. It was a Friday afternoon, and sensible peo-

PANIC AT THE BANKS

ple should have been planning for country rides and family picnics, to get drunk, go hunting or fishing or make love. Instead, the citizens were waving bankbooks and checkbooks and crying out, "We want *our* money! We want it *now.*"

To impress the crowds of worrywarts, both banks piled up rows of twenty-dollar coins, called double eagles. More were coming from the vaults. Gold was real and didn't melt like snowflakes. You could heft it, juggle it in the palm of your hand.

"Both banks I saw were packed tight as dried peas in a bag, and more shoving to get in. The lucky ones grabbed up their bags of gold and shoved their way clear to the doors. Outside on Main Street I could see people gathered like they were forming a lynch mob. Even those who didn't have two bits or two dimes to rub together on deposit, enjoyed the joshing and cursing of banks and bankers" (a letter).

Downey, the strong man, offered Temple, the kindly one, gold from his own vaults if Temple ran low on cash. Downey was still in the casual mood of—hell, it would pass over once people saw that gold coins would continue to be paid out. He alerted the business houses, all firms with legal tender, to empty their strongboxes, their safes, and get them to the bank. Downey's friends didn't let him down. They came with their sacks and japanned tin boxes to show confidence in the man and in the city.

By three o'clock, closing time, the vaults were nearly empty. The doors were pushed shut against an angry, confused, despairing mob, locked and bolted. The crowds muttered, then seemed to accept that the banks would be able to pay in the morning, and went about their business or to their homes. All were wondering how such a thing could be, and some began to think about tomorrow—would there be payment?

There was a meeting that night of bank managers, cashiers, stockholders and bookeepers. A few hours, they agreed, had seen the withdrawal of $125,000. Downey could hold out; Temple had to confess that a run on his bank tomorrow would ruin him. He'd have to close for good. Downey was well aware that one bank closing would only turn his own depositors into a frenzied mob demanding their money from him

An early California bank. The scales on the left were to weigh gold. Ladies felt the place was safe enough to visit.

A run on a California bank when the banking system was not as solid as the building. Harper's Weekly, 1875.

and pulling him down with Temple. How he wished Hellman were there to advise him.

The thing to do, most agreed, was to announce a temporary suspension of payment by *both* banks. They would negotiate loans from still solvent banks in San Francisco and reopen when the population had cooled down its fears and was able to think logically and realize that the banks had reserves and solid assets.

A cable went out to Hellman to hurry home. Downey knew Hellman would not approve of their closing to save Temple's bank. Still the deed was done.

> WE ARE COMPELLED TO CLOSE OUR RESPECTIVE BANKS FOR THIRTY DAYS FROM DATE.

The dreaded announcement appeared like a warning against lepers on both bank doors, and it was clear now to the citizens of Los Angeles that the eastern panic had come West. For the ordinary depositor it was disaster. The well-off banking transactions would go on (the newspapers were happy to announce) through the two big wholesale houses on Los Angeles Street. "Checks up to $250.00 will be honored. . . . In a few days trade will resume its customary channels and this passing ripple upon its surface be forgotten. . . ."

Not all the ripples, even if the press kept pointing out that the depositors' money had been converted into solid investments, into brick, stone, new business buildings, dwellings, improvements, cattle, sheep, more orchards. Land that had cost $20 an acre a year ago was going for $50 to $150 an acre today. Little solace to people who hadn't invested in land.

The weak personality in the banking crisis was the kindness, indifference or just stupidity of Francis Temple.

The biggest merchant in town, Harris Newmark, admitted, "Anybody could borrow money [from Temple's bank] with or without proper security. . . . unscrupulous people hastened to take advantage of the situation." Others said of Temple, with that sad shrug Americans have for men who don't measure up to making it, "Ill-fitted for a successful broker. . . ." "The unconscious victim of boomers and schemers."

Isaiah Hellman—"Money has to make money was Isaiah Hellman's motto"—made the trip back from Europe after getting cable news of the panic, in the then record time of twenty-three days. By September 29th, getting off the Telegraph Stage, he was back in his office at Downey's side in their Farmers & Merchants Bank and scowling at Downey with an "unpartner-like" look. Hellman had detoured just long enough to visit San Francisco, and there to arrange through his integrity, honesty and business success in the past, the loans he needed for their bank.

Also, the steamer *Orizaba* was making runs of gold coins to the bank, so it was clear Hellman knew what banking meant. He raised hell with Downey about the suspended payments, "I have always kept from sixty to seventy-five percent of the deposits in our vaults. . . . The bank should have been kept open."

As a result of their disagreement he demanded and got Downey's resignation. The doors of the bank opened at once, with Hellman himself smiling coldly behind the counter piled high with gold coins.

Hellman's touch worked. For *every* single dollar withdrawn, three were deposited. Next day it was five dollars *in,* to one *out.*

Temple's bank, however, remained locked and San Francisco wasn't giving him a red cent in help. Only someone like E. J. "Lucky" Baldwin might take advantage of him to strike a hard bargain. By taking chances and investing wisely, Baldwin was to become a Comstock silver millionaire and enter American legend. Until senility came years later, he was in reality a hardheaded opportunist.

He offered Temple a $210,000 loan at 1¼ percent interest *per month* in exchange for a mortgage on the Temple and Workman and the extensive Sanchez (a helping friend) ranch lands. Workman and Sanchez sadly agreed it was "the only game in town" and took it.

The Temple bank reopened with Francis Temple behind the counter piled high with gold coins. The citizens gave him three cheers, and three more, and palms were outstretched to shake the hand of an honest man and a banker. Such is the confidence in the sight of solid cash that when three o'clock, closing time, was banged out by the wall clock, only $20,000 had been withdrawn and $90,000 put *in*.

There was nothing more to do but give Francis Temple a big feed at the Pico House, a splendid banquet actually, attended by Lucky Baldwin and by forty of the big moneymen of Los Angeles. A local editor reported it as the "finest supper ever given in Los Angeles." Mayor Prudent Beaudry (again the wonderful choice of first names in that period) said the right words and the party—in Rabelaisian glee—didn't come to an end until one in the morning with three more cheers for Temple and Lucky Baldwin, "the banker's friend." Temple, in a piqué waistcoat, was a happy man.

Sentiment was stronger than sense, and Francis Temple, who had twice proved himself a dud in the handling of money, was elected city treasurer of Los Angeles. It was the one bright spot before the final ruin of Temple and the bank. Temple was like some God-cursed Greek figure, doomed by the fates, a frontier tragic hero whose life could not be budged from its ordained destiny to end badly. Temple was not of the stuff of the folk hero Simon Suggs, who warned that "it's good to be shifty in a new country." Temple was too casual, too easygoing. He did not heed the advice of J. P. Morgan, given during the Civil War: "We are going some day to show ourselves to be the richest country in the world in natural resources. It will be necessary to go to work, and to work hard, to turn our resources into money. . . ."

Temple lacked the all-devouring interest in money—the joy in balanced books, the viewing of a well-stocked vault. He liked being a banker—the respect, the title. Little more. What could he make of men who wrote: "Through all the grades I see the same all-pervading, all-engrossing anxiety to grow rich. This is the only thing for which men live here. Money is chiefly the object for which all men contend, its true worth and character. We live in a funny time—we nearly double our capital in a year" (Jay Cooke).

17 Francis Temple Goes Down

The Lucky Baldwin first-aid money transfusion to the Temple & Workman Bank served not as a life-giving fluid, but merely a shot in the arm. The town had now seen Temple go down twice, and the talk continued that while he was a kindly man, he was not much of a banker with which to trust your poke. People didn't rush to the bank to withdraw their funds, but slowly, and in bits, and without hurry, in almost imperceptible visits, many managed to close out their accounts or leave a mere token sum, a quixotic gesture that promised small losses.

In January 1876 the Baldwin money was running out and soon Baldwin himself had to cover withdrawals of $40,000, feeling for a moment that his coverage would in time be made up by deposits. But beyond that he informed Temple not a penny more. January 12th, danger signals up, the Los Angeles bankers had a meeting and Francis Temple put his plight to them.

Gentlemen, the bank can't go on. There was nothing left to do but sum up the bank's assets, study the bookkeeping and figure out what could be done in settlement. E. F. Spence, cashier of the newly formed Los Angeles Commercial Bank, and a real estate promoter, Dan Freeman, were given the salvage task.

So just a month after its gala reopening, Temple & Workman closed their doors for good. And the voices of panic were heard in the city. How safe was any bank? I. W. Hellman spoke up to defend the position of his Farmers & Merchants Bank. "I refer you to the formidable array of coin as evidence that we have been preparing and are prepared for any contingency."

The creditors of Temple's bank looked over the ruins and grew dour. Depositors, cutting their losses, were selling out their bank balances there at 60 to 75 cents on the dollar, and doing no land-rush business.

The assignees reported strange procedures as they brought in their statements of just *where* the bank stood. Assets on paper were $2.5 million, but it had to be pointed out that the assets were not real: "Some of the notes are not worth the paper on which they are written." There were shady unscrupulous debtors, overdrawn accounts and the uncollectable loans were unbelievable. A newspaper, the *Los Angeles Daily Republican,* pointed out that borrowers "who could hardly get credit for five dollars, are debtors to the bank for thousands of dollars."

The bookkeeping, while not dishonest, was pretty much hit and miss. The official report was grim: "There were no indexes to the books, and no posting has been done since 1872. . . . a number of notes due the

FRANCIS TEMPLE GOES DOWN

bank were almost outlawed . . . placed in the hands of attorneys for collection. . . . [But] If immediate suits were instituted against all the debtors . . . all the lawyers of Los Angeles county would hardly be sufficient." It had been banking immersed in futilities.

As for the assets of Temple and his father-in-law, while they were assessed at $700,000, they were mostly in landholdings on which Lucky Baldwin had first call with his first mortgage.

To prove that Temple actually didn't know what transpired, on March 29th the assignees swore out a complaint against Temple's cashier, Henry Ledyard, accusing him of embezzling the sum of $16,000. He spent the night in jail, but the case was dropped when all one could prove was that Ledyard was a pretty rotten bank manager, and for that he was not indicted.

William Workman was by then an old man. He had never interfered in the management of the bank by his son-in-law. Workman was an honorable man. He had led the first wagon train across the desert to the coast. He had made for himself and his family a good life at his Puente ranch. It was all too confusing to him how the innocent could become involved, to where one's pride and past deeds were sullied. On May 29th, William Workman put a bullet through his head.

The *Los Angeles Republican,* which represented, it felt, "God and prosperity," gave as the cause of suicide the fact that Workman "had been impressed with a morbid fear that the assignees would turn him penniless from his homestead, and to save himself from the disgrace, took his life. He was driven to his death by the scoundrels who managed the bank and they are responsible before God for his blood."

This sad death of a good man, the collapse of a major bank, brought back the panic, and Los Angeles felt that the boom years were over. The sure sign for that, as always, was the fall in land values. Unimproved land fell from $100 an acre to $30. The rise in the assessed value that had gone up $3 million a year leveled off. Half a dozen new towns set up around the rim of Los Angeles died without attracting their first owners. The Los Angeles Immigration and Land Co-operation Association, a long title for a short-lived land company, went down, with its subdivisions Artesia and Pomona going back to scrub and wild vetch grass.

As for Francis Temple, "broken by calamity" and humiliated, he was relieved of his public duties by a paralytic stroke, and retired to his La Merced Rancho. On his place he had had enough sense to avoid attachment, by the simple scheme of putting it in his wife's name. But there was no peace. Writs and attachments, legal executions followed. The sharp, merciless lawyers continued circling him like wolves a fallen buffalo. His mind began to go. In April 1880 apoplexy released him from all earthly debts.

The *Express* mourned his passing as one of the men who had contributed the most "to turn our city from a slow growing Spanish-American pueblo into a center of commerce. . . ." And today's commerce does remember him by Temple Street in downtown Los Angeles.

18 Water

By 1900 the water level of Los Angeles was so low that schemes were presented for going long ways to get it—steal it if they had to. The leading landowners and property holders, land developers, became aqueduct minded. By November 1913 an engineer, William Mulholland, built the Los Angeles Owens Valley Aqueduct. It crossed great mountain ranges and fearful deserts, a most marvelous engineering task. The naïve Owens Valley citizens, hardworking farmers, felt this was robbery; so there was a kind of a ranch war to keep the water, save the valley. Dynamite was used. But Los Angeles knew its power over the state and was ready to swallow those parts of California it needed. Los Angeles managed to get a law passed so that it could buy up almost the entire Owens Valley, including the towns. A horrendous crime to some, progress to others. With the adding of the Mono Basin, the waters rushed 338 miles to Los Angeles' thirsty needs. Besides this, the Metropolitan Water District of Southern California reached farther east and built Hoover Dam on the Colorado River's Black Canyon. Years and years of seeking water—by June 1941 a billion pent-up gallons of water a day was flowing west. Los Angeles stalked water the way a military strategist studied points of attack.

The hunt for water never ended. Northern California streams were tapped in exchange for portentous platitudes by speechmakers. A 444-mile aqueduct was no problem, not even pumping it up 2,000 feet to get it over the Tehachapi peaks, where the last native eagles with their amber irises watched the waters pass.

The Colorado River steal was bitterly fought in court by Arizona and Nevada, and after ten years, to the delight of lawyers on both sides, the California and Arizona case came before the United States Supreme Court. That was a sort of flatulent standoff, with neither side gaining any full victory. But enough of the Colorado waters flowed west for the nearly 8 million citizens in Los Angeles County to find water when they wanted it—from half a glass to swallow a headache pill for a hangover to thousands and thousands of brimming swimming pools. (By the end of this century Los Angeles expects to have a super nuclear-fueled plant able to convert the Pacific Ocean into fresh water.)

More water meant more building, fewer farms, orchards, wild country. Earthquakes never fazed developers and builders. They had their lobbyists and would in time win the battle against height and zoning restrictions. High-rise structures would shoot upward with no regard as to the fact that they could not always be rented. Insurance companies, union pension funds, even, it was hinted, Mafia "washed" money would turn Los Angeles into a city of lofting skylines. Buildings of forty and fifty stories were predicted (they came in the 1960s), even though scientists warned of the great fault that ran through the county which would produce a giant earthquake, and soon.

A front-page news item in the *Los Angeles Times* in the fall of 1973 shows that southern California's water problems continue to cause worries:

An Agreement designed to end a 12-year international dispute by improving the quality of salt-laden Colorado River water delivered to Mexico was announced. The settlement, which will cost the United States a minimum of $115 million in new water projects, was signed by U.S. and Mexican commissioners of the International Boundary and Water Commission in Mexico City.

The commission's order failed to specify all the water facilities the United States must build to achieve the agreement's goals, but officials said they include major projects in Arizona and Southern California. . . . the settlement would have no effect on the quantity of water available to Southern California cities and agricultural areas or to other states that use Colorado River water.

Seventy-five percent of the water used in Southern California comes from the Colorado. Of the 75%, about one-third is delivered to Southern California's populous urban coastal areas.

Those who saw the film *Chinatown* may not be aware that it was based in part on actual facts of skullduggery in getting water to Los Angeles. However, the melodrama covered up a lot of facts pointing to the *real* stealers, the city's "best people," who benefited by bringing water to their landholdings.

L ike Caesar's Gaul, the history of the *Los Angeles Times* is divided into three parts. Or rather, one can, as a historian, write about it fairly only as three different, distinct newspapers—each provocative, ofte.. insolent, usually insisting it was the whole truth. *Times* I was the fin-de-siècle newspaper of Harrison Gray Otis and his son-in-law. *Times* II was the publication of Harry Chandler and his son Norman. *Times* III is the present newspaper (1977), published by Otis Chandler, great-grandson of the founder. From personal acrimony to a good readable publication has come the richest press dynasty in the world.

Times I was taken over by Otis in 1881 and became a big, feisty, rather bigoted publication. Under Harry Chandler *Times* II saw itself as haute bourgeoisie and politically powerful. It was a self-righteous, dominating newspaper, backed by proper business interests. It had its favorite politicians and was hardly, liberals and debunkers claimed, a fair, farseeing publication that gave equal time to both sides—or fully reported the corruption in city, county and state politics. *Times* II didn't change much. *Times* III is one of the most successful newspapers in the country.

Times I began nearly a century ago. In 1881 Harrison Gray Otis moved down from Santa Barbara to Los Angeles. He was nearing his mid-forties, and had seen a great deal of life, experienced much. He had been born on a hardscrabble farm near Marietta, Ohio, and his first effort at an education stopped at fourteen when he left the country school to work in a Sarahsville printer's shop. He learned how to set type in the manner of a tramp printer, as Mark Twain did, filling a stick of text, running a flatbed press. He wanted more education, so he attended school at Lowell and finished a commercial course at Columbia.

At twenty, he married. One account calls his bride "a local belle." He went off to the Civil War, enlisting as a private. He was an excellent soldier and showed bravery and belief in the Union cause.

Like so many soldiers, he remained all his life attached to the memory of his war years. At one time he edited the *Grand Army Journal,* set type in the Government Printing Office, clerked in the Ohio Legislature. He viewed the democratic process with a cordial irony.

He knew politics and its nonaltruistic ways well, and got himself appointed treasury agent to the dismal Seal Islands in the Bering Sea, after failing to get something better. Here he existed for three grim cold years, preventing seal poaching. Escaping to a warmer climate, he got a position as editor of the *Santa Barbara Press,* and so entered the world of newspaper publishing.

He liked the power of writing about the better people of the little resort town of 2,000 people. Some insist they snubbed him and his family. He sensed there were other larger places to the south, as Los Angeles, for a newspaper man. Santa Barbara was too small and too ingrown. Los Angeles had a population of 11,000. The city then had at least half a dozen newspapers that came and went, among them the *Los Angeles Times,* produced by two printers. It was about to go under. Otis bought into it to become, as treasurer, one-fourth owner of a newspaper that was first issued in December 1881. It was a sort of afterthought of the publishers of the *Los Angeles Mirror,* which had come into existence in 1873.

Otis had a keen sense of money and was a remarkably good treasurer. He soon saw that the business end of a newspaper decided whether it lived or died. (A policy *Times* II and *Times* III were well aware of.) He seemed a hard man to get along with, at least from the murky evidence that one can dredge up of that period of his life. The partners were happy to sell out to him, and by 1886 he was sole owner, publisher and editor.

His interests were to make money, to promote Los Angeles and to keep radicals, unions and Democrats out of any position of power. Luck had put him into the proper place at the right time, for he prospered with a surge of population and advertising.

The difficulty of appraising Harrison Gray Otis fairly is caused by the fact that while a great deal has been written about him, it either falls into the polished worship of a great man, the hero of pioneer times, *or* he is presented as a villain, evil as sin and outlined in satirical clichés. Actually he appears to have been a man of his times, solid in his convictions, and very sure he was always in the right. He labored hard to get *Times* I off the ground. His daughters worked on the paper in the business office, his wife, Eliza, doubled as a reporter and authored the first column of comment ever done in the city. From all this, in time, grew the remorseless insistence of superiority for the *Times* dynasty to come.

The paper was housed in a wreck of an old brick building on the

General Harrison Gray Otis whose Los Angeles Times dominated the southern California political scene. (Ross collection)

Around 1890 Charles Ducommun spread himself in his third store. He was the type of successful merchant General Otis endorsed. Today Ducommun stock is listed on the stock exchange. (Ducommun photo)

OVERLEAF:
Downtown Los Angeles circa 1890 showing the popular American Victorian in style. (Ross collection)

corner of Temple and Main streets. The press was always in need of repairs and was run by waterpower, which came in pipes from the zanja (canal) that had been dug. Often fish got in the pipes and the power was lost, and the press stopped while the clogged pipes were cleaned. It never came to "picking fish out of the printing press," as one report had it.

Otis earnestly was for material progress. He had an appetite for power and expansion, and for him that meant boosting land development and projects that would bring more business to the city. The paper backed those who were the money forces, the political strength of southern California. And that included the railroads.

He got much advertising from them when there was a bitter and nasty fare-rate war between the Southern Pacific and its rival, the Atchison, Topeka, and Santa Fe. Their wars helped to swell the population when the rivals offered to carry passengers from Kansas City to Los Angeles for $1, and that meant more readers for the *Times*.

While that bargain travel price didn't last long, it was a time of moving west, of taking advantage of cheap rates, of what was advertised as "year round farming." There was the first great migration of farmers from Kansas, Nebraska and Iowa, as well as by the sick who had been told sunlight could cure tuberculosis, rheumatism, arthritic pain and assorted items just listed as "the miseries."

Land values went up again and again, and in 1886 land sales reached $100 million. And where did one find the most real estate advertising offered with no restraint? In the *Times*. How to tell the frauds from the truth has never been easy in land developments. (In 1976 the state was still suing and getting judgments against desert and mountain land swindlers of too eager buyers all over California.) How could one in boom times have obsessions with trivialities?

The right people, as Otis saw it, were those who invested in Los Angeles; the wrong kind were drifters, tramps, union organizers, unemployed bindle stiffs. Otis began to write of what he called a "Bum Blockade" to keep undesirables out. He, himself, had once been a tramp printer (worse—held a union card!) but that was long ago. He wrote strongly worded editorials: "People Who Should Not Come to Los Angeles . . . The *Times* Gives Honest Advice."

*Los Angeles' main drag—
Spring Street and First Avenue
teeming with horsecars and
wagons rather than autos in
1885. (Ross collection)*

He announced with no ceremony or protocol that he wanted "good, plain, middle class, God fearing men and women. And if they were Republicans, so much the better." He built a new *Times* building and set up on it a huge bronze eagle.

The editorial pages of *Times* I appear today, in the age of the soft sell, as bigoted. They did not pussyfoot around as to whom Otis wanted kept out of Los Angeles:

Dudes, loafers, paupers. . . . Folks who do not wish to obey high-grounded and wholesome laws. . . . People who have no means and no situation assured, and who trust to luck for something to do. . . . People too near death to be saved by anything short of a miracle. . . . Cheap politicians. . . . Men with shady reputations "back east." . . . People who are failures wherever they go. . . . People who are afraid to pull off their coats. . . . People who expect to lie on their backs and let the ravens feed them. (The ravens are all engaged.)

He encouraged the coming of

Workers. Hustlers, men of brains, brawn and grit. . . . Fruit growers and farmers. . . . Capitalists who seek large returns on honest transactions. . . . Men who have a little capital and a good deal of energy. . . . Men who have a good deal of capital who wish "to take life easy". . . . First class men in almost any line of business.

When a recession, a depression came to Los Angeles, Otis never lost the faith. The city during the boom time had grown to 100,000 population. When hard times lost half of them, he went to work to plug the leaks, appealing for courage, grit and faith, even while suicides, bankrupts and litigators made bad news. In 1889 he was still boosting:

Let our wide pasture be changed into highly improved farms. Let the arid wastes be provided with an abundance of water. Plant new orchards and vineyards. Build new railroads. Suppose we go back to work. We are standing still. We have been waiting to bring order out of chaos left by the boom. We have a very fine climate but we can't live on climate alone. What are our wealthy, intelligent, and once enterprising fellow citizens going to do about it?

And things did begin to look up. If *Times* I was prospering, still hard-hitting, separating the human wheat from the chaff among the arriving Californians, one wonders what Otis would have done about young Harry Chandler, who had arrived in Los Angeles in 1881, a tubercular teen-ager from the New England of Landaff, New Hampshire. He came either to be cured or to die. While a student at Amherst, on a dare, he jumped into a winter ice pond, a stunt which led to tuberculosis. That is the legend. Certainly he would not have made the desirable immigrants' list published in the *Times*. Yet, against all the rules set down by Otis as to who was to come to the city and who was to stay away, Harry Chandler became Otis' partner, son-in-law and finally the owner of the *Los Angeles Times*.

And was to continue with his own ideas *Times* II.

20 Harry

Harry Chandler was to be described in later years by friends as "a firecracker," but his first months in Los Angeles, at age seventeen, were miserable enough. He had almost no money, a hacking cough that forced him to move from the cheap boardinghouse he lived in, the cough keeping the other boarders awake at night. It looked like a quick death. ("Life is a lost gamble, the grave holds four aces"—

western saying.) At this point he met a doctor who had an idea that living in the open could bring about a cure of the white plague or at least a delay in the journey to a burying ground. The doctor offered to let Harry set up a tent in a high orchard the doctor owned at the head of the San Fernando Valley near Cahuenga Pass. There was no seepage of self-confidence in Harry. The cure worked, or at least it stopped most of the coughing. Harry put on weight and soon felt strong enough to think of earning some of the hard cash people were talking about, wealth and opportunity as being there waiting in the sunshine for the smart man. People who knew him them said he felt himself a singularly extraordinary person.

He went to work trimming and caring for the doctor's orchard in return for his tent and board. Then he suggested a partnership—he to pick and sell the fruit for a share of the income. The first year Harry Chandler made $3,000, in those days not too small a fortune. He decided to go east and finish his college education, but when his cough returned he hurried back to southern California. But not to the smoke-colored dawns of tent life.

He walked right into a newspaper battle between Otis' *Times* and a new paper, H. H. Boyce's *Los Angeles Tribune*. Boyce had once been a partner with Otis in the *Times,* but he was bought out. Harry got a job as Otis' circulation solicitor. The other rival paper was the *Express,* and all three leading newspapers were in a crucial race to survive, going all out to gain readers and to harm each other.

The papers were distributed by district workers who had contracts with the publishers, and owned their own routes. The newsboys worked for these contractors. The system takes the burden of distribution away from the newspaper itself, and of course for many years it got around the child-labor laws. Today the method avoids Social Security, bookkeeping and other payments.

Harry Chandler saw something else in the system—its power; the golden goose was the circulation franchise. Small monopolies, held by different men, but when gathered into *one* hand they were a powerful force controlling the newspaper distribution world. In a few months Harry managed to buy up, become the owner of, the franchises for the three newspapers in metropolitan Los Angeles. He was now in a position of aggressive self-assertion—able to increase or lower the sales of any of the newspapers. He could manipulate the number of copies he issued to his newsboys and had a few others ways of controlling sales. After carefully studying the field, Harry decided to back Otis and the *Times.*

The enemies of the *Times*—for several generations—have insisted that there was a full-length plot concocted by Chandler and Otis to ruin the *Tribune* and make themselves the beneficiaries of its passing. I have been unable to discover any documented evidence that ruin of the *Tribune* was the major plan. But the story is repeated in most unofficial versions of the *Times* history. According to this, Harry took his contracts to Otis and showed him that he controlled the circulation of all three newspapers. Otis agreed to pay for added service, and as one text has it, "The financial terms have never been revealed."

What is proven fact is that Boyce's sales of the *Tribune* went down, down. Harry reported to Otis that the *Tribune,* in debt, was for sale.

Otis offered to buy it and was told it had already been sold, the buyer unnamed. It was all suddenly bizarre and implausible to Otis.

So far, what I have set down is what people figured had happened. What is fact is that Harry owned all the Los Angeles circulation franchises. What is recorded journalistic history is that the *new* owner of the *Los Angeles Tribune* was at last revealed as Harry Chandler.

Otis in extreme provocation went into a rage. But he was wise enough to see that Harry still controlled the *Times'* circulation through his franchise. It was an added ironical fact that Harry Chandler was doing better—earned more money—in the newspaper business than Otis. By controlling the *Times'* circulation, he topped Otis' income by "$500.00 a month." Harry was proving to be a successful Yankee accumulator.

Westerners liked the saying, "If you can't lick 'em, join 'em." Harry and Otis worked out a partnership on the following terms: Harry was to scrap the *Tribune* in return for his assets on the *Times,* and as a safeguard he was to retain all the circulation franchises. If Otis had involuntary spasms of rage, he hid them. It was a good partnership, to be further cemented when Harry married one of the Otis girls and became a respectful son-in-law. Harry had no newspaper experience, but he was a quick student with a clarity of purpose: properly he saw, as did Otis, that the business office was the heartbeat of the paper. This, of course, will be denied by those who think in terms of format, news coverage, good attitudes to the community. But actually *Times* I in the Harry Chandler period, according to newspaper historians, showed mostly a sense of how to make money, how to join the booster community that invested in land and resources. Harry had a submerged puritanical vitality; *not* making money was the big sin.

It is public record that. Harry Chandler became a multimillionaire through land deals, stockholdings, corporations that grew and expanded. That Harry was a political power, used and backed candidates like a party boss, supported party machines, backed city hall groups that often in the end were not working for the public weal—all this may be true, but there is no clear-cut evidence any of this was illegal to the point of coming into a court of law for a conviction. It was an age that was heir to Jay Gould, Jim Fisk, Daniel Drew and John D.

A retired stockbroker who knew the Chandler holdings well told me: "They never did anything that all the other bigshots and promoters didn't do. It was a time when you could realize your full potentialities. Sure they used their political clout, and they could have backed projects in their paper in which they held interests. But who wouldn't? Harry was so smart he saw just how far he could go and not get his fingers caught in a jammed door. I always found him fair, but hard, no moss growing on Harry.

"You hear stories the Chandlers own the state. I ask how and where? As a stockbroker I want hard facts, and what do their holdings come down to? A list of them—sweet ones—that are public record, or that can be found by anyone someplace on file. What do they own outright, are they big stockholders in, or control? There's the Times Mirror Company that publishes the *Times.* Then there's the big eastern Long Island newspaper, *Newsday,* the Times-Mirror Syndicate, Signet Books, New American Library, Abrams art books, World Books, presses that print the southern California phone books, the western edition of the newsmagazines and other publications.

"Emmett and Chandler (insurance), Buffum's department store (Long Beach), Tejon Ranch Co., Rancho Santa Anita, Chandis Securities Co., Chandler Sherman Corp., Dresser Industries, Inc., Atchison, Topeka & Santa Fe Railway, Yosemite Park & Curry Co., Pacific American Investors, Inc., Farmers & Merchants National Bank of Los Angeles, Safeway Stores, Inc., Kaiser Steel Corp., Greater Los Angeles Plans, Inc., F. X. Pfaffinger Foundation, Associated Press. A few other things."

Harry Chandler was not uninfluenced by his father-in-law. Harry was anti-labor and anti-union. His philosophy was that growth was prosperity and Los Angeles was good for the *Times* and the *Times* was good for Los Angeles—an omnipotent pope, exasperating to some. The *Times* was no enemy of its advertisers and a boost in the news columns was a good thing to show the paper was interested in the welfare of other companies.

Harry was not a man easy to see in his office, or to whom you could become close. He believed in reason, not too much intuition. He came to the office at noon and worked until the early dawn. This was usually the rule on a morning newspaper. He said *"I"* not *"we"* or *"the Times."* He laid down the law to the state capitol and to the county supervisors; his influence extended into national politics. In his prime, he worked through his skilled political staff, Kyle Palmer, Chester G. Hansen, Bill Henry and Carleton B. Williams. *Times* political reporters were accused of pretty much picking and getting into line the candidates for county and state office that the Chandlers desired—even getting the message to congressmen and senators. It was no secret. The *Times* presented its candidates in print and backed them. Those who rebelled often went down to ultimate failure.

Otis had become General Harrison Gray Otis ("breveted Major General for meritorious conduct"), having commanded a brigade in the

October 1, 1910. The Los Angeles Times building is destroyed by dynamite and fire, the result of resisting unionization. Twenty died. Today the newspaper is still nonunion. (UPI)

POLITICS AND POLECATS

Spanish-American war in action at Caloocan in the Philippines. Some of the power and the running of things was going to Harry. Otis remained the publisher until 1917, and by that time he was well aware that his son-in-law was able to carry forward the expanding dynasty to his approval. Harry Chandler took over that year and continued to head the *Times* until 1944. Then his son Norman became its head. (Norman stepped aside in 1960 to make room for his son, Otis Chandler. That was another kind of ball game.)

What really settled the philosophy of the *Times*—set it in solid cement—were events in 1910 when Otis was still a force, running the paper. Otis had been behind the forming of the Merchants & Manufacturers Association, a powerful anti-labor organization whose chief function was to combat the coming of craft unions into Los Angeles. "Organized labor must never get a foothold in the city."

Unions from all over the nation contributed to fight the open-shop stand of the forces behind the *Times* crusade. The Structural Iron Workers led the fight. Neither side was sagacious and tactful. Pullman and Rockefeller forces had shot down their strikers ("Will they never learn their lesson?").

Not all Republicans agreed with Otis' ideas. Theodore Roosevelt wrote in *Outlook* magazine:

"He [Otis] is a consistent enemy of every movement for social and economic betterment; a consistent enemy of men in California who have dared resolutely to stand against corruption and in favor of honesty. The attitude of General Otis in his paper affords a curious instance of the anarchy of soul which comes to a man who, in conscienceless fashion, deifies property at the expense of human rights. . . . It may be quite true that the paper has again and again shown itself to be as much an enemy of good citizenship, honest, decent government, and every effective effort to secure fair play for the working men and women, as any anarchist. . . ."

Just after midnight, October 1, 1910, while the staff was getting out the morning edition, dynamite blew up the Times Building. A roaring fire followed. And in horrible ways, twenty-one people lost their lives. Time bombs that failed to go off were found on the doorsteps of the Otis home and that of F. J. Zeehandelaar, who headed the Merchants & Manufacturers Association.

One union lawyer was later to quote Talleyrand: "It was worse than a defeat, it was a blunder."

BOOK IV

CON MEN AND GENIUSES

21 Clarence Darrow on Trial

Otis at once accused the unions of planting the dynamite that blew up the Times Building. Defenders of labor blamed it on bad and defective gas connections in an old building and added that the *Times* was using the explosion to frame the unions for the tragedy. There were even those who said Otis had set off the explosion himself, to discredit union organizing, but it had gotten out of hand and turned into a raging fire—all sorts of absurdity and cupidity were hinted at.

Businessmen of Los Angeles raised a fund of $100,000 to investigate the dreadful happening and to seek out its planner or planners. Earl Rodgers, the noted criminal lawyer, was given the fund and, as evidence, some sticks of unexploded dynamite from a time bomb found on the Otis doorstep. It was easy to trace the explosive to a factory in San Francisco, and then to the McNamara brothers, J. B. and J. J., radical, fanatical unionists, ready to do away with a social organism like the *Times*.

There was also a stool pigeon involved, Ortie McManigal, a dynamiter of fervor and skill, working for the Iron Workers. Labor cried "frame-up!" and in bitter sectarian anger and righteousness funds were raised for the brothers' defense all across the nation. It was pictured as a fight of the unions against union-busting by capital and its unctuous bigots. The A. F. of L. took a hand to rally the workingman against the monstrous apparition of Otis.

Clarence Darrow was hired as chief counsel for the defense of the Mc-Namaras. He was the folk hero of liberal movements, the defender of the oppressed. But with an earnest exuberance, he was also able to get high fees from the rich when they were in trouble. He was a disheveled heavy man with a fringe of limp hair hanging over one eye, playing the country boy at times in bravura performances, but a very able lawyer with passionate commitments to his beliefs.

It was a bombshell of another kind that while the jury was being selected to try James B. McNamara, both the brothers asked to be permitted to change their plea to guilty, with no guile or eloquent evasiveness. Why? Lincoln Steffens, a popular journalist/reformer/muckraker (Teddy Roosevelt's coined term), is usually given credit for the sudden turn of events. Steffens' story was that he had gone to Otis and made a deal; if the brothers confessed their guilt to the bombing—one was to get life, the other a term of fifteen years in prison. Can we accept this version? Is it in character?

Harrison Gray Otis, one account states, "laughed uproariously" at the idea that the publisher had agreed to this compromise. What is the truth?

CLARENCE DARROW ON TRIAL

Harry Chandler insisted Steffens *never* met Otis, and that when Harry and the D.A. broke the news of the confession and the deal to Otis, his reaction was to shout, "I want those sonsofbitches to hang." All we can be sure of is that there *were* confessions, and a deal *was* made that eliminated the hangman's rope. Most historians accept the Steffens version—without proof.

Sensation followed sensation, for this was not the end of the matter. The district attorney had discovered, he claimed, that Darrow had drawn a great deal of money from banks in San Francisco and Washington, D.C., mostly in $1000 bills. For what? A prospective juror, George Lockwood, had come forward to state that Darrow's jury investigator had offered him $5,000 *if* he were accepted on the jury and voted Not Guilty. Lockwood was told by the D.A. to go along with the deal. Lockwood added he had also been told another already accepted juror, Robert Bain, had been bribed too. Darrow was indicted for jury bribery and brought to trial for the Lockwood case five months after the McNamaras pleaded guilty. The Bain case would follow.

Earl Rodgers defended Darrow, but Darrow made a poor client. As Steffens saw Darrow on trial, he was no Zola: ". . . at three o'clock he is a hero for courage, no nerves and calm [in] judgment, but at three fifteen, he may be a coward for fear, collapse . . . panicky mentality . . . he cannot conceal much, his face is too expressive." Rodgers felt Darrow looked "a portrait of guilt." Besides Rodgers, there were four other lawyers on the defense team, among them the young Jerry Giesler, later to become the most famous Los Angeles trial lawyer. They were all needed as the *Times* thundered on its pages to place Darrow, the Briber of Jurors, behind prison bars.

Lockwood testified that Darrow's juror investigator had told him that Darrow was letting him spend $5,000 on each juror who would take it. The investigator had turned state's evidence and admitted the bribing of Lockwood. He was a private detective and had been caught passing the bribe.

Rodgers—while a confirmed alcoholic—was still a spellbinder, an actor and he did his best to confuse the jury about the basic charges against

Darrow. He pointed out that a brilliant lawyer like Darrow, after thirty-five years in the courts, would not turn to someone like a shady little private detective and say, "just buy all the jurors you want. I put my whole life, my whole reputation, everything I have into your hands." He used every nuance of gesture and voice.

The trial had lasted three months and three days when Darrow rose to plead for his career. His was no act—at least not deep down. He wept, he wiped his face with the sleeve of his coat. Whatever it was that Darrow had in addressing a jury—guile, eloquence, psychological magic—he used it all. Today we have only his words; missing is the drama, the voice, the damp figure of rustic simplicity. When he finished, several jurors were weeping, the hard-boiled court reporter had tears falling on his notebook. Darrow was a trembling wreck, dazed, as if he had a fever, an enervation of will, unwound. In thirty minutes the jury came back with a verdict of "Not Guilty!"

There was then the new trial for the bribing of juror Bain. The alcoholic Rodgers at this time was not ready for frenetic action. He could only begin the trial, then was removed as too sick to go on. This gave Darrow a chance to make an indignant whacked-out speech condoning the blowing up of the Times Building as a *social* crime rather than murder. His inner thermostat seemed out of order. Several members of the jury later said at this kind of talk they changed their minds and decided to hold out for conviction. The second trial ended in a hung jury. It was not till ten months later that Darrow was freed of the precarious situation of going to prison, when the second indictment was dismissed.

Was the great Clarence Darrow guilty of the moral squalor of jury bribing? The fair-minded will never know the true facts. The radicals and the committed union man still insist that the two jurors and the investigator were tools of Otis and the *Times* in a plot to frame Darrow. The defenders of the Chandlers and supporters of the open shop—the enemies of organized labor—say the evidence was enough to convict, even if presented without corroborating witnesses and an informer turned state's evidence. Earl Rodgers had a favorite saying about witnesses: "There are three kinds: liars, damn liars and experts."

CLARENCE DARROW ON TRIAL

What can be proved is that Harrison Gray Otis and Harry Chandler were not pleased by the results of the two Darrow trials. The old soldier had not been lacking in courage. When the time bomb was found in front of his house, Otis failed to cooperate with the police guard assigned to him. He would not permit the man to ride with him through the streets. When asked why not, Otis replied: "Three reasons. First, I would not give the unions the satisfaction of seeing me seeking protection. Second, it wouldn't do any good. Bodyguards never save anybody. Third, I believe there is still a God in Israel."

He was always to show the bravery of a good soldier in battle.

A historian, no matter what his version or vision of things, should try to balance his picture of events and personalities. With Otis, this is difficult. What praise he got was the usual official honorings of his career and effusive apple-polishing, clumsy fawning that didn't fool him. Attacks on him were hard-nosed and pushed home without mercy. Irving Stone was to write of the results of Otis' organizing for the open shop that "by the decision of this one man, Los Angeles became immersed in a half century of bloodshed, violence, hatred, class war, oppression, injustice and a destruction of civil liberties which was to turn it into the low spot of American culture and democracy."

I shall skip the most fanatical attacks on Otis. Here is only a sample from a speech given by Hiram Johnson in Los Angeles:

But we have nothing so vile, nothing so low, nothing so debased, nothing so infamous in San Francisco as Harrison Gray Otis. He sits there in senile dementia with gangrene heart and rotting brain, grimacing at every reform, chattering impotently at all things that are decent, frothing, fuming, violently gibbering, going down to his grave in snarling infamy. He is one thing that all California looks at when, in looking at Southern California, they see anything that is disgraceful, depraved, corrupt, crooked and putrescent—that is Harrison Gray Otis.

I have found no record that Otis ever sued for libel.

No wonder that Ogden Nash in his poem "Don't Shoot Los Angeles" wrote:

CON MEN AND GENIUSES

Is it true what they say about Los Angeles, that
Los Angeles is erratic,
That in the sweet national symphony of common sense
Los Angeles is static?

Harrison Gray Otis died in 1917, and as one tribute had it:

full of years and honors, having reaped the rewards of a strenuous and
remarkably successful career. His dominating characteristic might be
summed up in one word,—Loyalty,—loyalty to his country and to the
cause of humanity. Enemies he had who were many and bitter. A man of
such positive and aggressive character, taking a leading part in affairs that
concern vast numbers of people, could not expect to be free from enmi-
ties, at least during his own lifetime. It remains to an unbiased posterity—
to the calm and judicial arbitrament of history—to do such men justice.

The city had hardly time to mourn his passing. Los Angeles had been
preparing for war. It had believed Woodrow Wilson when he had said,
seeking reelection, "We are too proud to fight." (Another Wilson election
slogan in Los Angeles: "He gave you extended Parcel Post.") But events
had moved swiftly, and a draft army had been built up. Boards were
busy in the city and county, drafting men.

One official report of events gives the mood of the times and the effects of rumors and gossip:

Many of the regiments from Los Angeles County were quartered in
Camp Kearney, near San Diego. . . . The Balloon School at Arcadia
was in full operation, and half a dozen of the air monsters could be seen
hovering over the field or in practice flight. The dispatching of troops
from the camps for eastern or coast points of debarkation was without os-
tentation, and the time of departure, the route of travel, the point of destination, etc., were closely guarded as war secrets. This was undoubtedly
justified by the fact that there were German sympathizers, spies and
anarchists abroad in the land, who would not have hesitated to dynamite
a train or adopt any other desperate expedient to interfere with military

preparation. It might be noted in this connection that there were bands of I.W.W. conspirators firing haystacks and barns of the farmers in various portions of the state. Many German citizens and known sympathizers with the enemy were interned in government camps, and the incendiary bands of I.W.W. conspirators were finally run down and placed behind prison bars.

In March the Southwestern Shipbuilding Company was organized, with William F. Howard at its head. The next month the company started its plant on the southerly end of Terminal Island, at the mouth of San Pedro Bay. The company was awarded a contract for building twenty-three 8,800-ton ships for the Emergency Fleet Corporation. October 19th the first ship—the West Carnifax—was launched from the ways. The plant had been built in five months and nineteen days, and the first ship had been completed and launched in seventy-seven working days. This undoubtedly broke the record for ship yards and ship building. A second vessel—the West Caruth—was launched December 31st. Meanwhile the Red Cross activities were continued with unabated energy by the women and such assistance as they needed from the men. The community practiced all sorts of economies in food, such as the use of sugar and other commodities needed for exportation, and cut down luxuries and extravagance all along the line.

Both the accounts of I.W.W. action and spying were blown up from very minor events, actions. And there were no shortages for the well-off of any commodities. What did shock the city was workers, shipbuilders, buying and wearing silk shirts. The American worker in southern California, as elsewhere in the nation, was supposed to wear a blue work shirt, carrying his lunch in a tin lard bucket and not listen (the *Times* warned him) to talk of union organizers. This was the time for all to sing: "Lick Kaiser Bill! Hang Him on a Sour Apple Tree!"

22 Early Movie Days

Los Angeles, from 1900 until 1918, when the nineteenth century really ended, was mainly interested in growth, in swallowing land and planting orange trees. Then came shipbuilding during the war years and just before that, the growth of something called "The Movies," which were being made on the streets of the city and/or on large open-air lots, where actors, with their white made-up faces, gesticulated wildly.

Rose Parade winners of 1908 reflect the spirit of the time. The auto car attracted as much attention as the beauties. (First Federal Savings Bank)

Built in 1901, the cable cars of Angel's Flight transported Los Angeles citizens up a 33-degree grade run on Bunker Hill for nearly seventy years until the line was scuttled. Current plans call for reconstructing the line as a historic monument. (UPI)

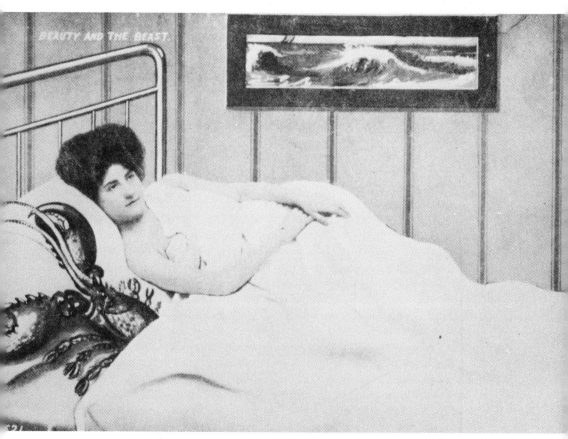

A picture postcard sold on the Santa Monica pier with a hint of sex and the Pacific Ocean.

CON MEN AND GENIUSES

Helen K., who worked for a dollar a day in early Mack Sennett, Thomas Ince and D. W. Griffith films, recalled for me in a letter how it was growing up in Los Angeles in the first decade or so of the twentieth century.

Looking back, the real charm of the city was the slow pace, no choking traffic, no freeways, and the pedestrian—slower to react than today's wary citizen—had a chance of survival. Oh, there were cars, the actors had early French and English autos, and Douglas Fairbanks (the father, not the son) used to take me for a ride in his Duesenberg. My father once had an Apperson Jackrabbit before his Pierce Arrow. But it was still a town big enough for excitement.

The marvelous trolley rides made in my childhood! Those big red trolleys that went everywhere. For a nickel you'd go riding out into the country, and if my Aunt Trudie was in love with a railroad man, we'd go as far as the Santa Fe Station. No one had yet invented the traffic light. The only parking problem was that maybe a horse trough on Hill Street would be in the way of your Model-T. Best of all my early memories was our home—the big fourteen-room Victorian General Grant house, all fretwork and cupolas and Tower of London chimneys. Porches with rockers all around, sliding doors of fumed and golden oak, high ceilings, thick walls that made it cool in summer and warm in winter, and heat coming up from gratings in the floor. I remember Teddy Roosevelt in the parlor rehearsing his speech of 1912: "We stand at Armageddon and we battle for the Lord!"

Papa, as a popular lawyer, liked an impressive house. Mama had some inherited New England furniture. But mostly our house was in a style called California Mission; settees, black walnut shapes, and something called a davenport (a primitive sort of sofa). Our doorways had portieres and strings of beads hanging from them, bought by Aunt Trudie in the old Chinatown where the Union Station is now. My father had a Morris chair and wore a fez and smoking jacket when he puffed on a claro cigar on the sun porch. The bathroom had stained-glass windows and a tin bathtub on brass lion's feet. The cosmetics my mother used were merely rice powder, a secret little box of rouge, extra hair called "rats" and that was it. Most of the bathroom cabinet held paregoric for aches and pains, an anthelmintic for my sister's worms, and my aunt's supply of "women's aid herbs," like Lydia Pinkhams.

Most families had an aunt who had lost her one and only true love. In our case, my aunt's boyfriend, a captain of Los Angeles' own "Old Seventh," had died in Cuba, with Teddy Roosevelt, of poisoned Chicago canned beef. When high on "female medicine," she'd say, "Oh, hell, I died that day. *Je ne cherché qu'un.*"

Aunt Trudie often worked in the movies at Thomas Ince, and was having her teeth fixed by a little bald-headed dentist at Broadway and Fifth streets—upstairs. I'd go along in case she was drugged by the dentist's use of the gas he gave her, and some white slaver kidnapped her and sold her to a brothel in Argentina (a plot of one of her films). The dentist had a drill which he operated with a foot pedal, and it was a gruesome thing to watch and hear. Aunt Trudie had a lot of gold inlay work done; plugs of gold were hammered into a drilled-out cavity by a little hammer in the dentist's hand. That was the dental science before World War One.

Aunt Trudie worked in movies with Chaplin who used to pinch her ample rump, and with Marie Dressler and Mabel Normand. But she never got past being part of a fashionable crowd in a ballroom or café scene in her big picture hat and her hobble skirt. I, myself, worked in movies as an extra, with a girl called Smith who became Mary Pickford. But I wanted to be a painter, so didn't really care if I was always given the edge of the scene to sit or stand in. Coming home from the studios by trolley, we'd stop off to do the shopping.

Aunt Trudie was an expert shopper. She could sniff a fish with all the drama of Clara Kimball Young breaking up a marriage. (Her ideal actress and a great scene.) Twenty-five cents of fine meat from the butcher would feed the six of us. No baker dared not give us thirteen to the dozen, and the grocery and general stores were a delight of smells; prunes, dried apples, cracker cookies in barrels. I would dive for dill pickles at a cent each, deep down in thick brine. The coffee grinder was a huge engine with the wheel of a steamboat, and gave off a true java smell you don't get in cans.

In my innocent kid days, we'd load up at the soda fountain near the Laughlin Building on Broadway, with a marble counter and the attentive Greek owner and soda jerk. There would be soda pop of a poisonous color and sarsaparilla. But the real production was what was called "The Los Angeles Soda," to which Richard Barthelmess introduced us. Two scoops of soft strawberry ice cream, a couple of serving spoons of some sticky orange mixture, thick as tar—all in a large glass. Then The Greek (he must have had a name but we all called him The Greek) would turn to his soda machine, a huge, rare marble and metal art object, with a nude brass woman as the "Spirit of Soda Water"—plus three silver faucets with black onyx levers. The Greek would turn a valve, then wait, for the soda was being made, he assured us, in the next room by pouring acid over marble dust. He'd grip the glass in its silver holder under a faucet, courageously pull a lever and a gush of bubbly water would churn into the ice cream and goo mixture. Skillfully, with short jerks, he'd fill the glass with bubbles on top, to which he'd add a dollop of whipped cream and one scarlet cherry, which an actor named Milton Sills once told me reminded him of "an angel's testicle."

D. W. Griffith was an ice cream soda nut, as were several other early film people; Mae Marsh, Bobby Harron and Lillian Gish, so the tiger rug and the champagne film era wasn't as chic or as sinful as has been remembered.

We felt damn modern, but not Bohemian. My mother, Los Angeles born, rebelled against the high button shoes that came up over the ankle, and she threw away her buttonhook by which one closed the shoes and began to wear what the Los Angeles sporting set called "Irene Castle pumps." My father wore stiff wing collars most of his life, but insisted that the celluloid collar was inflammable and dangerous to life. He never would wear a soft shirt that had an attached collar, or any shirt that didn't have detachable cuffs. He swore he had once seen a young dude light a coffin nail (his name for cigarettes) in the Alexandria Hotel bar and set his celluloid collar on fire.

I remember President Wilson getting off his train at the Arcadia Station, and me, in white lace, white shoes, white hat and fluffy lacy drawers—with other high school girls—waiting to greet him. We used to dress that way for Liberty Loan drives in Pershing Square, and "Farm or Fight" parades, and at shipbuilders' sites—at one of which Harry Lauder, the Bing Crosby of his day, showed up. The war was a great social success in Los Angeles.

EARLY MOVIE DAYS

At midnight, November 10th, the newspapers headlined the war was over. All night the newsboys cried *Extra!* in the streets. My father, in his nightshirt, went down to buy a paper and we all sat around a table in the parlor and read the brief announcements, every hour buying a new extra which said little more.

The next day it was madness downtown, all around town. Soldiers, sailors, shipyard workers in their overalls, curb to curb. Everybody with a bell or horn or banging on pots, soldiers being kissed and a great crying out, "The war is over!" and "Armistice!"

Armistice Day was a day that stands out bigger than most events of those years. That day my father was very serious about the future: "It's a new age appearing—and I don't know, I don't know if we're going to like it. We'll be filling a dozen more Sawtelle Soldiers' homes before this century is out. We've tasted victory. Christ, it's a bitter thing winning a war, after a while, when you keep trying for more victories." My mother told him not to take the Lord's name in vain, and go find Aunt Trudie who was off someplace, carried away with a sense of celebration. My father didn't trust President Wilson to make a proper peace. His legal knowledge sensed intellectuals made poor politicians. "You need hard scoundrels, sly, dishonest enough to cut corners and greedy enough to be smart enough to know you have to share the loot with everyone."

As for Aunt Trudie, she ended up bathing in her slip—no truth she was nude—in the fountain in the lobby of the Fremont Hotel on South Olive. When someone brought her home, she insisted she wasn't bathing, "just sipping champagne and wading." So ended an era for me and Los Angeles.

PEACE

WORLD WAR ENDS AS GERMANY SIGNS ARMISTICE!

[Extraordinary Service Bulletin by the Associated Press.]

WASHINGTON, Nov. 11th, (Monday)---The world war will end this morning at 6 o'Clock, Washington time, 11 o'clock Paris time. The armistice was signed by the German representatives at midnight. This announcement was made by the State Department at 2:50 o'Clock this morning.

The announcement was made verbally by an official of the State Department in this form: "The armistice has been signed. It was signed at 5 o'Clock a. m. Paris time and hostilities will cease at 11 o'Clock this morning, Paris time."

The terms of the armistice, it was announced, will not be made public until later. Military men here, however, regard it as certain that they include:

Immediate retirement of the German military forces from France, Belgium and Alsace-Lorraine.

Disarming and demobilization of the German armies.

Occupation by the Allied and American forces of such strategic points in Germany as will make impossible a renewal of hostilities.

Delivery of part of the German high seas fleet and a certain number of submarines to the Allied naval forces.

Disarmament of all other German warships under supervision of the Allied and

(Continued on Second Page.)

On November 11, 1918, Los Angeles, before the days of radio, is told the World War is over.

23 The Strange Father of Wilshire Boulevard

HGAYLORD WILSHIRE cannot be described or pinned down by any ordinary pattern set up to capture the doers and makers of Los Angeles. There is a hint of him in Robert V. Hines' *The American West:*

"The search for a representative West or a typical westerner has always depended on what the researcher sought. There are in fact and legend many Wests . . . . There is the historical West . . . . There is also the West that existed in people's imagination. . . . Frequently, however, the myths and realities are so intertwined that it is hard to distinguish where motivation comes from."

H. Gaylord Wilshire was born in Cincinnati, Ohio, in 1861. He was called in his time a con man, swindler and quack health-fad promoter. He was a Socialist candidate for public offices, banker, lecturer, publisher, inventor, subdivider, gold-mine owner, several times a millionaire and a few more times dead broke. All of this labeling is true. Also, the fact that one of the most fashionable streets and shopping centers in the world, a western Fifth Avenue Rue de la Paix Bond Street, is named after H. Gaylord Wilshire (no record I have seen tells us what the "H" stood for). The name Wilshire Boulevard, also known as "the Miracle Mile" and "the Fabulous Boulevard," is all that today recalls his once conspicuously active life to most people. Few know how the street came to bear his name.

He put it there himself. On December 21, 1895, he filed a subdivision plat in the office of the Los Angeles County Recorder. The plat stated that his subdivision was to be called "The Wilshire Tract," and to take in the areas from Parkview to Benton Way and from Sixth to Seventh streets, with a 120-foot-wide street to run east to west down the center of his subdivision to be named "Wilshire Boulevard."

A born exhibitionist, he came from a wealthy family, his father being connected with John D's Standard Oil Company, railroads and gas companies. Gaylord was a Harvard man and in 1884—not at all deficient in various schemes—was in California growing oranges and walnuts. Three years later he became an ardent Socialist, helped establish a Socialist newspaper and ran for Congress. He got only a little more than a thousand votes. In 1891, set in the traits of his personality, he went to London and stood as a candidate for Parliament from Salford, but left before the election, perhaps by request of Her Majesty's stuffy government, which did not recognize him as a British subject. Back in California,

THE STRANGE FATHER OF WILSHIRE BOULEVARD

Gaylord ran for Congress and started a weekly newspaper *The Challenge,* which the Post Office illegally but effectively suppressed by withdrawing publisher's rates from it—so much for the freedom of the press in the 1890s.

Gaylord offered William Jennings Bryan, then famous for his frenzied Cross of Gold speech, $10,000 to debate on the subject of Socialism. Mr. Bryan declined.

Gaylord not only inherited a fortune and got rid of it, he made new fortunes and lost those. He saw nothing wrong in simultaneously being a Socialist and a millionaire in a foulard ascot.

In need of money, Gaylord courted and won a rich London widow, and got rid of her wealth very quickly. He lacked what the Los Angeles Chinese called *feng-shui* (the balance of things). He sold mining stock worth $3 million and dissipated all of it.

He neither drank nor gambled (with cards, that is, dice, roulette or on horses). There do not seem to be any passionate attachments to women in the available records, nor any sexual scandals in his life. There is mention late in life of a second wife and son, but few personal details about his private life seem to exist.

In London Gaylord had become the friend of that other eccentric Socialist George Bernard Shaw, and by letting his beard grow, Gaylord began to take on a Shavian look. He often postured himself in Shaw poses, and printed his picture and Shaw's side by side. There are reports of interesting debates between these two active exhibitionists who made public protestations of eternal amity. Gaylord insisted, "Shaw and I were never altogether at one upon our socialism, and I am sure that neither he nor I are at one with anyone in particular." One wonders what Gaylord would have thought of Shaw's later admiration of Mussolini, Stalin and Hitler? He, Gaylord Wilshire, was more a man of the world than G.B.S., and faced the hard world as the sheltered Shaw never did. There is gossip that Shaw called him "a second-rate first-class man."

In Hyde Park where Gaylord gave public talks to the gathered people, he was always attired in formal claw-hammer dress coat, spats and silk topper and carried a gold-headed cane. But he never preached to a mocking crowd. They listened.

He had a reputation as a great wit and possessed a full sense of humor, but none of this seems to have survived in print.

By 1925, he was aging but about to promote his most amazing and grandiose scheme, a quack electric health product produced by his I-ON-A Company of Los Angeles. No clear explantion of the name exists.

Gaylord held no degrees in medicine, nor knowledge of therapeutics. But his device was advertised in no inchoate terms as a cure for Bright's disease, cancer, paralysis and, oddly enough (for such a high-powered item), able to turn gray hair back to black *and* to give a permanent wave to women! The world in blight had found a savior.

Committees were set up to investigate these claims, and they found the gadget from the I-ON-A Company to be a little over six pounds of twenty-two gauge insulation wire made into a belt. There were also a few bits of hocus-pocus hookups that served no purpose, but for one, which lit up a flashlight bulb to signal that the magnetic appliance was doing its healing work and curling hair.

The cost for this brilliant innovation was $58.50 for cash customers, but it could also be bought on time for $65. It cost Gaylord $5 to make each belt.

There were many "testimonials" to its effectiveness: "On crutches. Suffered from arthritis for eleven years. Used I-ON-A-CO. . . . lime has dissolved . . . regained health completely . . . white hair has become black!"

It's most amazing cure was for Canine Chorea (St. Vitus's dance) in a dog owned by William Sisk of Hollywood "by sleeping within the influence of an I-ON-A-CO."

Gaylord printed long testimonial lists of his product endorsed by well-known physicians. Investigations by the American Medical Association found that none of the doctors quoted had ever heard of I-ON-A-CO.

THE STRANGE FATHER OF WILSHIRE BOULEVARD

In 1927 H. Gaylord Wilshire advertised that I-ON-A-CO was "approved by the Rockefeller Institute for Medical Research." In June, Rockefeller lawyers were on Gaylord's tail with lawsuits. But with Voltairean irony, on September 8th, the obituary column of *The New York Times* contained the following:

H. Gaylord Wilshire, editor of the pre-war *Wilshire Magazine,* died yesterday of heart disease in his apartment at the Hotel Westover . . . in his 68th year. . . . Among other items in his life . . . in 1906 he entertained Maxim Gorky, the Russian Socialist, here on a visit, and the same year he tried to found a servantless Eden . . . on a profit sharing basis.

He had come a far way from that day in 1895 when he had filed in Los Angeles a plat for a subdivision that would be dominated by the 120-foot-wide street named Wilshire Boulevard.

24 The Silver Screen

The beginning of motion pictures was simple. When the Kineoscope Company opened its peep show on Broadway in 1894 to first show people in movement by a procession of photographs, Hollywood had a population of 200. It is ironic that Kansas prohibition pioneers, Mr. and Mrs. Horace Henderson Wilcox, founded Hollywood, a place that would later be blamed for producing the most decadent versions of American drinking and sexual activities in films that became, all over the world, a version of the United States—fully accepted as true.

It was not until 1904 that filming actually began in Los Angeles when a camera in old Chutes Park recorded a dirigible on exhibition there. David and William Horsley came from New Jersey to make cowboy pictures on Beachwood Drive. In 1908 Colonel Selig (the military title was never fully explained) rented a house at Eighth and Olive streets and turned out the first full-length feature film in the city, *In the Sultan's Power*. By 1909 the New York Motion Picture Company sent out its Bison Company to grind out westerns in Edendale, at the rate of one every day and a half.

The reason given for this move of the eastern film makers to southern California is usually given as a search for strong sunlight and an escape from bad weather. This is only partly true. Thomas Edison had perfected a hand-cranked motion picture camera, which he leased to film makers. They, to escape the rental fees, began to make their own bootleg cameras, infringing on Edison's patents. He, knowing of long court delays and the poor record of justice to inventors, had the bootleg cameras hunted down and smashed on the spot. So it was just as much to escape Mr. Edison's reach with their versions of his camera as the all-year-round sunlight that drove moviemakers to California.

The greatest boost to Hollywood came in 1910 when Biograph's D. W. Griffith, the films' first and perhaps only American film genius other than Chaplin, came west, as did such later names to fame as Mack Sennett and Mary Pickford.

It was the same year that Hollywood ceased to exist as an independent city, since being deliberately deprived of an adequate water supply forced it to become part of Los Angeles. The population of Hollywood was 4,000, plus some few actors, directors and hangers-on who were "mostly cavorting at the Alexandria Hotel," making something called movies. In ten years' time what had been Hollywood had a population of 100,000. In 1913 came Cecil B. De Mille, Jesse Lasky (a former vaudeville trumpet player) and Dustin Farnum to shoot *The Squaw Man* in a barn at Gower and Sunset. Sam Goldfish (later Goldwyn), a glove salesman, was soon to follow.

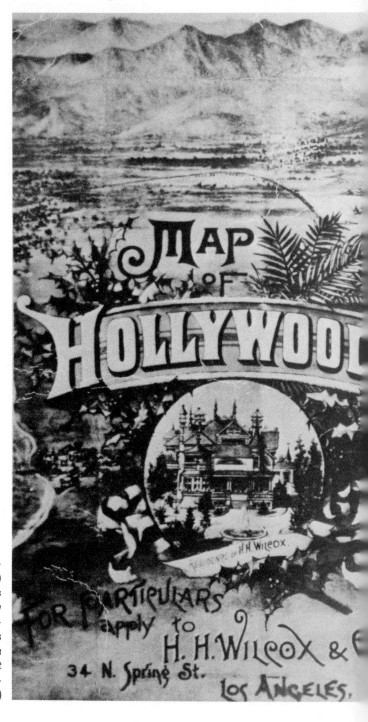

An early map of Hollywood (circa 1900) before the movies came. Actually, today there is no legal section of Los Angeles called Hollywood or a post office by that name. (Ross collection)

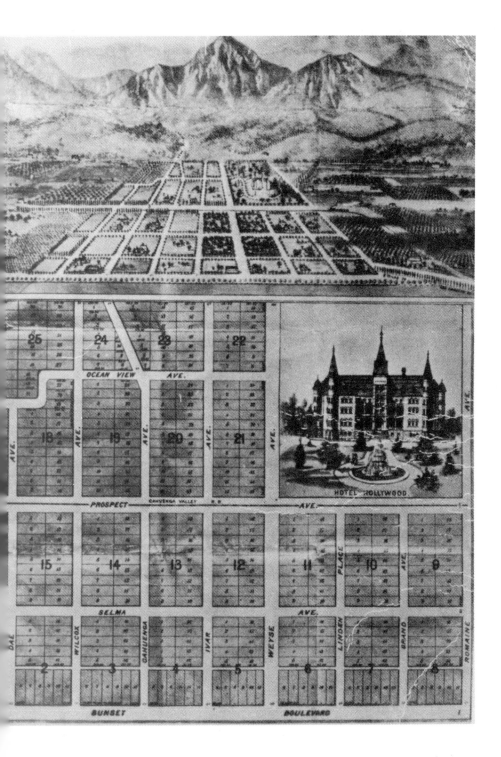

OCEAN VIEW AVE.

PROSPECT AVE.

CAHUENGA VALLEY R.R.

HOTEL HOLLYWOOD

SELMA AVE.

SUNSET BOULEVARD

CON MEN AND GENIUSES

Griffith in 1914 brought motion pictures and Hollywood to maturity with his long feature-length picture *The Birth of a Nation.* A master of movement, the use of hundreds of extras and if not the inventor, as often claimed, of the *close-up,* the *focus-in* and the *focus-out,* the *iris shot,* the *split screen,* he nevertheless created a remarkable picture using all these devices. His use of *crosscutting* for action suspense gave pace and movement to what had been static copies of stage techniques.

Being a southerner from Kentucky, Griffith's attitude toward the Klan and blacks was not in the liberal mood. When the picture opened on February 8, 1915, in Los Angeles, at the Philharmonic Auditorium, there was talk of race rioting and an army of police were mobilized. However there was no rioting, no organized protests. The film went on to a box-office score of about $20 million, an impressive gross in an age when a dollar was a dollar and when admission prices were a fraction of what they are now. The optimists in the L.A. Chamber of Commerce noted that *The Birth of a Nation* made "Los Angeles the permanent and recognized seat of the motion picture industry."

Cecil B. De Mille told me, when I was writing the dialogue for his picture *Greatest Show on Earth* in 1951, "Well, a forty-year run is about as permanent as anything is these days."

The other film genius 1913 produced, the little knock-about comic from a traveling English pantomime company, went to work for the Keystone Company, and two years later Charlie Chaplin was getting $10,000 a week—and was soon to make millions producing, directing and writing his own feature films.

25 To the Hoover Era

On the death of the *L.A. Times* founder, Harrison Gray Otis, his son-in-law Harry Chandler had taken over with hardly "an extra twitch of a muscle in his face." He was to carry on the *Times,* carry forward the policies of the general, a bit smoother, in a somewhat more polished, but hardly changed, philosophy—conscious motives, unconscious drives. The paper and he would get richer, and he was breeding a dynasty. Son Norman would replace him someday, but not *too* soon. Harry was made of an oak-like New England stock, had an inheritance of patience and serenity and an eye for investments. He supported Harding and Coolidge. But his best bet was on Herbert Hoover, President by a businessman's mandate, a moralist with no mystical hallucinations like Woodrow Wilson.

But sometimes even Hoover had a habit of appointing commissions that didn't sit well with the powers that ran Los Angeles. A commission was usually set up to take a long time, file a report—and let the situation evaporate. That was the kind of commission Harry liked.

If the Chamber of Commerce group and the anti-labor Merchants and Manufacturers Association saw all liberals as anarchists and Marxists, monsters of revolution, the liberals in turn saw the men who ran Los Angeles as Babbitts (the ultimate insult in the 1920s by the intellectuals in reference to the men of business). In his book *Dynamite* Louis Adamic roared out against "the people on the top in Los Angeles" with a hurricane of abuse, blowing so strongly that one critic wondered, as the western expression was, *what wild hair he had up his ass?* He decried

the promoters, who are blowing down the city's windpipe with all their might, hoping to inflate the place to a size that will be reckoned the largest city in the country—in the world. . . . These men are the high priests of the Chamber of Commerce whose religion is Climate and Profits. They are—some of them—grim, inhuman individuals with a great terrifying singleness of purpose. They see a tremendous opportunity to enrich themselves beyond anything they could have hoped for, and they mean to make the most of it. . . .

During the depression the Wickersham Commission's report on law enforcement, prepared at the request of President Hoover, found that

Los Angeles police . . . still use the old-fashioned methods in dealing with crime . . . expressing a theory of law enforcement more openly opposed to the Constitution than any I had yet encountered. . . . There had been a series of abnormal pressures. . . . The first . . . exerted by a dominant financial group, fanatically anti-labor, which utilized the police as an adjunct to its open-shop industrial policies.

It was a time of capricious changes. The stock-market crash, unemployment, the Dust Bowl and, worst of all, F.D.R. on the horizon.

The city wanted no desperate hungry men, no public protests from the victims of the Crash. The state police could keep the Okies in line, but Los Angeles had poor who showed their hunger, their rags in public.

Louis Adamic reported that Los Angeles police records in one year in the 1930s showed nearly 15,000 arrests for the phony charge of "vagrancy." Adamic wrote:

Shabby-looking men are stopped in the streets, dragged out of flophouses, asked if they have work; and if they answer in the negative, are arrested for vagrancy. . . . Few persons in Los Angeles know about these things. The press of course is mum on the subject; for the tourists must not get the idea that anything is wrong with Los Angeles.

The Chandlers, tuned to the constants of human behavior, came through the Hoover depression well, and while a buried news item on Christmas Day, 1931, stated, "Among the 1300 men working (in state labor camps) for food and tobacco are former army officers, professional men and college graduates," the editorial page, on the other hand, gave a cheerful holiday greeting to Los Angeles:

Merry Christmas! Look pleasant! Chin up! A gloomy face never gets a good picture. The great battles are fought by Caesars and their fortunes, by Napoleons and their stars. Faith still does the impossible. Merry Christmas! You may be down on your uppers; but that is better than being up on someone else whom you have downed on his uppers. Maybe you did lose money a year ago; then you did not have as much to lose in the Guaranty debacle. Merry Christmas! Catch the tempo of the times. You have your life before you; and, if you are growing old, the greatest ad-

A view of the traffic on Broadway in 1925 caused by the city's rapid growth.
(UPI)

venture of all is just around the corner. Earth may have little left in re-
serve, but heaven is ahead. Merry Christmas!

The affluent middle class was dissolving; fathers of families were selling
apples, sit-in strikes happened, then came driving sheriffs away from
selling off farms for defaults on mortgages to banks; all this pointed to a
need for change. A year after its Christmas greeting, the *Times* was clob-
bering a candidate up for election:

Governor Roosevelt (F.D.R.) seems unduly excited as to whether he or
some other Democrat is to be beaten at the polls by Hoover. You can bet
your best hat that Hoover will be the next President of the United States.
There is always considerable harmless entertainment in panning the oc-
cupant of the White House; but the American public has no real intention
of changing horses in a stream as tumultuous as this.

The *Times* was wrong. It felt both Franklin and Eleanor were distraught
neurotics—*until* Pearl Harbor when the flag went up.
The 1930s saw Los Angeles as the breeding ground of many schemes
to fend off the effects of the depression and create, instead, a state of affairs that would aid those citizens in despair and often hungry. That most
of these plans were based on heartfelt feeling for humanity, rather than
on the logic of an already failed economy, did not detract from their aim.
Some, of course, were greedy schemes of promoters, but most were
serious fantasies for improving a world not really interested in those un-
fortunates who hadn't gotten theirs.

There was Mankind United, and the Decimo Club, and most of all,
EPIC (End Poverty in California), Upton Sinclair's crusade to help everyone to a better life. He ran for governor on its platform, as a Democrat,
and it looked as if he would be elected. In panic, the film studios began
to fake "newsreel" shots of the influx of tramps and criminals into California for the handouts if Sinclair was elected. Actors dressed up as
hoboes to be filmed in freight yards as arriving with a lugubrious happy

shuffle to enjoy Sinclair's freebies. Sinclair was defeated. But the Townsend Pension Plan lasted a little longer. It offered "$200 a month to oldsters." (The words "senior citizen" weren't in use yet.)

The Ham and Eggs group offered "$30 Every Thursday." The catch was that both plans called for the state to make the payments by passing laws to that effect. The Los Angeles corporations controlling the state didn't approve—so no law was passed.

> Two hundred dollars a month,
> Youth for work, age for leisure,
> Two hundred for the oldsters,
> To be spent in ceaseless pleasure.

The middle class and the bond- and property-owning class, besides fighting back the hope of state aid and beating the Okies out of setting up their sleazy, smelly camps too near the cities (clubbing them and exploiting them as cheap labor), had the problems of failures of great big blue-chip companies. In Los Angeles there was the receivership of Richfield Oil, the failure of the Guaranty Building and Loan Association and liquidation of Pacific Mutual of California. Whole sections of the state that had been swallowed had to be vomited up. The major scandal was that of the looted Julian Petroleum Company that had raked in money from all over the state. A district attorney was found guilty of taking a bribe. Several of Julian Petroleum promoters went to prison for very short token terms. And a big banker who was involved was shot and killed in a Los Angeles courtroom. A radical sheet printed an item: "Fortunately Hubert Eaton has established Forest Lawn and there is room for an important banker with a bullet hole in him."

Los Angeles took to Roosevelt's New Deal; it was a pattern of hope when 40 million Americans became instant paupers. Los Angeles had its share of suicides (20,000 people in the nation ended their lives during the first couple of years of the depression). The unemployed stood at a steady 20 million. Los Angeles' Skid Row at least had good weather and free soup. The song "Buddy Can You Spare a Dime" didn't seem amusing to Jack L., a cartoonist, as he remembered it all:

No, it was no frisky time—the depression in Los Angeles. Hoover just looking dazed over that damn high collar of his, and saying, "We are at the end of our string. There is nothing more we can do."

I was married, had a new baby—we were all living over a garage on Beachwood, cooking over a hot plate *if* we had food. Roosevelt in 1933 certainly was a shot in the arm to southern California. I went to lean on a public works shovel, and we ate beans and beans and rotting oranges. All those letters were stuck up all around Los Angeles. NRA (that came with a blue eagle—and boy were we *blue*). CC was for the young to go hoe pine seedlings; WPA too. And then the FAP (Federal Art Project). I got to painting pictures on post office walls, with Lorser Feitlson, Helen Lundeberg, Stanton MacDonald-Wright and I think Jackson Pollock was also up there on the ladders with us. And the Marxists from UCLA slipped us mimeographed manifestos. The murals we did are all covered up now, or smoked up by smog, but we did some good stuff.

There were other angles to view Los Angeles during the 1930s. Wrote a local critic, Paul Jordan Smith:

Our population is a rare mixture of evangelical mountebanks, new thoughters, swamis, popular novelists, movie persons, solemn pamphleteers, realtors, Ku-Kluxers, joiners of the thousand-and-one fraternal orders of goodwill and everlasting sunshine, artists, consumptives, music lovers, retired farmers and beer magnates—mostly American to the core, and as typical as signboards and peanut stands.

It is now my firm conviction, Mencken notwithstanding, that out of this motley throng . . . there will grow the most splendid center of genuine culture and enlightenment on this continent. For, with all its uncouthness, the place is alive with illusions, and illusions are the stuff of art.

Like most working citizens of Los Angeles in the 1930s, Jordon-Smith couldn't help ending up with a booster's tag line. But by 1970, Jack Smith, writing for the same newspaper, his column in the spot once held down by Jordan-Smith, could state: "Scarcely anywhere in Christendom are illusions so easily and cheaply obtained as in Los Angeles. If we are really in Christendom at all."

Certainly a Smith of a different color.

The Okies might starve, the Skid Row bread-and-soup line grow and a sense that the national dignity was blowing away with the clouds out of the Dust Bowl, yet California, hard hit, managed to come through the worst years without major riots, protest marchers and a feeling that all was lost. There was an active Communist Party and Marxist-dominated union organizers. People didn't pay rent, lived in shacks labeled Hoovervilles, got rousted by the police, state troopers and the ranch owners' goons. But living was cheap, and artists, actors and writers in Los Angeles managed to do some good work on federal projects. The *Times,* too, did well in those woebegone years. It had its political favorites set in City Hall, in the corridors of justice and in the D.A.'s office. It was no hidden support, but direct public endorsement of men it thought best. The Los Angeles of the 1930s continued in corruption, reaching high into Police Department and City Hall.

One morning in January 1938 Harry A. Raymond stepped on his car's self-starter and the car and garage blew up and Raymond with them. But he managed to survive his serious injuries. Raymond was an investigator for a reform group called CIVIC. It was proving the city was a jolly gathering place of gangsters, former bootleggers in new rackets, highjackers busy stealing, from the ports to the warehouses, all with police awareness—and that pimps, madames and whores paid for police protection, to run wide open, and Mayor Frank Shaw was slack, or worse. Facts began to gather that Raymond had been bombed by members of the Los Angeles Police Department, as CIVIC was coming too close to their involvement in rackets and crime.

District Attorney Burton Fitts issued a strange statement that there were some men who would set off a charge of dynamite under themselves, just to blame it on other people. Mayor Shaw, a *Times*-backed man, was not too happy about all the hullabaloo. He was very close to contractors who got most of the city work, to suppliers, to insurance companies and to banks that did city business. It would not be politic to uncover the rottenness in the Police Department or its use of dynamite on a private citizen. It was proved that police higher-ups had kept Raymond under surveillance and that his house had been bugged. An acting captain of police, Earle Kynette, who led the harassment of Raymond on orders of police headquarters, took the Fifth Amendment when cornered about his activities.

The *Times* felt that the mayor and the police were being harassed and it sprang to their defense.

Has it ever occurred to any of the investigators of this Roman holiday that we are making ourselves slightly ridiculous? As large cities go, Los Angeles has heretofore enjoyed a pretty good name in the country at large. We have spent considerable money trying to maintain and to deserve that reputation. When we permit it to be thus publicly inferred to the world that conditions here are so incredibly rotten as to require all our own facilities, and a good part of the State's, even to find out how bad we are, what is it going to do to that reputation?

A very mild investigation took place. Raymond recovered, and some minor police figures stood trial. Two were found guilty, and whatever connection there was between criminals, the police and City Hall was clouded over. Four newspapers (the *Times* refused) backed a recall movement for Mayor Shaw. As for the citizens of Los Angeles—*what shall we do about the world?* Accept it was their verdict.

Things went on as before. Reform, as usual, went into atrophy. The Police Department did not really get a superior chief until a man named William H. Parker came in: while he cleaned up the more blatantly dishonest police sections and held down the bribes from bookmakers, gamblers, madames and whores, even he did not do away entirely with the abuses of the Los Angeles police. The attacks on minorities continued.

Harry Chandler was getting to be an old man, but he did not change his views, or his support, of those he wanted in City Hall. And those he backed to dominate the Republican Party listened to his advice.

26 Oil and Olvera Street

Los Angeles has lived with the extravagant clichés created about it. While most of the nation thought that oranges and motion pictures (with some lemons in *both* groups) were the major industries of California, it was and is, actually, oil. Politically, Big Oil, with its headquarters in Los Angeles, has more crunch in swaying the state's laws, and the men who make the laws, than the fruit growers and the film industry. The people accept it as BIG in a kind of awed euphoria.

In the 1890s, before the autocar was a form of popular transportation and before Henry Ford had begun to make Everyman's car, the Model-T, oil was refined into kerosene for lighting lamps. Called coal oil, its smelly not unpleasant odor filled the homes of those of us who were once young enough on country farms to emerge from the oil-lamp age to gas, then to the final mazda of Thomas Edison's electric bulbs. I knew farms and ranch houses where the familiar smell of lamp oil remained with me as a kind of nostalgic booster, as strong as Proust's memory of things past when he dipped his cookie into that cup of herb tea.

It all began when E. L. Doheny and his partner, C. A. Canfield, noticed that some loads of sand dripped a greasy black substance. They trailed it to its source, dug a shaft with a pick and shovel and sent a bucket down 160 feet to strike oil. It was that simple—a giant step toward the motor age—and the disappearance of America's greenery.

"Black gold" was the first cry and many people began to poke holes in the earth in the hope of making a strike. By the 1890s, the oil developments were ruining whole sections of Los Angeles County, hundreds of derricks were going up, the primitive steam drills, before the days of the high-speed rotaries, spudding in, piles of pipes destroying property, mule teams hauling them; making a blight of the neighborhoods. Heavy steel rigs with multiple teams tore up the roads, leaving oil puddles and greasy areas wherever they stopped. Sump holes smelled and huge steel tank wagons went by like long funeral processions, eight mules, four abreast at times, straining at their dripping loads. Nearly 1,500 derricks rose where Los Angeles' lawns and flowers had once been. Seventy years later some of the first wells were still producing.

Many districts were soon exhausted, and in time the industry shook out its losers. Doheny and others expanded to new fields—Signal and Baldwin hills, all the ridges seemed filled with derricks. Long Beach fields came in, and offshore islands were productive.

By the time of World War I, the automobile was the means of family

E. L. Doheny, the Los Angeles oil magnate. (Ross collection)

In the 1920s, Los Angeles had oil wells to burn, as this one does to entertain a crowd on Signal Hill. (Security First National Bank)

OIL AND OLVERA STREET

transportation—and active productive wells with their bird-billed pumps were familiar sights on many Los Angeles streets. Most of the last oil wells were removed from the streets only a few years ago; even today, I daily pass a productive old well still pumping on the corner of Beverly Boulevard and La Cienega. On Pico Boulevard there are curious, well-painted, landscaped structures, with high fences which look like narrow apartment houses out of science fiction. They are camouflaged oil wells, masked as ordinary reality.

Los Angeles oil millionaires never became as flashy or such public clowns as the Texan variety. Some endowed undersea study, aided colleges, set up private museums ("a good tax dodge") and usually spread themselves in grand mansions and in travel—the women, often victims of couturiers, the men, bon vivants at Monte.

The original discoverers seem to have had a curse put on them for inflicting their drills through the skin of an earth undisturbed since the last ice age or volcanic upheaval. Charles A. Canfield's wife was murdered in 1906 by their coachman, Morris Buck, who was convicted of the killing and hanged, while E. L. Doheny got caught up in the Teapot Dome scandal. His son, E. L. Doheny, Jr., in some outré drama, was murdered in 1929 by his male secretary, Hugh Plunkett, who then killed himself.

But most of the oil-rich Angelenos (a term very popular in the society columns) lived well in some prudence and decorum with little more to bother them than divorces, the wrecking of expensive cars and membership in the Los Angeles Athletic Club (founded in 1880 with forty-one charter members who, someone figured out, were worth $25 million en masse).

The wrecker's ball, or conversion to nunneries, has overtaken most of their ornate mansions. Doheny's Graystone, a Beverly Hills palace, was bought by that community to keep it out of the real estate market.

Even more active than oil drilling around the city are the sales of oil stock. A retired stockbroker I know told me of many doctors as investors:

In a community where medical fees are sky high, and costs of illnesses can bankrupt the average citizen (hospital rooms run to more than a hundred dollars a day, and an aspirin is billed at $5), a pack of medical men in Los Angeles have incomes of $100,000 to $200,000 and $300,000 a year. Stock salesmen are delighted at these high incomes and the irrational optimism of their owners. Los Angeles doctors are a stockbroker's best pigeons. You can't form a company to go after an oil lease for drilling without doctors coming to you with check in hand. I've known doctors who have put as high as sixty thousand a year into a drill site in partnership with other doctors. In this shareholding of wells being dug, they never give up. Do they find oil? Sometimes. But costs and restrictions don't make it the gold mine you think of, as owning part of a producing Los Angeles County well. Lots of the doctors just see it as a tax loss.

Actually, to historians, the La Brea Tar Pits of prehistoric animal fossils is more interesting than oil drilling. In 1916, Captain G. Hancock and his mother, owners of the site, donated the park to the county. It was part of the 4,439-acre Rancho La Brea, purchased in 1860 by Captain Hancock's father, Major Henry Hancock, for $2.50 an acre, priced later at $2,500 a front foot on Wilshire Boulevard. Hancock, a surveyor out of Harvard, the Mexican War and gold panning on the American River, built a home on what is now Wilshire Boulevard. He shipped asphalt from the pits to San Francisco for sidewalks and street paving. Los Angeles manufacturers used the tar for fuel and roofs were covered with it.

After the turn of the century, Hancock completed seventy-one producing oil wells on Rancho La Brea. When these became depleted, he turned to buildings. After geologists found the first tooth of a saber-toothed cat in 1902, scientists came to inspect the tar beds, and still do. Will Rogers, commenting on some sharp dealings, once said, "Maybe Los Angeles should adopt the saber-toothed tiger for its city seal."

Real estate rivaled oil in making money.

The City of Los Angeles spreads out like a fungus growth across an immense area. Islands of architectural interest—usually a single building,

OIL AND OLVERA STREET

sometimes a group of buildings—occur almost everyplace in this vast real estate surrounded by miles of dull repetitive structures. . . . (From the preface of a *Guide to Architecture in Southern California,* 1965.)

Even a friendly publication cannot resist the term "fungus growth." Among the mass-built tract houses, the remains of many "Spanish styles" still stand, but not the first flat-roofed adobes of the pueblo. "Spanish" survivors of the 1920s are a cross between the romantic, but rather false, rusting iron grills and red clay roofs of early days. These tile-embroidered erections are based on the 1915 San Diego Exposition. (The last large "Spanish" building is the now nearly deserted Union Station and the early motion picture styles of the *Mark of Zorro.*)

The building styles of Los Angeles are as far apart as the novels written about southern California—from *Ramona* to *The Loved One.* English visitors have always been delighted and amused by Los Angeles, as was Waugh when he mocked Forest Lawn in *The Loved One,* a tribute to the tastes and vicissitudes of the body-burying racket. And Noel Coward, who said on his last visit to the city, "There is always something so delightfully real about what is phony here. And something so phony about what is real. A sort of disreputable senility."

He could have been referring to the transformation in the late 1920s of Olvera Street into "a picturesque Mexican marketplace."

I have asked my friend the Mexican-American poet Inigo Mori to write of the Plaza restorations:

Christine Sterling was a gringo lady described as tiny, blue-eyed and a redhead, when in January of 1928, she first saw Olvera Street adjoining the Los Angeles Plaza, the street a revolting alley with a gutter of raw sewage and a sinister look about the Chicano loafers that loitered there. On what had once been a proud Avila house—perhaps built in 1818—the city had put up a sign of condemnation, as the structure being unfit for human habitation, even Mejicanos, Hispanos. Mrs. Sterling of English descent, out of San Francisco, was shocked the city did not do something about its early heritage, a survivor of colonial oligarchy. There are certain types of women in fortuitous circumstances, having buried husbands, who come out for the welfare of stray dogs or cats, begin crusades to drive sex education from the public schools, or spend a lifetime collecting milk glass and wooden butter molds. We of Chicanismo know them well. Sometimes, as with Mrs. Sterling, their drive takes them into a civic project to dress up *los de abajo,* if they are picturesque. (In the 1960s a crusade to put diapers and pants on all male animals, from pet dogs to cows, was taken seriously by the city, and by its dwindling newspapers, until it was exposed as a hoax.)

Mrs. Sterling was a practical, humorless Angelo. She had begun to try and get some of the Mexican-Americans into trying to recapture "the color and charm of the pueblo." She was under the impression that old Sonoratown was a kind of Spanish Shangrila, rather than the gamblers, grogshop and whore-house section of the old town. She went to Harry Chandler, commandant of the *Times,* and enlisted him in the plan to turn Olvera Street into something she thought of as its original form. One of the newspaper's staff writers, John McGroarty (he had done the local propitious version of *The Mission Play* given for tourists), sat down and turned out a story of "The Plaza Beautiful." There were meetings and funds were called for. It seemed at first a slow start, a pilgrimage going no place, until Mrs. Sterling began to exploit the sign condemning "perhaps Los Angeles' oldest surviving residence. . . . which had served as Commodore Stockton's headquarters in his invasion of 1847 . . ." when he brought the *pachucos* under Old Glory. She rented the remains of the Avila place from the owners, who were some of the remaining Rimpau family. Mrs. Sterling erected a twelve-foot billboard on the building:

WHY SHOULD THIS BE CONDEMNED?

Mrs. Sterling had cunning skill in using the press, and in interviews she put across her idea of reviving the alley to something she imagined would have the true romantic flavor of the barrios and colonias of the past. She gathered a group of interested people who began to contribute objects that might once have been Mexican and were certainly, in a more careless classification, to be called antiques.

Repairs were made to the place. The patio, or where it had been, was turned into a tree-filled vine-covered garden. With some bribing with grain as bait, wild doves were induced to take up residence. One reporter called it a "haven of tranquility." The Chicanos who weren't going to get stalls there shrugged it all off as Yankee nonsense.

This had all been done by Mrs. Sterling. She faced the City Council and not only persuaded them to forget the condemnation of Avila House, but also to send out a prison labor gang to clean up the muck. With the *Times* behind her, Mrs. Sterling raised $25,000 for restoration. A board of directors was set up of well-known names about town, with no Chicanos of course.

It all became part of the State Historical Monument group, and Mrs. Sterling from 18 Olvera Street, the Avila House, ran things with a firm hand, inspected and policed shops and booths, tasted the food and, free of malice or humor, felt history had been preserved. Two million visitors come to Olvera Street each year to move among the concessionaires and visit the canopied booths. The food is a fair perversity of Mexican cooking, the "native" objects sold are rush "Indian" baskets, painted *maracas* made of gourds, various versions of *piñatas* shaped into burros, roosters, sheep, bulls. One can buy Pancho Villa straw hats, the Mexican shoes called *huaraches, calavera* masks, decorated skirts, belts and buckles. There is displayed leather work, pottery, cactus candy, chocolate fudge, pumpkin sweets. There are candlemakers, glassblowers and a blacksmith. Street musicians wander around, but you will not hear the "Corrido of Gregorio Cortez."

There are, of course, those cynical, tasteless people who say that to make it all really authentic, it needs a few clapped-up whores, some knife-carrying gamblers and the smell of poverty, privies and pigpens. For these, go to the barrios, the Chicano ghettos of Los Angeles—not at all the kind of people who have pride in the backing of more and bigger parking lots near the Plaza.

27　Aimee's Temple

No genre retelling of Los Angeles' past would be complete without the lacerating intensity of Aimee Semple McPherson. She, of all the Bible pounders, pulpit stars past and present, is still the best remembered. Ranging from good old-fashioned hellfire preaching to grabbing up what she wanted from theosophy, simplified metaphysics, New Thought and Billy Sunday's stagecraft, she made national religious

AIMEE'S TEMPLE

history. The late Bishop Pike once told me, "Sister Aimee makes Billy Graham look like a Sunday-school boy who forgot his lessons. She had a remarkably penetrating psychological insight into the spiritual needs of simple people."

It was in 1922 that Aimee first appeared in Los Angeles, arriving in a broken-down jalopy with two children (there is very little known about a missing Mr. McPherson). As to worldly goods, she had about $100 in cash. She came to Los Angeles with something called the Four Square Gospel—as a shield against the universal holocaust and sin—which she had been preaching since 1918 without much success in San Diego. Besides the Gospel, she was strong on faith healing, the miraculous intervention of God, the second coming and redemption, and with infectious enthusiasm she was aiming at conversion, mass conversion. She had in the past dropped texts from airplanes to attract attention and didn't feel it was wrong to hold revival meetings in boxing halls. But somehow, apathetic San Diego did not reward the pretty red-haired woman with the Lord's plenty.

By the time Aimee reached Los Angeles, she had perfected her evangelistic style. And Los Angeles took to her "like duck to cracked corn." Her volatile preaching, like burnt offerings of hope, joy and the Kingdom of Heaven, brought forward thousands. In only three years she managed to get offerings of $1 million and was personally worth $250,000. They came to offer her folding money—the lonely, the baffled, the borderline cases with madness or grievances. Also the crippled and those who needed cures, all flocked to the titian-haired God giver. She dressed in faultless white, waving the holy texts, promising redemption to all the imperfectibility of human nature and accepting offerings in return.

Angelus Temple rose, "a strange mixture of tent-show style, crossed by Moorish and architectural gibberish" with 5,000 seats. From there Aimee broadcast her message through a fine radio station costing $75,000. A school was established that turned out, at its prime, 5,000 eager young evangelists a year, sent out to spread the word of God, *and* Sister Aimee. There was a huge movie theater organ, louder than most, and a brass band "worthy of a marine regiment combined with a circus parade troop. The female choir was beautiful with marcelled hair, makeup and costumed like a M-G-M musical chorus." Sister was like some great seed in joyous germination.

Aimee opened branch churches called Lighthouses, 240 of them, all taking their cues and orders from the Holy Mother Church of McPherson. Thousands read her magazine, *The Bridal Call*—"Grant peace, good blessing, kindness and mercy . . . and all life will give thanks to thee, Selah!" When the depression came in 1929, she had 12,000 fanatically loyal members of her Temple in the city, with reserves of 30,000 in southern California counties.

Aimee felt this was Hollywood and she took a lesson from Cecil B. De Mille and even outdramatized that maker of sanctimonious Bible corn.

Sister was the star of her production at the Temple of a mauve-lit version of "Sodom and Gomorrah," with a nice eye for orgy detail. She also dressed as George Washington praying in the "snow" at Valley Forge (still dear to many American hearts, but an event which never took place). Aimee as God's wrath chased a red Devil, complete with horns and tail, across the stage of the Temple with a pitchfork. And the howls of Old Scratch proved she wasn't faking the scene.

There were thousands who said she was "a genuine faith healer, why I seen the lame walk and the sick perk up, get color back in their cheeks. One man took off his truss and he just thrown it up yelling halalooyah like all blazes" (an interview).

Aimee, as she coyly admitted to the press, was aware "woman, like man, does not live by bread alone." There was much gossip of her interest in the male of extraordinary qualities. On May 18, 1926, she had disappeared while wearing a Mack Sennett type bathing suit on the Ocean Park beach at Venice, California. The news was that Sister had been drowned in the surf and her body carried out to sea. Thousands of her flock appeared on the beach, there to drop onto the sand on their knees to pray for either her return or entrance into Heaven. A plane was hired to fly low over the beach and sea to drop flowers. A great meeting

AIMEE'S TEMPLE

was held at the Temple after a follower who had been hunting the body was drowned. The place was filled for a Memorial Service. The plates were passed and $35,000 collected.

The prayers were answered; their fervor raised Aimee from the dead in, of all places, Agua Prieta in Mexico, just across the border from Douglas, Arizona. She had been kidnapped, she claimed, by two men "and a bad woman" and held for ransom, but escaped.

And there she was—clothes neat, clean, uncrumpled, her hair perfectly done. No heroine ever made an entrance into a city as strange and as glorious as Aimee returning to her flock. The press, world wide, filed nearly 100,000 words on the return of Sister Aimee. A fleet of airplanes this time dropped flowers on the train returning her to Los Angeles. A carpet of red roses had been laid down on the station platform for her to walk on. A parade formed and 100,000 people in the streets cheered and prayed out loud. Her white-robed Temple band, oompahing joy, led the way. Two dozen cowboys rode as her escort. Whole squads of police were needed to keep order. "The crowd was the largest ever to welcome anyone in the history of los Angeles."

The Temple had its own back. Aimee stepped forward, "a vision of red hair and white dress," arms sweeping up in a gesture of "you are my people and God's people—in His sympathy for all our dilemmas." There began a chant that echoed through the Temple loud enough to shake out angels from the rafters.

> Coming back, back, back,
> Coming back, back, back,
> Our sister in the Lord is coming back!
> There is shouting all around,
> For our sister has been found;
> There is nothing now of joy or peace we lack!

If only the newspapermen, suspicious of all spiritual values, had not been so nosy. They showed that the kidnaping story Aimee told was nonsense. They traced the fact that after "the drowning" she had, as a later generation would put it, shacked up in a "love cottage" with a husky male radio operator who had once been employed by her at the Temple broadcasting station. (Did she know John Donne's line: "Love a sovereign state of two?")

Los Angeles enjoyed being in the middle of a sensation, and local politicians knew how to exploit it. Aimee was arrested. She was charged with providing false information, information designed to keep the law from the due process of doing its duty. She was brought to trial and legal hassles dragged on for more than two years.

The Temple cheering squads encouraged her to stand the strain by yelling:

> Identifications may come,
> Identifications may go;
> Goggles may come,
> Goggles may go;
> But are we downhearted?
> No! No! No!

Behind the actual legal appearances, she was being given the works by the usual bland Protestant ministers. She wasn't their kind, she made religion a great nihilistic stage show, an interesting living pageant. The clergy showed her no Christian mercy, tenderness, no tolerance. They filed documents for her conviction, presented petitions and passed resolutions condemning her. And they suggested that even He would not have asked them not to throw the first stone.

Today, hunting through old records, one wonders just *what* she was guilty of? She had not committed any crime. Perhaps fibbed a bit, fornicated with a man to whom she was not married. A judge of the Superior Court was accused of "accepting a fee" from her. In the end, justice looked foolish and all the charges against her were dropped. (District Attorney Fitts: "If the public feels like I do . . . they are sick and disgusted with it.")

But eventually it harmed her as a symbol in white, the color of purity.

AIMEE'S TEMPLE

Her followers were lower middle class, not factory workers, but little shopkeepers, gas station attendants, struggling real estate and second-hand car salesmen and their wives. They were a section of society that felt exploited, overtaxed, harassed by installment buying at unfair interest rates. True or not, they felt cheated by insurance companies, escrow and banking methods. Uprooted too, they were from many parts of the country and usually poorly educated, if at all. Aimee gave them a vision of a loving God, of a Jesus no prouder than themselves, but of divine origin. She gave them a feeling that spread-out, busy Los Angeles could be home. Best of all, the Temple served as a sort of huge Lonely Hearts Club, gave them a forward push of personality. They could meet people like themselves, feel a great and strong bond in their love of Aimee. Aimee, for all her opulent razzle-dazzle, never poor-mouthed or maligned anyone, never spoke in tones tearing anyone down (but the Devil). If she milked her people for liberal donations, they got their money's worth in faith, in prayer, in comradeship, instead as so many did, in whiskey and brothels.

By the late 1930s the Temple had lost its power to draw younger new followers in any great numbers. The scandal had done its work and Aimee's haranging voice had taken on a shrill edge, aware that she was on exhibit to the thrill seekers, for the first things any visitor wanted to know about Aimee were the details of her "kidnaping" and her "love cottage." Membership for the Temple and its branches fell to 16,000. These followers—in many cases—crept closer for spiritual shelter and settled in the neighborhood of the Temple.

Aimee still preached, had her pageants and parades, broadcast the faith that comforts. But she must have become deeply depressed. In 1945 she was dead of an overdose of sleeping pills.

Perhaps she had come around to Ambrose Bierce's definition: "Religion: A daughter of Hope and Fear, explaining to Ignorance the nature of the Unknowable."

28 Fade-Out: Desmond Taylor

Not since Dickens' unfinished *The Mystery of Edwin Drood* had the world been so intrigued by a killing as in 1922. This one took place in real life—if what was known as Hollywood was real life.

At that period it was popular to live in places known as "courts," areas rimmed by bungalows.

FADE-OUT: DESMOND TAYLOR

In such a bungalow on the night of February 1, 1922, at about 6:30 P.M., William Desmond Taylor was about to sit down to dinner. He was a prominent motion picture director, gifted with the fluid quality of charm. He had been working on his income tax return for the year 1921. Money was worth about ten times what it is today; his yearly income of $37,000 was very good. He set aside his tax accounting as his black houseman, Henry Peavy, announced that dinner was ready. Henry did not live in, but left after cleaning up after dinner and would return to prepare breakfast about 7:30 in the morning.

Taylor, a handsome Englishman (almost typecast), was a middle-aged bachelor who led a free and easy life much involved with women, mostly actresses from the film industry.

He seemed, from his two-carat diamond ring and thin platinum watch, a successful Hollywood producer, with no interest in any other life-style. Actually, as was to be revealed bit by bit, he was a man of mystery with an irregular past.

In 1908, it was later discovered, he was called William Cunningham Deane Tanner, lived in New York City, carried on a successful business not in any way connected with theater or film. His income then was $25,000 a year. He had served as a captain with the Canadian Army in World War I and he seemed settled into a proper upper-class New York clubman's life, with a wife reported as "charming" and a beautiful daughter. Yet in the autumn of 1908, after a pleasant day of activity at the Vanderbilt Cup Races on Long Island, he sent for his personal things (kept in a hotel room he maintained) and with $500 drawn from his office account simply vanished from business, family and friends.

Evidence was produced later to show he was in Alaska at least three times; what he was doing there was never revealed. In 1917, nine years after vanishing from New York, he appeared in Hollywood. With the swiftness possible in those pioneer days, he became in a short time a top director. It may seem odd that a man with no theater or film background could accomplish this, but it had happened to many people: a boilermaker (Mack Sennett), a truck driver (Boris Karloff), a glove salesman (Sam Goldwyn), a vaudeville trumpet player (Jesse Lasky), a schoolgirl

screenwriter at fourteen (Anita Loos), a nice Jewish boy who became the
first western star and who couldn't ride a horse (Bronco Billy Anderson).

Motion pictures were still not fully respectable. It was a pirate world of
stolen dramas, bootleg cameras, of true shoestring operations. Taylor got
there just as the first multimillions began to roll in.

An important footnote is that in 1912 Taylor's brother, Dennis Deane
Tanner, also did a vanishing act, leaving a wife and two children behind.
Dennis' whereabouts and just who *he* became is one of the mysteries in
the events about to take place.

The bungalow court was mostly occupied by people connected with
the growing film industry. Edna Purviance, Charlie Chaplin's buxom
blonde leading lady, and once his very close friend, lived on the other
side of Taylor, just a wall away, for it was a double bungalow. Across the
way were Mr. and Mrs. Douglas MacLean, he a light comedy director.

At 6:45 P.M., give or take a few minutes, the chauffeur-driven car of
Mabel Normand, the hard-living comedy star developed by Mack Sennett, drove into the court. Mabel was the wild kind of girl, outgoing,
beautiful and careless, given to a reckless and happy way of life. When
she entered Taylor's house, he was talking on the phone—the door appeared to have been unlocked.

The houseman, Henry Peavy, left the two and went out to gossip with
the chauffeur. He testified that he left for home at about 7:30 P.M., and
also reported that the director and the film star were drinking cocktails.

According to what Mabel said later, she had come to visit Taylor at his
request as he was very anxious for her to read a book. The press later
gave the impression that the book was a volume by Herr Doktor Sig-
mund Freud, as explosive an item then as LSD during the hippie generation. Mabel declared to the press that the book was *Rosmundy* by Ethel
M. Dell, the Jackie Susann of her day.

Mabel left at 7:45 P.M. Taylor was to call at nine o'clock to ask her what
she thought of the book, leaving her less than two hours to read it. He
escorted her back to her car, watched the car drive off, returned to his
bungalow and, as the journalists put it, "was never seen alive again ex-

FADE-OUT: DESMOND TAYLOR

cept by his killer, or killers." Night descended on southern California like the fade-out in a motion picture.

Fade in: The dutiful Henry Peavy appeared for work at 7:30 next morning to prepare breakfast. As he opened the door with his key, he discovered the body of Taylor lying on the floor, face up, with his feet pointed toward the door. As Henry remembered it: "I turned and ran out and yelled. Then I yelled some more."

Quickly people gathered, and the police and doctor arrived. The physician noted much too casually that "death was from natural causes, a hemorrhage of the stomach"—that was his diagnosis without, of course, an autopsy. The men from the coroner's office arrived and disagreed. Taylor, they showed, had been shot by a .38 caliber revolver of an obsolete pattern, the slug having entered the left side at the elbow and gone on to lodge in the neck on the right side.

The position of the dead man on the rug was also rather odd. He looked laid out as if for burial. The shirt, tie, collar and cuffs were unrumpled. It was decided that the shot had been fired at close range. His watch, the diamond ring and $78 in cash were untouched. The watch, a jeweler said, had run down at 7:21 P.M. and had not been stopped by the shot. Nearby on the desk was the unfinished income tax report, a pen and an open checkbook.

Mr. MacLean remembered that he had heard a shattering report some time after eight the night before. Mrs. MacLean added that she recalled a figure standing in the light of the open Taylor door, coming out at that time, saying some words of farewell over his shoulder as he went off.

Howard Fellows, who drove Taylor's car, said he had called the house and received no answer at 7:55 P.M. At 8:15 P.M. he rang the bell and still got no answer, so he put away the Taylor car and went home. He may, or may not, have been the man Mrs. MacLean saw. The police set the time of the killing between 7:40 P.M. and 8:15 P.M., the usual unscientific guess. Mabel Normand at home, expecting a call from Taylor at nine o'clock, never got it.

The murder of a prominent film director caused a nationwide sensation. The press, local and national, always presented Hollywood as if spelled Sodom, and it was notorious for its sensations in reporting crime rather than facts. Example in the Taylor murder: Did a detective pick up a handkerchief with the letter "S" lying near the body? He said he put it on a table, but it was never found again. Fact or a reporter's invention?

It was Edna Purviance who telephoned Mabel that morning and informed her that Taylor had been murdered. Mabel at once rushed over to the bungalow and was loud in her demand that certain of her letters and telegrams to Desmond Taylor be returned to her. She knew, she added, just where they were kept. She admitted she wanted them to "prevent terms of affection from being misconstrued." Later she denied she went to the bungalow to get the letters; she said she had been asked by the detectives to appear so as to show them, she claimed, how the furniture and art objects had been arranged when she last saw them.

Given permission to get the letters, she went up to Taylor's bedroom, opened the top drawer of his dresser, and announced the letters were missing. A scene pure Mary Roberts Rinehart. It was gossiped about in Hollywood that the manager of the Lasky Studios where Taylor worked had been there already and removed, among others, Mabel's letters. Yet on February 10th, the public administrator said he had found the letters at the Taylor place concealed under "a double lock." What would Mabel say to this?

Mabel Normand announced: "I would gladly set them [the found letters] before the world. . . . I have nothing to conceal." However, the contents were never given to the public after the D.A.'s office confirmed that they contained "nothing helpful" to the investigation of the murder of Desmond Taylor. A letter that did cause a sensation—*the* letter of the case—was one found by a police officer rummaging in Taylor's library. As he picked up a book at random, a letter dropped out on which was an embossed crest: M. M. M. It read: "Dearest, I love you. I love you. I love you." Ending with several X marks and an extra big X, signed, "Yours always, Mary."

M. M. M. Mary?

FADE-OUT: DESMOND TAYLOR

Mary, a popular and demure movie star—not one of the dashing, out-going types—announced that the true relationship between herself and the dead man was that they were an engaged couple but had kept it secret. Later it was also revealed that in a riding boot in Taylor's closet were found what a press story called, "A dozen fervent letters written in a simple code . . . signed Mary . . . the outpourings of a young girl's heart to the man whom she obviously loved." There were no other quotes from the letters. Kept back for some time was the fact that the police found "two strands of blond hair" on the murdered man's body.

Miss M—'s later career, some film historians felt, suffered from her relationship with the Taylor case, and she appeared less and less in pictures.

Certain serious events that occurred before the murder were pointed out to me by Ben Hecht when I was beginning to collect material for this book, incidents that might have solved the killing. There had been a series of burglaries of Taylor's bungalow. Jewelry was stolen and Taylor's private brand of cigarettes taken. Pawn tickets made out to William Deane Tanner had been mailed back to Taylor, so he could redeem the stolen items. Important too: six months before his murder Taylor, returning from Europe, had accused his secretary (some said valet), E. F. Sands, of forging Taylor's name in buying clothes and lingerie for women. Sands then vanished and was not to be found.

It was Ben Hecht's theory, as a former police reporter—and others agreed with him—that E. F. Sands was actually Taylor's brother, Dennis Deane Tanner, who in 1912 had left his wife and two children and vanished in the manner of Taylor himself. As Ben Hecht surmised, "It's clear now that Taylor paid a monthly allowance to Dennis' deserted wife, a payoff of some kind. And a man in Denver, after the killing, identified Sands as Taylor's brother." He said he "knew them both very well." He added in a press interview, "When Sands is caught, the mystery of Taylor's murder will be clear. . . . Revenge is the motive behind the murder of William Desmond Taylor." But the police never followed that up or made any real effort to collar Sands.

One of the few references by Taylor to Sands that I have discovered is

Taylor's comment—reported by a witness to the police—that when Taylor was told Sands might have escaped from California, Taylor said, "I would go to any trouble, or expense, to extradite him, not only from a neighboring state, but from any country in the world. All I want is five minutes alone with him."

To the film actress Claire Windsor, Taylor's reaction to Sands was even stronger. He told her, "If I ever lay my hands on Sands, I will kill him." Both statements are not the normal reaction to an employee who had merely charged some lingerie to his boss's account and stolen a few trinkets which were redeemed.

Sands as Taylor's brother and his murderer is not the only plausible theory. Among all the kooky ones that have been dreamed up "a good bet is a woman he did the dirty to" (Hecht to me).

The D.A. did send out an offer of immunity to Sands to come in and testify, to help find the actual murderer. Sands, however, wherever he was, remained mute.

There was a letter from a former British officer stating that while Taylor was in London with him after the Armistice, he had pointed out a man in Canadian uniform and said, "That man is going to get me if it takes a thousand years to do it. I had him court-martialed for the theft of Army property."

Several men were rumored as being that court-martialed soldier and had also been heard making threats against Taylor. But in the end that story did not lead to one identified person. By March, more than 300 people in the nation had confessed that they had murdered William Desmond Taylor.

An ex-convict did name a motion picture actress as the killer, and the Taylor houseman, Peavy, in 1930 was reported to have stated flatly that "a famous actress killed the equally famous director. . . ."

Later he was not so certain—but believed he knew who did the killing.

However, the D.A. did get possession of two diaries of a young woman whose lawyers insisted their contents be kept secret.

For years—without any evidence at all—the actress M.M. was con-

FADE-OUT: DESMOND TAYLOR

nected in many people's minds with the convict's story, the houseman's statements and with the diaries. She once went to court to get legal action against being mentioned in this manner, but the case never came to judgment.

Taylor remains through it all a mysterious, nebulous personality, and a few remaining fuzzy strips of motion picture film, all that is left of his work, and they give us no clues at all. Hardly anyone involved led a normal exemplary life, which delighted the public and gave them an excuse to feel shocked and then resentful. The Taylor murder was but one in a series of scandals that were to help destroy the Hollywood film industry.

29 Pictures in Sunlight

Lorp street

I have avoided becoming a character in this story of a city where I have lived for so much of my life. But if the book is to have any intimate picture of the death of the Moby Dick that was the motion picture industry at its greatest, most glamorous success, it will have to be told in "close-up" (as the film scripts put it). In 1927 the nearly busted Warner Brothers (four) in a desperate attempt to stay afloat issued a novelty film

PICTURES IN SUNLIGHT

called *The Jazz Singer,* with Al Jolson, a Broadway star, singing his best-known songs and featuring a three- or four-minute scene in which he is heard talking to his old mother. (Just twenty years later I was to write *The Jolson Story,* in which Jolson actually appeared as himself in the black-face scenes.) The picture was a huge sensation, a novelty that killed off the old silent films, many of its stars, directors and producers and created a demand by the studios for writers of dialogue.

When I entered Hollywood we were about to go to war. The stars were the last of the fabulous great personalities: Clark Gable, Garbo, Bette Davis, James Cagney, Humphrey Bogart, Gary Cooper, ruled by the last of the wild buffalo gods, who were aging fast but still aware of their sadistic powers. ("Is there a black list?" I once asked Harry Warner. "Of course not, we do it all by phone.") Harry Cohen, I was told, was the most despised, the most shaggy of the town's monsters. Yet I got along very well with him when I wrote *The Jolson Story.* He was rude and vulgar, but he was also a true personality and had a keen sense for making films people liked. Cecil B. De Mille, I found, took one's measure to see how much abuse you'd take, and if you faced him down he was a lamb. I worked for months on his picture *Greatest Show on Earth,* and it was always "Mr. De Mille" and "Longstreet"—a wary truce. When I worked on *Duel in the Sun* with David O. Selznick, he was already a man on a slide—a rather clumsy, tragic figure, who had risen high and would fall away to a has-been.

I attended Louis B. Mayer's sixty-second birthday party. So did everyone that day in the big dining room at M-G-M. We all drank to the "raunchy little monster" (quoting Wallace Beery). He was mean, hard, a rough-and-tumble fighter who had ruined many people of talent when crossed. While I was working at the studio I saw him pushed out by a younger climber, Dore Schary, a public liberal. Hedda Hopper, the gossip columnist, renamed the studio Metro-Goldwyn-Moscow.

"The system of survival is the thing," Bogart told me with his famous lisp one afternoon at the Lakeside Club. "It's to hit 'em first." The lunch is always confused in my mind, because across the way Oliver Hardy

EFORMERS OPEN BARRAGE ON STARS' PRIVATE LIVES

eatures—Drama—Radio

Los Angeles Times

Music—Books—Art

SUNDAY MORNING, JUNE 3, 1934

PART II

ROVING SHOTS AT THE UNSUSPECTING CELEBRITIES AS THEY RAMBLE HITHER AND YON

Film scandals and other gossip in 1934 took people's minds off the Depression.

Al Jolson, Douglas Fairbanks, Eddie Cantor, Ronald Colman and Samuel Goldwyn posing at a Hollywood studio in 1932. (Wide World)

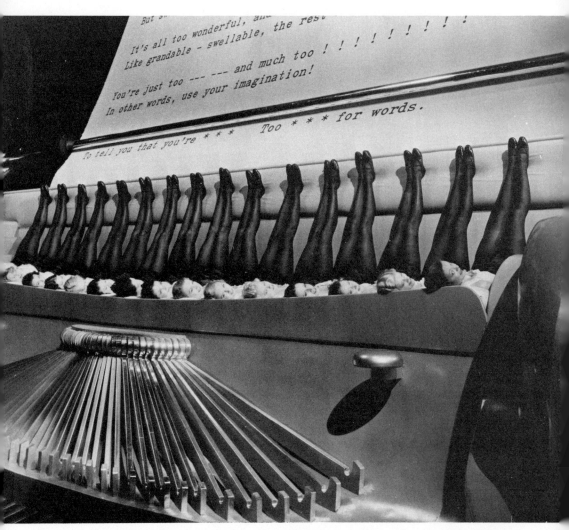

While working at Warner Brothers film studios in 1942, William Faulkner noted: "Everything in Los Angeles is too large, too loud and usually banal in concept." Here, a scene from a film musical of a living typewriter. (Academy of Motion Picture Arts and Sciences)

without his little mustache was kissing the hand of a young blonde and sighing in her ear—a surrealist scene that has haunted me.

"It's a jungle, kiddo," Bogart said. "And don't you ever forget it. It's all politics and shoving the other guy. Not talent. Sock 'em first or they'll eat your gizzard on toast."

It was, and is, a cruel industry in a cruel town. D. W. Griffith, who had brought the Hollywood film to maturity, was unemployed, sitting in a lonely room, drinking; F. Scott Fitzgerald, coming partly out of his crack-up, was begging for screen-writing jobs, with his daughter at school and wife in a sanitarium. I remember the gin bottles piled up outside his cottage window out back, all empty.

The war pictures Hollywood made were dreadful trash. John Wayne, swinging his torso and haunches fought heroically on a dozen war fronts, rose to glory and fame on studio sets. Errol Flynn did the same for the British. Flynn was a charming man, well bred, rather sad ("my mother disliked me"). He was a gentleman without making an effort, well read and the writer of several books. "In like Flynn" became a kind of indecent joke. But actually Flynn, whom I got to know very well, was never the great lover. He was really the victim of women; he believed his publicity and took female flattery seriously, gracefully, but took it.

John Barrymore was then on his last legs; I was writing his radio material for him, the only form of work he could get in his last years. He was a magnificent Art Nouveau object crossed with a Second Empire wreck. Unwashed, legs swollen with dropsy, ulcers bleeding, he was drinking and there was talk of dope, as drugs were called in those days. He would come into the radio studio with some addled sexual conquest, or a new wife, and move about in a daze; then, waiting for a first reading, he would sometimes come fully alive and recite something from _Hamlet_ or _Richard III_ with a vigor and sense far from the dying old man he was. He retained his looks—a bit puffy—until the end.

My favorite tippler was W. C. Fields, who was as mean and as erudite as legend made him. I once heard him say, "It's a Christian's duty to give a glass of water to a drowning man."

CON MEN AND GENIUSES

If all this seems banal, rather like a columnist's gossip, that was the true horror of Hollywood in those days; it *was* exactly that, a cheap and vulgar world of tinsel, its victims trapped in unreality—and mink. It was the product of an industry that owned the theaters and was needed in wartime, when all craved entertainment and people stood in lines for blocks to see *anything* the studios offered.

Nasty political squalls from the left and the right were battering at film studio doors in the late 1940s. Labor racketeer and union leader Willie Bioff had blackmailed studio heads for a million dollars or so to keep the unions from calling a strike. Willie was to step on his car's self-starter one morning and be blown into a Keystone Cops explosive finish, only *this* was for real.

The Screen Writers Guild, which I joined in 1940, was a union that had just defeated a captive studio company union, Film Playwrights, and it was becoming more and more dominated by the aggressive left-wing writers out of New York "on their Chippendale soapboxes" (Charles Grayson), making converts of native rebels. Later it was widely and wrongly accepted that the Screen Writers Guild was a Communist-controlled union. The actual facts were different. John Wayne, Ward Bond and a group of their friends supported an organization, a kind of true-blue American group, that took on the task of deciding *who* was a commie, a pinko, a liberal, a radical, a fellow traveler.

Members of the guild and the industry were soon shouting "fascist" and "commie" at each other. Anyone who wore a hat could be called fascist, and anyone who had once given a dollar to a Loyalist Spain fund to feed women and children (as I had done—*one* dollar) stood in danger of being blacklisted as a card-carrying Communist. Cecil B. De Mille once showed me my F.B.I. dossier which noted the fact that I had once had lunch with Albert Maltz at Paramount, he soon to join the Unfriendly Ten.

At a Screen Writers Guild meeting the tactics adopted by the Marxists as a minority group of 40 to 60 was to outwait the 200 or 300 other members who had come to the meeting and then left at a decent hour. The left-wing then continued the meeting and passed resolutions of their own. They were at last defeated when the guild began having a late-hour member present with 300 properly signed proxy cards in his pocket.

Then came the time of the Unfriendly Ten screenwriters, as the press labeled those members who were called before the Un-American Activities Committee sitting in Washington to testify whether or not they were card-carrying Communist Party members. They were asked whom else they could name as having attended party meetings, supported party projects, talked the party line. Most of the writers called the ten (actually a dozen or more) took the Fifth, and some spent a year or so in federal prisons.

A greater harm was done those who were suspected of being fellow travelers; radicals and liberals who were *not* party members. The true-blue groups went into action. Some writers and actors ate crow and were anointed as repentant. Many people not remotely connected with the party or its philosophies were ruined "by association" and driven from the industry. Some committed suicide.

Ironically, the Unfriendly Ten under other names often continued to work slyly on screenplays. As Harry Cohen told me, "When you need a sonofabitch with an Underwood, you need him." It was reported in print that Dalton Trumbo, one of the jailed, actually won an Academy Award Oscar for a screenplay he did for the King Brothers under a pen name. The Oscar still has not been delivered to the author of that screen play.

The 1950s saw the first decline of the great film studios. Better, more daring films were being made abroad and shown in Bel Air and Beverly Hills living rooms. Early Fellini was about to appear, and the English were producing amusing little films with Alec Guiness and Peter Sellers.

The real killer, however, was television, if not to kill at least to deeply wound. TV products were no worse than the studios' and were for free. Its banalities were an extension of motion picture fare. Instead of seizing the TV industry when it could, the studios waited too long for it to go

CON MEN AND GENIUSES

away, and in the end surrendered their old films for continuous rerunning.

Hollywood films are no longer made for theaters by the three or four hundreds, as once issued in a good year's output. Today perhaps thirty or forty major films are produced, many made by independent producers financed by some surviving, just surviving, once major studio. Name stars mean very little. Perhaps Marilyn Monroe died in vain.

Millions have been lost in "blockbusters" that failed: *Cleopatra, Dr. Doolittle, Darling Lily, Star, Camelot,* against one *Sound of Music,* a rather dull and saccharine picture but a box-office success. The public has supported brutal, cynical, perverted pictures like *The Exorcist, The Godfather, The Dirty Dozen.* Violence and more violence, bloody crime, slob horror; depraved taste done in a costly manner by skilled but cynical craftsmen without any moral sense. Sam Peckinpaugh has been acclaimed as a master of sheer violence and is very much admired by theater owners for pictures like *Straw Dogs.* The director expresses his unrivaled philosophy which mistakes violence for strength.

Overuse of four-letter words and some near-nude footage are featured in almost all major productions, except the bland, too cute Disney fantasy parodies of life.

However, it is not the studios or well-known directors who make the most successful films, but rather the unknown creators of pornographic films. "Hard porno" is the town's name for *Deep Throat, The Devil in Miss Jones.* The pioneer "flesh flic," however, was the Swedish film *I Am Curious (Yellow).* After its success, the race to be the most raunchy and depraved began.

Meanwhile M-G-M is in the hotel business, the Twentieth Century-Fox lot is a monstrous high-rise development, a traffic bottleneck called Century City. Universal caters to tourists—a ride around and thrills. Columbia and Warners have combined, making one small of what once was two bigs. And rumors are that one major lot may be turned into bowling alleys, or a giant McDonald's hamburger grease pit.

30 William Faulkner and Sinclair Lewis in Hollywood

S outhern Californians will admit, those who are literate, that northern California has produced writers, while Los Angeles has merely
hired gagmen and screenwriters. There have been no mature native authors like Bret Harte, Jack London, Frank Norris or John Stein-
beck to write of the barley fields or cities of the south. Visitors, yes, and
best-selling craftsmen producing a salable product. Guests, too, like

CON MEN AND GENIUSES

Thomas Mann (in exile), John O'Hara (between trips on the wagon), Ernest Hemingway (to go duck hunting with Gary Cooper), but no Los Angeles Dickens or Proust.

I, as the writer of a weekly book column for Readers Syndicate, was a way station for visitors—publishers usually gave authors coming west introductions to me, often with a side warning, as one publisher wrote me, "Keep him sober and out of the slammer."

In 1942, hearing my friend William Faulkner was having a hard time of it and needing money, I arranged with James Geller, story editor at Warner Brothers Studios, for Faulkner to come to the coast to do some screen writing. He had been out before in the 1930s for a short spell, and I had been on friendly terms with him since 1937, when his books weren't selling.

Faulkner took no interest in Los Angeles. He was hard up—no matter what the critics thought of his books—and he was here to make some money. For his first assignment the studio gave him my novel *Stallion Road* to turn into a screenplay. One morning, as he came into my office in the writers' building, Bill gave me a sad but belligerent eye. "I don't read much of yo' young writers, but they are paying me for this, so I'll read it."

He began the job with no beguiling protests. But he was going off on periodical drunks during his entire writing period in Hollywood. The story editor would plead with me to have him turn in at least some script pages for the front office to see, even if he wasn't on the lot. When Bill did come back, he had a contrite and humble look.

One day I was called into the office of the jumpy little producer who had been assigned to the picture. He threw a bound bundle of yellow onionskin sheets at me, said my friend Bill had written an impossible screenplay on *Stallion Road,* and would I forget his version and write my own screenplay?

I read the screenplay that afternoon, an original Faulkner manuscript—now in the Faulkner Collection, University of Virginia, and still unpublished. I thought it was a magnificent thing—wild, wonderful, mad.

WILLIAM FAULKNER AND SINCLAIR LEWIS IN HOLLYWOOD

Bill had gone off on a Faulknerian tour of his own despairs, passions and storytelling. Today, even in Los Angeles, it could be made as a New Wave film. It had an enduring and authentic fluid flow, a disquieting persistence.

Bill went to work, with collaborators, on two screenplays, *The Big Sleep* by Raymond Chandler and *To Have and Have Not* by Ernest Hemingway, both Bogart films. He loved horses, and I told him as long as he was giving the director what he wanted, he could afford to keep a horse in California. He bought a mare. I never rode with him, but people who did said Bill was a pretty poor horseman. For all his love of horses and dogs he was not a sportsman, and in fox hunts in Virginia—one of my former secretaries wrote me—he actually fell off his horse very often.

Bill's social life in California seemed to be kept down as close to zero as he could get it. He lived in a Faustian loneliness of his own making. The U.C.L.A. and U.S.C. college intellectuals (he called them "endowed loafers") tried to capture him. His fame was spreading in the 1940s, but he avoided contact with what passed for culture on the coast. I attended two dinners he could not refuse at the home of James Geller, the studio's editor in charge of writers. Christopher Isherwood was present at both; he and Bill didn't exchange a word all night after the first introduction. Bill spent the evening drinking in a sort of pious complacency. He sat silently, clutching a tall highball glass, while talk of art, literature, income tax and film making went on all around him. From time to time he held up the glass to be refilled with bourbon and a little water. The inanities of the table conversation he ignored. His was an easy, prolonged drinking, no effort and seemingly no reaction. Most guests expected, they told me later, some dispensation of irony, or a funny Negro story.

Bill was, I had long sensed, a kind of actor, and he would present several facets of his country-boy character when trapped for a Hollywood interview. His favorite answer as to why he wrote, or what literature was, became a formula answer: "The drama of the conflict in the human heart." I heard so many versions of this I wondered that he dared repeat it so often. His other favorite was, when asked what made a writer: "A little whiskey, a little tobacco, and paper." He gave several readings of that line when he had to say something.

It was near the end of his Hollywood stay that I finally penetrated some of his defenses and disguises. I saw a man of great talent (and time may prove, a genius), an encumbered heart, a provincial with a certain naïveté, not given to any surface exuberances. Magnificently sensitive to the true stuff of life, he could make simple things nearly epic: the sound of grease in a hot skillet, the shade of a certain plant at a certain hour, the feel and smell of a hot day, the direct sexual reaction of a woman, the pattern of the perverse demons that haunt us all. William Faulkner was the historian of the consequence of errors, of climate and hereditary pride. Los Angeles had no theme or story to offer him. He himself was irrational and bizarre on the outside, a silent man, who saw the world as a sad spectacle, an audible country sick with heat, lust, greed, for he had a fine native ear. The correlation of words and eye he drew down into his own unadulterated self and ejected as his strange prose ("I am a strangulated poet").

We would sit in the late afternoon at the studio, not talking at first, yet aware. His sadness came naturally to him; he saw, he told me, that the world needed a minimum of integrity to function. "Ecstasy and disgust," he went on, "are often two spellings of the same word. Most writers perpetuate the juridical lie. . . ." (I'm referring to some scribbled notes I kept.) "Life is a mass of irrelevant detail," he said, "And the writer presents it in a little order with a bit of poetry. Poetry, now, that's the highest form of art. I wrote some in my youth. It wasn't much. When a man finds poetry isn't for him, and the short story isn't everything, then all that's left is the novel."

But I suggested that that, too, was one of his set interview pieces. He really admired the great novels he had read as a young man. He did not read much contemporary writing in California. Except for Hemingway and Wolfe, I never heard him mention a modern writer with any degree of pleasure.

Like most readers, I wondered if he had from the first planned his

WILLIAM FAULKNER AND SINCLAIR LEWIS IN HOLLYWOOD

strange world of Yoknapatawpha County, its hillbilly Greek shadows, its sly redneck country Romans, his symbols into which the critics read so much that is universal. In what Bill said when I hinted about the subject, it would appear he had planned nothing, had written of himself and his background and had let his people make their own themes. "To feel happy without feeling guilty, now, yo' can say that's what I hoped to find in my writing. The critics—I used to read them, I don't no more—they found all that metamorphosis and labyrinth of purpose. Maybe they were right. Oh, I tried later—sure—to make some of it fit together. I wasn't Zola or Balzac, who had it all blueprinted for a series of books. I didn't have their brilliant impromptus either. I just wrote. Ideas are necessities not luxuries. It's people I write about. Good and bad, I don't make them good or bad. Can't explain some of them, why they are as they are. People are an indestructible element. Yet they're going to sicken, going to die, going to be forgotten, but leaving a sign of themselves sometimes. . . . The flesh has its own spirit, I feel, free of the mind."

He didn't care to discuss the distortions or involutions of his sentences or his symbols. I think he sensed he didn't really fully understand them himself. Writing was a grand audacity, full of discrepancies, but the only thing he wanted to do.

My last scene with William Faulkner in Hollywood was like his last novel, a kind of minor comic masterpiece. I was standing in front of the studio waiting to be picked up for the ride home. A battered car appeared with Bill at the wheel. A two-wheeled horse trailer was attached behind. In it was his horse, the most pregnant mare I had ever seen.

"That's a mighty pregnant mare, Bill."

"Gotta get her to Mississippi. No mare of mine is going to throw a foal in California."

With a grind of gears he moved on toward the hills where details of the day were fading into fragmentations of browns and golds.

I saw Bill only once more before his death. Years had passed; he had won the Nobel Prize, had been sent to Japan by the State Department, was a novelist-in-residence at the University of Virginia, had been a guest at West Point—that was his bowler hat and furled umbrella period. He hunted with Virginia fox hunters. He was much photographed.

I had been puzzled by his Nobel Prize speech; it did not express his true dark philosophy, nor was it the introspective, subtle language of the man I had known. It neither sounded like him nor conformed to the antagonistic brooding of his own personality.

So the last time we met—in a dark mellow eating place—I told him my doubts about the speech. He sat a long time smoking, then looked at me and placed a hand on my knee. "We really live in the world of our mind, we only move about in the visible one."

For the literary records, I am guilty—indirectly—for the production of his worst novel, *A Fable*. It resulted when I introduced him to a kooky film producer named William Bacher, who sold Bill on the idea of Christ as a soldier in the 1914 war as a screenplay. When the script was rejected, he gave William Faulkner all rights to the pompous stuff. I tried to talk Bill out of the idea that it was magnificent material, but Bill was stubborn.

To finish off all the literary friendships this book will contain, I must mention Sinclair Lewis' last trip to Los Angeles.

There had been talk once between us about a novel of an American artist; I was to furnish the artist's studio background. Nothing much came of that; I finally wrote the book myself as *The Lion at Morning*, incorporating some of Lewis' ideas.

Many people in Hollywood and elsewhere were offended by Lewis' manners, his dismal drinking, his overextended clowning, even his appearance, a spoiled face of advanced acne necrotica seborrhoeica. I found the true man lonely, badgered, but alive, and with a sadness that clung to him at all times, sober or drunk. Unlike my contact with William Faulkner, with Hal (his friends never called him Sinclair) there was a letting down of guards and a lot of casual, often amusing small talk.

I had known him since 1930. Lewis in Hollywood in the late 1940s tried to keep up his pose of being a great writer and continued to insist that there was no perfect equivalent for "reality" in literature. But his

WILLIAM FAULKNER AND SINCLAIR LEWIS IN HOLLYWOOD

novels no longer received critical cheers, and he resented this, but was, I think, well aware that they were not the prime stuff of his youth.

I suggested to Lewis that he meet William Faulkner at Warner Brothers and join us at lunch with Humphrey Bogart at the Lakeside Club, but Lewis shied away. He was like a child in his personal relationships—sort of, "you like him better than me, you see more of him than me when we're both in town." He could be pugnacious and infantile, but he had warmth. Faulkner never projected exposure of any emotion.

The last time I was with Sinclair Lewis was in 1947. Robert Nathan, the popular novelist, was giving a party for Thomas Mann *and* Sinclair Lewis—a poor idea to begin with, to merge two hypersensitive personalities. It was a cool night, and Nathan, a gourmet, a lover of good wine, music and the best people, had attached a huge tent to his house where the dinner would be served, and baskets of cherry-red charcoal drove off the night air. There was a gathering in the house proper, a collection of those changing names and faces that make news in southern California, natives with bellicose eyes, well-known writers passing through, refugees in power or in poverty, introverted, oblique and subtle, Hollywood hacks smiling sadly at those who didn't make $2,000 a week.

Very gala at its beginning, the dinner soon suffered a chill. The refugees had put Thomas Mann—gray, steel-hard as a Prussian helmet, silent—in one corner of the big living room and surrounded him like a guttural Old Guard making genuflections to a founder of a hierarchy, protecting him from the outside world. In another corner sat Lewis, his head shaking a bit, his facial scar tissue roast-beef red, surrounded by the Hollywood hacks, as if pointing up to the refugees *this* is one of ours. The two groups would not mix or mingle; the guards hovering between self-sustained importance and pride would not relax their circle of protection. Robert Nathan went back and forth like an emissary, hoping to arrange some truce, some field of meeting. But the owners of the adoring Teutonic voices were like a barrier of covered wagons drawn up in a circle to defend their leader against an Indian attack by Lewis and his American horde.

CON MEN AND GENIUSES

With a crucified expression, Lewis rose, shook off his attendants and said to me, "Let's get away, get boozed; let's get drunk." We called a taxi and went down to the tomb-like bar of the Beverly Wilshire, where we had a few more drinks to add to the ones imbibed at Nathan's. I suppose we did get high. The bar was dimly lit, and there were about four other drinkers who looked already drunk themselves, sad too, as if aware of the impermanence of all human endeavor.

Lewis set down his glass, empty, on the bar, faced around and began in a thick German accent I can recapture only in part: "Mine name, Gott sei dank, ist Thomas Mann. I haft joost been honored, meinen Herren, by the Nobel Prize, Gluck auf, und six cases mit Pilzener Bier. . . ."

And he proceeded to deliver his version of Thomas Mann receiving the Nobel Prize to the indifferent stares of the drunks and a scowling but puzzled bartender. I paid the bar bill and we left. A brusque, baffled, unhappy somnambulist, Sinclair Lewis (I sensed) saw the comic and stupefying vistas of Los Angeles' literary scene.

I never saw Lewis again after that night. And so no more of the higher literary life in Los Angeles from me on these pages.

BOOK V

POSTURES AND POSES

31 The Self-Indulgence of Beverly Hills

R ich people who move to California do not go to Pasadena to live unless they have had money for at least two decades; the rest go to Beverly Hills. The more ornate Beverly Hills has been marked down in print as being named after Beverly Farms, Massachusetts, the hometown of its founder, Burton E. Green. Irving Stone repeated this when he wrote of the city. Actually, Mr. Green got the name from read-

POSTURES AND POSES

ing a newspaper account of President Taft's visiting "Beverly Farms" in Massachusetts, and Mr. Green so liked the sound of Beverly that he changed Farms to Hills and sold the name to his associates in the land dividing business.

One story told about Beverly Hills that is not a myth is that you can be stopped, even arrested, for walking in the residential streets of the city. I have been picked up three times by the Beverly Hills police for walking, and as I don't drive a car and have no driver's license, I have been driven home to be identified.

Actually, Beverly Hills is no Winesburg, Ohio, or Sodom-among-the-Palm Trees. It's a polarized society of brains or money—often both—the lawns are well taken care of, its children are better educated and it shows off its wealth in a direct Philistinism. Otherwise it has the same domestic problems—marriages, divorces and rebel generation—as the rest of the United States—and inflation worries, a bit beyond any American town its size. It also has more names the newspaper reader recognizes as makers of fleshy gyrations and foolish sensations, but only because some of its people are either in *Who's Who* or in show biz.

It is like a European nation with no outlet to the sea, in the sense that Beverly Hills is *not* part of the city of Los Angeles, which surrounds it on *all* sides but has so far been unable to annex it. The talk that taxes are lower in Beverly Hills is a sort of myth, for while the rate may be lower, the house and land values are overinflated and realtors tell soft plausible lies about this. A $200,000 Beverly Hills house (practically a slum price for Beverly Hills, a real estate broker tells me) would, outside the magic boundaries, be wearing a price tag of $60,000 to $75,000. The average old Beverly Hills house in 1976 was valued at $250,000 to $300,000 and thirty years ago, when already old, could have been bought for $22,000. I know people who did buy for around that price. The place is nourished by appetites that want a Beverly Hills address.

There is a dreadful pecking order that goes by names of desired districts in southern California. To live *inside* the Bel Air gates with posted guards or in Beverly Hills or Holmby Hills is an AAA rating, even if your house is a wreck, the plumbing and wiring are gone and the decomposed

THE SELF-INDULGENCE OF BEVERLY HILLS

hillside is crumbling away. To live in Glendale and Eagle Rock, the younger with-it set tell me, is to live among squares. Pasadena, until a few years ago, was solid and safe for one's money, well-being, social status and Herbert Hoover's philosophy. Now it has smog and the problem of blacks darkening its place as an exclusive town of unprogressive social standing. "The best families are fleeing, splitting in their Rolls or Lincolns, with the family silver and grandma's painting by John Singer Sargent on the back seat. I mean Panicsville" (interview with a Pasadena high school girl).

Los Angeles has the second largest Jewish population in the United States (New York is number one), the last count coming to about 500,000. Anti-Semitism is subdued but for a handful of addled boys playing at Nazis. The Jonathan Club, the California Club, the L.A. Country and the L.A. Athletic Club are segregated oligarchical clubs. (Unlike one New York club which, when criticized for bigotry, decided "to let in *one* Gimbel.")

The plush Jewish club—complacent and exclusive—the Hillcrest, sitting as Ben Hecht once said "on a pool of oil and sour cream," is strictly for very well-off Jews ($15,000 a membership if you can wait out the waiting list).

The only exciting Jews that I found in Los Angeles were in Boyle Heights and the Fairfax section, mostly poor, striving, struggling, laughing, speaking Yiddish, eating pungently and living, as one young storefront rabbi told me, "a philosophical ritual mishmash and wise farting." Here there is a supporting of Orthodox *shuls* and ancient faith. As the young rabbi explained to me, "The temple bacon-eating Jews, the fancy reformniks of Beverly Hills, the Magnin crowd, to me are not really Jews. They run social clubs, not shuls, and their rabbis, call *them* rabbis? shave and play golf. Wouldn't surprise me if they aren't even circumcised. Come, attend a few of our Hasidic meetings with the dancing, shouting, the joy of chanting, you'll see it is the poor Los Angeles Jews who get the fullness of fun out of their faith here. And they don't have their names on the doors of the *goyim*'s Music Center." There are quite a few Jews like this young zealot, but they don't get press coverage.

32 Times II and Times III

Times II began its reign with a woman sharing the power—*la reine le veut*—of the publisher. For when Harry died at eighty, in 1944, Dorothy Buffum Chandler, the wife of Norman Chandler, helped run the Chandler empire. She was once called by Oscar Levant at a party "the Gertrude Stein of downtown Los Angeles."

The tone, the quality of *Times* II was great deal the result of her hard and ardent work. The arts, and what passed for local society, were her special fields. She was president of the Hollywood Bowl Association, executive vice president of the Southern California Symphony Association, a guarantor of the Los Angeles Civic Light Opera, served on the Board of Regents of the University of California and on the Board of Occidental College, besides being the managing director of the doing over of the Civic Center. Her clout was being able to get huge sums of money from those wealthy folk who wanted to be listed with the best people, to have their names set on some façade or other, particularly the rich philanthropic Jews of the community.

Times II welcomed all groups, spread itself with editions that reached deep into Orange County, Birch Society territory to be, and north past Santa Barbara. *Times* II continued to exert its power politically and remained the ruler of the city and state in politics according to observers. But the Democrats managed to outnumber the Republicans, so that there were often marjorities for Truman, Kennedy and on the state level for bland fellows like Pat Brown.

Times II preached a philosophy: Possession isn't all bad, pride in Los Angeles is for the good.

In 1960 Norman Chandler stepped aside for his and Buffy's son, Otis. It was Otis who brought together the people and the policy to create *Times* III, the present newspaper. The true cause for the change was the recognition of the handwriting on the wall, or rather the sounds and pictures in the air. Television made over *Times* II into *Times* III. News was stale stuff in a morning newspaper—people had had it all the night before both before and after the Late Show.

The *Times* turned itself into a daily magazine. Count the real news columns, then count the fillers—the columnists, local and canned, the pictures, the features, the comics, crossword puzzles, bridge skills, astrology, the theater, film and television gossip, beauty hints, food sections. And often half the front page is not news at all, but articles, sometimes very good ones researched by an expert staff. In fact, if you wanted just news in the *Times,* you could read a good condensation of it on page two and set the rest of the paper aside.

But *Times* III is read for other sections. The business section, written with penetrating acumen, is one of the best in the West. Ellen Harris' in-depth consumer research is the only really excellent work in the West being done to protect the public in what it eats and uses. She presents an opening up of topics that *Times* II would never have touched. The paper now reports clearly and directly on lesbians, homosexuals and abortions without rancor or leering and will use words like *ass* and *sonofabitch* in a report, and this in a newspaper that once painted out the navel in a model wearing a bikini for an airline ad (1970). It now runs a section ad-vertising (with art work) erotic and porno films with their text suggesting perversions, come-ons for the kick seeker and the offbeat sexes. Its Hol-lywood gossip texts were much more repellent until dismissed in 1975.

Seen for what it is trying to do, *Times* III is an excellent paper. It may, as my retired journalist friend says,

lack a great prose style, solid literary writing, and a coverage of how the other half lives and exists, with just a few stories on blacks or Chicanos. Its biggest problem oddly enough—to me—is in not encouraging a really solid rival morning newspaper which would keep it on its toes, trying harder, hitting stronger, digging deeper. Now that it's alone in its field, the major newspaper of the *whole* of southern California, it's flabby with fat, for it doesn't have to test its muscles with somebody racing elbow to elbow with it.

And there is no sign there is any change around. *The New York Times* threw a scare into it with talk of a West Coast edition. But what came was a miserable few photo-copied pages; they were no more *The New York Times* than a pea is a watermelon. They were stupid to think we really are all kooks and nuts out here.

"Does the *L.A. Times* appeal to the up-coming generation? It hardly knows how to report them—mostly with a kind of nervous magnanim-ity—it can't attract youth. The best thing about the present *Times* is that it's honestly square. . . .

One may not agree with all that by an old journalist, but certainly *Times* III is a unique survival, keeping a nervous equilibrium, a strong

TIMES II AND *TIMES* III

survivor in a world where hundreds of fine daily newspapers have died or been digested by rivals.

Most large cities are more and more rationed to one morning and one evening newspaper. There is a worm in the bone of American journalism. The future? *Times* IV? The news, what there is of it, is first on the sappy laugh-fests on television, accepted by a mass public. So *Times* III is becoming more and more a very good cross section of daily magazine features.

Harrison Gray Otis used to quote Charles Dana of the New York *Sun:* "Journalism consists of buying paper at two cents a pound and selling it at ten cents a pound. . . ." (inflate the prices, and it still keeps a news-paper in business).

Times III's power has moved beyond state boundaries and is kow-towed to by important figures in the national and international scene, as witness the following *Times* announcement:

A few days before Henry Kissinger was nominated secretary of state, Mrs. Norman Chandler wrote him in San Clemente on behalf of The Amazing Blue Ribbon 400 asking if he would be guest of honor at the group's October meeting. After announcement of his new appointment was made, Mrs. Chandler followed up her letter with a phone call. And received a prompt and affirmative answer from Dr. Kissinger.

He said he'd be delighted to appear before the group . . . in a news format question-and-answer session. He also told Mrs. Chandler, "I'm better when you ask me questions."

33   The Minority Blues

In its rush to absorb and expand, Los Angeles has never had time to take any strong, prolonged interest in its minorities. The tumultuous slogan was "shape up or shut up." This was in many cases not a direct cruelty. Minority big shots were as bad as the whites. And it, the society, accepted the black or Mexican-American exploiter, often as a brother in southern California progress. The Uncle Tom bankers, doctors and insurance executives were no worse than their white counterparts, but no better, and so left a nadir of bitterness and anger. Nor did Mexican-American labor handlers (*patrones*) show any feeling for the field hands, the *manitos,* they exploited for the benefit of the growers' associations that ill-fed and ill-housed the Chicanismo. The accepted excuse as one white rancher told me: "They are better off here than in Meh-he-co [Mexico] 'cross the border. Feed 'em better too—sheet—they'd swaller dog food you give it to 'em. Here they got some change too in their jeans. Sheet—you put in toilets and they wash clothes in 'em. They always lived in dirt. You know that. I'm a fair hombre. I don't screw 'em like their own field recruiters do."

The first exploited people were the original inhabitants of Los Angeles, the Indians. The Spanish were mainly interested in their souls, and having baptized them, their duty was done, "but for impregnating the squaws."

By 1830 there were 764 whites counted in Los Angeles to 198 Indians.

When in 1834 the missions were transferred from Church to lay administration, the Indians drifted into town. They were segregated in a district called the Rancheria of Poblaos. They took to drink, bathed, washed their clothes and drank in the *zanja* water. A new ghetto across the river was set up for them amongst the melodious and sad refrain of the wind in the cottonwoods. They continued to steal, kill stray cattle, drink. It was pointed out that they spread venereal disease to the eager whites hunkering down the squaws.

The ghetto was razed, and the problem left to the Americans taking over in 1850.

The only use the city could make of the Indians (it was not a time of feeling guilty about the treatment of minorities) was to arrest them as drunk and disorderly and put them into chain gangs to do "public work." As the need for farmhands grew, the City Council passed a law offering the Indians at public auction to the best bidder for private limited slavery. The pay was usually in alcohol, the deadly *aquardiente.* There was no program for education, for bringing the Indians into the culture. Horace Bell who observed all this wrote: "The slave at Los Angeles was sold fifty-two times a year as long as he lived, which did not . . . exceed one, two or three years. . . . Thousands of honest, useful people were absolutely destroyed in this way. . . ."

The Mexican-American population, no matter how it lived in its poverty pockets, grew. For the first decade of the twentieth century, thousands came across the border to pick fruit, hoe and carry railroad iron cheaply. World War II found several hundred thousand citizens of Los Angeles of Mexican descent. The local police treated the young (*los jovenes*) who stood up to them brutally. Discrimination created gangs of youths called pachucos, and they fought back the police rousting the best they could. Mass arrests took place. Innocent or guilty, just watching, or walking out of one's ghetto barrio could bring the police into action with clubs, fists, beatings in cells, to cries of *"Jesús, María y José me favorezcan!"* By the 1940s, the rest of the city fell into a habit of anti-Mexican talk and even hatred. The once despised Okies had now been absorbed by the city and county, and they and their children turned on the Mexican-American youths in their zoot suits, their duck-ass haircuts, long pocket chains, broad-brimmed hats, as somebody made to kick around as they once had been themselves.

The first big Zoot Suit Riot broke out between sailors and pachucos in the beach dance halls in 1942. The whole weekend exploded as soldiers, sailors, marines, willing civilians, all joined in beating any dark-skinned citizen. They invaded the Mexican section of the city, looking for victims. The mob gleefully held the streets, while the police stood by, waiting for orders. Youths, one report read, were "dragged from theatres, stripped of their clothing, beaten and left naked on the streets. . . . dragged from out of restaurants and off streetcars, mauled and beaten by mobs." It was four nights of a one-sided street war by a mob in armed forces uniforms. The police acted by arresting the Mexican Americans already beaten, stripped and bloody. One thousand police took to the streets, and the Navy put Los Angeles off limits.

THE MINORITY BLUES

It was too late to stop the atmosphere of violence. Murdered was a youth named José Diaz. His body was found near a deep puddle known as Sleepy Lagoon, where Chicano kids swam in the muck. His skull was crushed and his body badly battered. Tests showed he had been drunk. On rumors of some recent gang fights in the neighborhood, the police arrested 300 Mexican-American youths. As Ben Hecht was to observe, "If each Chicano got in one blow on José, they would have destroyed the evidence." Twenty-three youths were held for trial on the charge of first-degree murder. There was little evidence that any were connected with the crime. But the city was there to punish, and seventeen were "convicted of varying degrees of responsibility," a rather strange verdict, ingenuously puzzling.

A year and a half later—justice was as slow as an oxcart in the case—the appellate court reversed all the convictions and "severely castigated the trial judge and jury and the prosecution for the methods used to secure the verdict."

Several vindictive people who remember the event still feel "they should have gotten the limit." As for who actually murdered José Diaz in the notorious Sleepy Lagoon case, no one knows to this day.

In a recent survey done by Mexican-Americans (1973) they pointed out a common misconception of the Chicano: "He is seen as a rural person recently arrived in the United States from Mexico. But, in fact, there are more Chicanos (over a million) in the highly urbanized greater Los Angeles area than the total population of at least 10 states; half of those people have pre-1930 roots in the United States."

Late in 1973 the press began to report that the Mexican-American section of Los Angeles was again working toward incorporating East Los Angeles into becoming the seventy-eighth city in the county. If they succeed, they will have created the largest city in the nation controlled by Mexican-Americans. Its population of 105,000 would be 83 percent Spanish-surnamed.

East Los Angeles' title as the "second capital of Mexico" stems from the fact that metropolitan Los Angeles has the largest number of residents of Mexican descent of any city of the world outside Mexico City and Guadalajara. East Los Angeles is the heart of that community.

Riots in the 1960s along Whittier Boulevard, the area's major commercial strip, symbolized a frustration and blind anger over myriad social problems that spurred the latest and most serious effort to incorporate East Los Angeles. Two previous incorporation efforts failed. A 1961 campaign was defeated in an election. An effort in 1964 petered out when a petition drive lost steam.

It is doubtful, I was told by some political people, that the WASP political powers that control Los Angeles will permit a section of the city to go back to its original settlers, to see them create a modern version of El Pueblo de Nuestra Señora la Reina de los Angeles.

The Chicano Brown Beret movement has developed better political ideals and goals, but is continually harassed by the police who, it is claimed, foment riots at Brown Beret park meetings and picnics, to arrest its leaders and scatter the people with tear gas. When Mexican-Americans picketed a new multimillion-dollar avant-garde-designed Catholic Church in Los Angeles as a waste of money when many Mexican-Americans were in dire need of food and clothing, the cardinal turned away from them and had the police make arrests and bring charges of inciting to riot. There were several convictions.

The same year, 1942, of the murder of José Diaz it was the turn of the Japanese-Americans to feel the brutality of wartime hysteria. There were 110,000 Japanese in southern California on the west coast, 75,000 of them American citizens. People saw them as sinister enemy agents, Mr. Motos with odd covert behavior, working for the Emperor of the Rising Sun. A joke of the time, I remember, was of a woman asking her Japanese maid, in jest: "I suppose you have been ordered to cut our throats while we're sleeping?" The maid answered, "Oh no, the gardener, he do that."

It was decided to move the entire 110,000 to concentration camps, distinguished as "relocation centers." The Japanese-Americans were all removed from their homes and businesses, and their property and bank accounts were seized (in the 1970s many were still trying to recover some of their bank assets). President Roosevelt authorized the exodus to the wild and flimsy mountain camps in nearly inaccessible areas. Here, in primitive conditions behind barbed wire and guarded, they were little better off than the Jews under Hitler. However, in fairness, it must be said that F.D.R. never considered The Final Solution of Auschwitz or Buchenwald. Reading of the expulsion of these American citizens and their families and friends from their homes and rights, it is sad to recall that both the Attorney General and later Chief Justice of the United States, Earl Warren, and the liberal's god, Walter Lippmann, favored concentration camps for the Japanese-Americans. Altruistic idealism in print is not enough. The Supreme Court upheld the treatment.

Life in the wilderness barracks continued until 1945. The discomforts and great hardships applied to women, children and infants, as well as to men. As one letter writer set down in an appeal, "Nothing is too fantastic in real life." Losses in goods and investments were heavy, many never to be repaid or recovered. The 1948 Evacuation Repayment Act made only a partial compensation to people who lost nearly everything.

The southwest Los Angeles 10th District has a population breakdown approximately as follows: black, 50 percent; Asian-American, 12 percent; Mexican-American, 12 percent; Jewish, 20 percent; other Caucasian, 5 percent, and American Indian, 0.5 percent.

Once growers on the land, the Japanese-Americans lived mostly on the plain, not on the hills, and are the most aggressive of the nonwhite minorities in Los Angeles County. They exist as three generations, each generation growing taller than the parent one, so that members of the third generation, the *Sansei,* are often four inches taller than their grandparents. The first generation, called *Issei,* now deep in their seventies, came mostly after the Great Earthquake (or Fire of 1906, as they like to think of it in San Francisco). As aliens, they could not own land until after World War II. Farming, fishing and gardening took care of their needs;

they sold guavas, loquats, kumquats and less exotic produce. They brought over picture brides, and their children are the *Nisei,* the second generation. As children, most of them went into the concentration camps.

Some of the Nisei who were old enough could join the armed forces, and the 442nd Regimental Combat Team did take part in the insane, rugged, murderous fighting from Salerno to the Vosges Mountains. As one survivor told me on a tape recording: "It was our stupid generals in Italy—us fighting their murderous mistakes. But we went through it and some of us lived. They called us Buddha-heads, but we didn't mind. It was a kind of title of honor. My old man and old lady were in one of the ten camps Earl Warren approved of. My old man, old lady, had to leave for a camp on forty-eight hours' notice, with only two suitcases permitted. The seafood business was sold for nothing. He lost his whole fishing fleet. Eyetals, Yugoslavs took over, and his insurance policies lapsed. When I came back, I wrote Washington to shove its medals up its ass. You know how much the Japanese-Americans lost by that evacuation? I give you figures, the official ones. Four hundred million dollars. You know what the federal government offered in restitution? About twenty-four percent of the total. And even that hasn't been fully paid by the flannel-mouths who run things. . . ."

There is a little Tokyo in Los Angeles. But it's mostly a shopping center, a tourist trap, a daytime place for banking, eating, seeing a samurai film, for meeting other Issei and Nisei friends, and not very interesting to the Sansei, the third generation, the children of the Nisei. (Sansei are often the product of intermarriage.) They live all over the country and feel little racial prejudice, unlike the blacks and the Mexican-Americans, who call themselves *"los Americanos olvidados"* (the forgotten Americans). To most Sansei, all the past is anachronism. Unlike their grandparents, they can be patronizing rather than deferential.

American soldiers from the wars in Asia brought in many Japanese war brides. It has been figured out that nearly a quarter of all Japanese in the United States are war brides. What keeps the Japanese-Americans out of big managerial positions in industry in Los Angeles is what keeps out the

Jews and the blacks—missing is that country-club fraternization and mixing, social contacts from which so many positions are filled. "The restricted exclusive WASP country club," my Nisei friend told me, "is the solid foundation of true fascism in America."

The enemy of the black, the Chicano, the Filipino, was not the country club but the police. In the 1960s Los Angeles Police Chief William H. Parker was, to judge by reports of C.O.R.E. (Committee of Racial Equality), an efficient and Prussian-type police head, "who could have commanded a panzer division, right down to the cold glassy stare." Parker was a humorless, honest, but not a tolerant man. His police were brutal against minorities. As the local chairman of C.O.R.E. put it, "the L.A.P.D. had an advanced technology, a superior force in . . . equipment, technique, but a rotten record on minorities." As Chief Parker put it, speaking of the Mexican-Americans, "Some of these people were here before we were, but some of them are not far removed from the wild tribes of Mexico. As for the blacks," Chief Parker sat back and announced, "the main source of Los Angeles crime just happened to be in areas populated heavily by Negroes, and Negroes just happen to be figuring in most of the city's crime." True of course—but he offered no suggestions to change the situation.

The present police chief, Edward Davis, insists on the need to set up a portable gallows at the city's airport to hang highjackers right on the spot.

34 Lady Macbeth of Los Angeles

T here is a type of female novelist whose books are best sellers, a person who is a creator of volumes of wild imaginary dreams, usually sexual, showing little deepness of understanding or intellect. But, flowing along with easy simplicity, their books are devoured mostly by people who move their lips while they read—stories fully satisfactory to those whose daily life is as dull as themselves. Louise Peete could have been a very successful author of this kind of best-selling book. Her world of fantasy, however, revolved around susceptible victims that she bedazzled by her stories.

No hack writer would have dared to present the drama that Louise Peete committed the *same* crime twenty years apart, in both cases using the same method of entrapment of her victims and disposing of them in the same way. The fact that her crimes are spaced twenty years apart is due to the length of time she served for the first crime; from the moment of her release, she began the commission of the second one.

Louise Peete could invent a situation, explain a contradiction on the spur of the moment; even experienced law officers, questioning her, were amazed at her ability to spin yarns and inventions, which she continued to do even when she was aware that she was already trapped and that her stories were no longer being believed or making sense.

She was neither a great beauty nor overbright, but plump, pleasant, attractive and had that charisma of being liked and confided in at first meetings.

Her background is obscure, and details vary. But she seems to have come from native American stock, her folk neither wealthy nor endowed with high position, and was married three times. In 1913 she was involved in the death of a friend, a desk clerk in a Dallas, Texas, hotel, who died of a bullet hole in his head. His diamond ring was missing. The diamond was "recovered," his death listed as "suicide" and Louise moved on. The next seven years are not on record.

Los Angeles was booming in 1920 when Louise Peete appeared again in legal history—to visit a house on South Catalina Street, a house just a block from Wilshire Boulevard.

The house was owned by a Jacob Denton, a man interested in mining claims and stocks. Aged forty-six, he was rather handsome, twice married, once divorced and at that time a recent widower with a daughter, Frances, by his first wife who was living in Arizona. "A rough diamond" was one unoriginal description of Jacob Denton.

The house was of an attractive English Tudor style that fought off the false Spanish so popular then in Los Angeles. It contained about a dozen rooms. Denton, planning on going east for a while, wanted to rent the house, and Louise said she was interested in a lease. The interview between them went well. She attracted Denton as being lively and bright. She told him of her husband, R. C. Peete, an ailing, poor man, in Colorado, and their five-year-old daughter, Betty, who needed California sunshine.

There was talk of a lease but it was delayed, and the Peetes moved in while Denton retained for himself one room until he was ready to go east. He seemed in no hurry to leave the company of Mrs. Peete.

The last time anyone who knew Denton saw him alive was at a beach party some of his friends gave. He attended with Louise (no mention of Mr. Peete). The hostess of the party said of Louise that she was a "charming woman, one that would attract a man's attention." She also noted, "Louise was very much attentive to Denton. . . . She seemed to be seeking his favor."

The rough diamond and the glib talker had hit it off. Later, when she was called his housekeeper, she told the press, "I deeply resent having been referred to by *that* title. I leased the house . . . just as anyone would lease a house."

Untrue. Actually, no lease was ever signed, and later reporters privately agreed that the two had become lovers with, or without, Mr. Peete's knowledge.

Denton had many business connections and people who had appointments with him called—but he never showed or called to cancel. Louise insisted he had gone off to the beach or journeyed to San Francisco. She took over Denton's car and even got an endorsement on it for an accident policy in Denton's name. She asked the insurance agent where she could buy some bags of cement "to cover some cherished possessions" of Denton's second wife, who had died recently. Cement hardly seemed the best way to preserve anything of value. Wanting a new car, Louise made some appointments for the salesmen to meet Denton. But it

LADY MACBETH OF LOS ANGELES

turned out, she said, he had gone to Arizona and then on to San Francisco. She explained he had been wounded in an arm, was in pain and the limb was infected. And he wished to avoid any public notice. The trashy novelist was at work, plotting. "Mr. Denton is *so* ashamed of the wound . . . doesn't want people to know of it."

The salesman was puzzled. Denton hadn't been injured when in another deal he had signed an agreement to turn in his old car and pick up a new one in the East.

In the middle of June Louise told the car salesman that Denton's arm had had to be amputated in San Francisco. He was going east and they could turn the new car over to her so it would be there on Mr. Denton's return. There was however a little problem of financing the new car.

She said Denton had left her power of attorney to sell or rent the Catalina Street house. The price was $27,000, and her commission would be a clear $3,000. Meanwhile, she moved Denton around the country; he was in Missouri, she told some, in Seattle, even others were told he was holed up in the Lankershim Hotel in Los Angeles. His arm was gone. She had to help him write checks and open his mail. Poor man, "the way he feels about the arm, doesn't want to see anybody, that is anybody but me."

Frances, Denton's daughter, was a problem. She wasn't getting the monthly allowance from her father. Some friends of Denton's were puzzled by Louise's stories and worried over him.

Louise showed up at the Farmers and Merchants Bank with the key to Denton's safe deposit box. But the woman attendant there said no; no access without a written order from Mr. Denton. Louise produced a check signed by Denton made out to her for $300. However, the signature did not match the Denton signature on file. Louise's talent for glib spur-of-the-moment storytelling came to the fore. Ah yes, she had been signing checks for Mr. Denton, he asking her to do it as he, poor man, with his arm amputated could not. He did, she added (a novelist's bit of realism), "touch the pen." However, Louise was told the bank would need Mr. Denton's own confirmation as to the new signature. Louise told the woman at the bank she hadn't heard from him in a few days. He *did* wander, and he was having some kind of a romance with a "Spanish woman." A rather disagreeable woman, this Spanish one. She was in the house, too, often. Once the two were in a lovers' quarrel most of the night. The next morning they left the house together. Mr. Denton "had a patch on his eye."

The vault attendant never forgot this strange melodramatic story told to her by Louise. It was the first appearance onstage of the mysterious "Spanish woman" that was to be featured later on in Louise's version of the secret life of Jacob Denton.

Friends of Denton hired a lawyer who, in turn, hired a private detective, and both ran up bills, seemingly content just to observe events in the Tudor house. In August, Louise, fearing complications in selling the place, rented out the house on Catalina Street and sent small checks to Denton's daughter, Frances. The Peetes moved to Denver.

The new tenants were surprised one day by the lawyer, Mr. Blodgett, and the detective, A. J. Cody, who came calling, saying that they were at last worried over Mr. Jacob Denton and would like to search the premises.

No one objected and the hunters began with the basement. Under the cellar steps there was a kind of boarded up closet obstructed by a large box labeled MRS. R. C. PEETE. Moving this and the boards, they found old stovepipes laid on a canvas-covered mound of garden earth. With the aid of a spade, a man's foot was uncovered. The police were notified and the body of Mr. Denton was unwrapped from bedclothes and the ropes crossing the body from toes to top. The earth had been loosely shoveled over the body. In a house search, a .32 caliber revolver was found, one shell discharged.

Later, when the chief autopsy surgeon examined and X-rayed the body, a bullet hole was found in the neck that fitted a .32 slug.

The Los Angeles district attorney's office sent a man to Denver to talk things over with Louise. Not, she was told, to accuse her of the murder.

LADY MACBETH OF LOS ANGELES

No, no, she was assured, but would she return to Los Angeles and help run down the person who had killed her dear and good friend Jacob Denton?

It is clear that the law knew by then the vanity, the ego of their leading suspect. And she, living no doubt in that fictional and, to her, satisfactory world of lies, deceit, imagination and invention, saw herself as too smart for all of them. She had planned the story of the Spanish woman, the battles between Denton and his paramour. Yes, she would return to Los Angeles and help.

Louise was put on a train by Los Angeles lawman William Doran. When trailed by a bevy of newspapermen, Doran arranged to have Louise and poor Mr. Peete go into hiding with him at the Glenn Ranch in the San Bernardino Mountains.

Here in comfort, with hot food, in the clean, bracing air, Louise began to talk. Rather she rambled on, invented details, poured out talk at a great rate, clearly enjoying the situation, working her imagination to its limit and a bit beyond. Two shorthand writers tried to keep up with her flow of explanations. The soil in the cellar? Mr. Denton felt there was "too much earth in the yard," he'd save it for later. (The cement idea was never put into use.) Yes, she had asked about boarding up the cellar against intruders, as part of watching out for Mr. Denton's interests. "Someone had tried to break in." True, she had cashed small checks as they came in for Denton, and she had endorsed them. Forgery? No, "not when he told me to do it."

There were matters of forged leases, even trying to bribe a detective with an offer of a diamond (gem never produced). And the mysterious Spanish woman was in the story again.

The Denton jewels? The Spanish woman, *she* got them. "You can't always tell about foreign women," she added. "Mr. Denton told me she was his wife. Just tell people I've lost my arm and I'm married again." (No one, at this point, seems to have brought up the fact that Denton's body had been found with both arms in place.)

Mr. Doran, perhaps a reader of popular novels, said to Louise, "This sounds to me very much like fiction. . . . The whole situation is absurd. Have you ever heard anything to equal it?"

Louise had to admit, as the author, "No, I never have."

It was clear now the state had a good case. Louise was taken to Los Angeles and the press quoted her as saying, "I have not told all."

The day Harding won the American Presidency by a 6 million plurality, the Denton murder case went before the grand jury.

35 Justice and Mrs. Peete

Louise was to be represented in court by a public defender. The Hearst *Examiner* printed a letter signed "The Spanish Lady," which said Denton had met his death by accident.

On January 21, 1921, Louise Peete went on trial for the murder of Jacob Denton, an event locally outranking the fact that Woodrow Wilson had been defeated in his plan to get the country into the League of Nations.

At the end of three weeks of trial—when things looked bad—Louise's lawyer decided not to put her on the stand, not with all the evidence against her—all her bold and foolish fiction. The jury was out four hours. The verdict: "Guilty as charged, of murder in the first degree and we fix the sentence at life in prison."

Headline: **Mrs. Peete Does Not Even Wince at Verdict of Guilty!**

Twenty-two years later, in April 1943, Louise was paroled from the Tehachapi State Prison for Women. She was permitted to use the name "Anna B. Lee." Her hair was now of grayish tone, she in her sixties, but looked much younger even if plump. She still had her old gift of charming people with her talk. Her Parole Board member, Mrs. Latham, liked her. When Mrs. Latham became ill, Louise went to live with her. In September Mrs. Latham died, and before Louise left, she stole a .32 caliber Smith & Wesson pistol.

"Anna Lee" went to work for Mr. and Mrs. Arthur Logan on Hampton Place, Pacific Palisades, near the coastal city of Santa Monica. It was a fine house, five rooms, a garden with an avocado tree. Mrs. Logan worked in war industries at Douglas Aircraft. But she had been active in real estate.

Mr. Logan was ten years older than his wife, seventy-four, a poor seventy-four. He was ill and feeble, and Louise spread the story around that he was also senile. Yet he was still able to pick up the daily mail at the post office and walk out along the Pacific Coast cliffs at a good pace.

Louise moved quickly to upset the household. She offered to get the legal information needed to commit Mr. Logan to an institution, this just *five* weeks after she moved in. A petition was filed and Superior Court found Arthur Logan "mentally ill, dangerous and insane." He was ordered to Patton State Hospital. Louise had worked her best bit of fiction on Mrs. Logan who was away all day riveting warplanes and had to take Louise's word about her husband's dangerous condition. But Mrs. Logan could not bear the ordeal of her husband being in an institution, so nineteen days later she brought him back home, just before Thanksgiving. It must have been a Hitchcock film dinner around the turkey.

Mrs. Logan gave up war work to have more time for Mr. Logan, and went back to selling real estate. Louise became a kind of partner in some of Mrs. Logan's deals, as she talked pleasantly of thousands of dollars she would put up as her share. She never did. Louise, as "Anna B. Lee," got married in 1944 to an elderly messenger for a Glendale bank. A man with a good reputation and a clean life, Lee Judson did not know of Louise's past or her over twenty years in prison for murder. We know nothing of this marriage but its outcome. She kept Judson as a husband secret from the Logans and moved in with him at the Glendale Hotel. The Logans thought Judson was "just a friend." Louise was forging Mrs. Logan's name on documents. She tried to borrow money from Judson's nephew—she needed money for real estate deals.

On May 29th, she went to visit the Logans, and no one ever saw Mrs. Logan alive again. (It was just about twenty-four years since Jacob Denton was last seen alive by his friends.)

On June 1st, Louise and husband Judson moved into the Logan home, and old Arthur made them welcome. He did not seem to miss his wife. He told a neighbor that Mrs. Logan had been injured in a car accident and was in the hospital. Louise winked, and said there had been no accident—just the old man getting dotty and hard to manage. The accident story, she explained, was to lure him into the psychopathic ward at the General Hospital. Once the old man was again in an institution, she finished up some business for Mrs. Logan, forged a signature and collected $910. Again, as in the past, friends were put off from visiting Mrs. Logan by the story that she was badly disfigured, the result of a mad attack by Mr. Logan. (A new version of Mr. Denton's missing arm.) Friends were told that Mrs. Logan was having plastic surgery because of the attack, also that she was in a hospital in San Bernardino or in Oregon, even that she had cancer. She spread the news that Mrs. Logan had ordered a coffin for Mr. Logan who was dying at Patton. "It's going to be a family affair" (the burial). She also tried to legally take over Mrs. Logan's car (as she had done with Denton so long ago). Poor Mr. Logan, believing he was deserted by his wife and friends, died at last, having no will left to live. Louise turned the body over to the Loma Linda Hospital "for research purposes."

Several weeks later, Captain Thad Brown, chief of the Los Angeles Homicide Department, came calling, and there were Louise and her husband busy breaking into the Logan strongbox.

The detective listened to all the old stories of the Logan conflicts, then asked, "Are you still on parole. . . . Who signed your parole papers?"

It turned out Mrs. Logan hadn't signed them since May and, yes, Louise had signed them for her. "She asked me to." As to where Mrs. Logan was now, Louise answered cheerfully, "She'll be here. . . . I know she'll be back."

Under arrest, Louise was exposed for the first time to her husband not as Anna Lee, but as the convicted murderess Louise Peete. He was co-charged with the killing of Margaret Logan, after Louise led the police to a grave under the avocado tree in the Logan garden.

"Did you dig the grave yourself?"

Louise nodded, "It seemed like hours and hours. I ruined my hands."

Mrs. Logan had been shot in the neck (as had the late Mr. Denton) but not fatally. She had been clubbed to death by the pistol butt of the Smith & Wesson found among Louise's things. Mrs. Logan, while having been savagely beaten, had no old facial wounds that Louise had talked about as being caused by the late Mr. Logan.

Lee Judson was exonerated after his wife, Louise, was held for murder. In January 1944 he went up to the thirteenth floor of the Spring Arcade Building and hurled himself down the stairwell to his death. Louise said, "He just couldn't face dishonor and disgrace. . . . Everything that happened to him, even his death, happened because of me." No heroine of a bad novel could have said it better.

On April 23, 1944, Louise Peete stood trial for murder. It was a repeat performance and there was not as much public interest in her as there had been in the first trial. Some said it was because of the war and the resulting scarcity of newsprint, so much space was being taken by war news and talk of invasion of Europe.

Against all legal advice, Louise took the stand. It was a rambling non-stop verbal bout of storytelling. Several fictional versions of life with the Logans; stories, much detail of how Mr. Logan, gone mad, used the weapon on his wife, and how Louise tried to protect Mrs. Logan from being killed. Yes, Mr. Logan was the true killer, and she merely tried to protect the Logan good name by covering up.

It was not a very believable version of events. Asked, "Will you please show the jury how Mr. Logan held the gun?" she said, "I will *not* touch the gun."

The deputy district attorney addressed the jury with these final words, "Mrs. Peete, who was a Dr. Jekyll and a Mrs. Hyde, must have sat in her prison cell figuring out what went wrong the *first* time, and plotting this new crime."

The jury, out three hours, agreed and found her "guilty of murder in the first degree, without recommendation for mercy."

Louise stood up, "Is that *all?*" To a woman reporter she cheerfully added, "Don't weep for me, dear."

Back in her cell she finished reading Lin Yutang's *The Importance of Living,* a corny touch no serious writer of his craft would have dared to add to her final coming to judgment.

With the death penalty mandatory for her, California was deprived, some said, of her coming out of prison as a *very* old lady and repeating her pattern to kill. Louise never seemed to regret her cold, murderous acts or to grasp the fact that her crimes were not realistically practical, properly planned or carried out. And that shallow graves too often give up their secrets.

36   Native Earth
and By-Products

Downtown Los Angeles died in a matter of decades—or rather became very sick. The city merchants and real estate owners never
gave up the idea that downtown would be brought back to life.
But first the Model-T, then the huge volume of auto traffic took families,
then business out to the far-flung fringes of the expanding, land-swallow-
ing city. The theater decayed, once grand eating places closed. Depart-

NATIVE EARTH AND BY-PRODUCTS

ment stores opened branches as polite shoppers began to shun the downtown shabbiness, the panhandlers and indecent exposure artists, the winos and kooks sleeping off jags of cooking sherry in Pershing Square.

There was never any steady upward march of land values. It was more like the Pacific Park roller coaster. There were boom times of high prices and exhilarating prospects. It took, on the average, twenty years for the losers, the bankrupts, or their heirs, to begin another land boom in Los Angeles—to stake out plats of new subdivisions. Some won, some lost. It has been shown by sales of land and permits for building structures that the big boom years were 1855, 1875, 1887, 1906, 1923, 1949 and 1963, give or take a few years in the fundamental seesaw insanity of land values.

The 1920s produced newcomers to Los Angeles at the rate of 100,000 a year, and the World War II shipping and aircraft industries brought hundreds of thousands of new population. Many were blacks escaping the South. Others were hillbillies and mudsills, retired citizens or busted speculators ready to try again.

The city kept gulping down land, everything it could settle into and claim. The game was *annexation* and *consolidation* of towns, villages, as orchards turned to streets. What had begun as a Spanish pueblo was approaching 500 square miles in area.

To the visitor after World War II, it seemed that every new building was for a bank or an insurance company. Branch banking, like an octopus, kept putting out its tentacles (Bank of America, 1,000 branches in the state), banks seemed to take over every corner. Title insurance, financing, escrow service, credit companies, even bail bondsmen, created a rash of businesses connected with banking and savings and loan services. The downtown bail bondsmen under neon lights, *"24 Hours a Day,"* offered service to the battered, the hustler, the thieves and rapists, the businessmen in trouble, the society embezzler or extended schemer of crooked books, offered bail at a pleasant, hefty rate of interest. The bail bond business was often called by some a racket and was often tied in with judges who aided the bail industry, as palpable to some in its feline savagery as a foreclosing bank.

In the 1960s, 260 acres a day in the county were turned into building tracts. It used to worry a lot of sensitive people.

The fruit also suffered. In 1947 the two counties of southern California were growing 135,231 lemon, orange and grapefruit trees. By 1960 there were only 49,663 such trees still alive, and the figure was dropping at an amazing rate. There was a continual deterioration of nature all around the city. I have not been able to get anyone to give me today's figure (1977). The excuse some give for the loss of trees is not just the greedy land developers and bulldozers, but a virus disease, *tristeza* (Portuguese, meaning "sadness"). In the 1940s it did great damage to orange trees. But even when disease-resistant stock was developed, the land was too valuable to the builders and speculators to put back in fruit.

Fires burning up brush are another source of destruction and usually rim the city during the dry season. The blazes break out on the dry slopes, ravines, in the growth called chaparral, which fuels an advance of a ground-running fire often to forty miles an hour. It can, with the right wind, jump 600 feet over fire roads and canyons. There are always trained fire fighters on duty, with reserves of men—"trusties" is the term—from the county prisons, also Indians who make a profession of fire fighting, coming from New Mexico and Arizona. Chemical- and water-dropping planes exist. But every year the fires come, like a primitive ritual demanding sacrifices. Once luxury estates in Bel Air presented a row of chimneys, charcoal ruins, twisted pipes, looking as if just bombed by the U.S. Air Force. The difference is that instead of rice and natives consumed in flame, there is cremated an occasional Picasso, a cellar of Château Rothschild and other rare wines. Aldous Huxley lost his house, a collection of autographed rare books and family heirlooms in the complete destruction of his North Beachwood home by a sudden surge of fire.

At L.A. Jaycee luncheons the fire topic is avoided. Scientists have been working on fire-resistant plants. The most promising are from areas along the Mediterranean and from Australia. The rockrose (not a rose at all), the saltbush (*Atriplex halimus*) and the yerba santa (*Eriodictyon californicum,* a California native) are the three most promising. None have yet made much progress against the tough chaparral. The fires will continue, the hill dwellers agree, as they stare out of their huge picture windows.

An advertising account manager who lives near me lamented, "Real estate selling is an overbloated industry in Los Angeles—land values are inflated sky-high, taxes are murderous, upkeep supports a wealthy society of plumbers, electricians, appliance repairmen, keeps them in the upper brackets. Gardeners who can't garden. Pool men, painters, paperhangers, earn more than most college Ph.D. holders. To own property here is to sink one's facile optimism to zero." Many people agree he is not far from the truth. Realtors, as they prefer to be called, and their dubious improvisations, are all over Los Angeles County like gophers. Their lingo in their advertising is pure Orwell-Newspeak:

> Custom Cedar Barn. 2 beamed BRs, den, 3 bas., mds rm.
> Biltins, 2 FPs, brick, wood, stained glass goodies, peg flrs.

Los Angeles banks exploit the buyer and the seller, is the complaint. The buyer is loaded with finder's fees, escrow costs, title searches, extra "points," and both buyer and seller pay city, county, state tax fees and high legal costs. On one $44,000 house sale, this came to $1,500 extra (not counting the agent's commission). I know of another case in which a buyer of a hillside home found she didn't own her garden after the bank title search proved a myth; it belonged to the people next door. And several cases are known where a "termite certificate" aided in the sale of a house later found to be infected with the little fellows. Hillsides are sometimes not safe; they shift; sun-rooms, porches drop off, and the guarantees of some developers for clubhouses, swimming pools, golf courses, exist only in promises.

The biggest selling points in Los Angeles, after overluxurious bathrooms, are the simple announcements by a realtor as he inserts a key in a front door: "This is the old Garbo house" or "Gable, Clark you know, built this . . ." Historic sites, plentiful as the ten thousand items of furniture from the *Mayflower,* are the two dozen homes I have been shown that were "Gary Cooper's" or the hideaway love nests of the adultery-prone stars of films and television.

There are real estate brokers who will not handle any house valued for sale under $200,000. As for interiors, costly taste is often irrational and vulgar when serviced by some type of interior decorator that seems to flourish in surroundings pushed to total inadequacy. "The trick, darling, is to find everything they own just *too* outré for words, so drag it out, sell it to some other customer, and move that house's contents to the first house. Load 'em, load 'em, I tell my people. Lads, I say, they adore old milk cans, ancient slaughtering blocks, cobblers' tables, *anything* made of brass. As for modern, I have a raft of artists splashing huge abstractions on canvas, acres of *merde,* and I can't get enough hatch covers off ships for coffee tables in Bel Air.

"Hemingway was wrong you know. It isn't just that the rich have more money: they have bad taste and a fear of being thought old-fashioned if they resist our suggestions—that is what makes Los Angeles' potbellies so nice to exploit" (from a tape recording).

Against the belief of what the rest of the nation thinks, however, most southern Californians live in simple overvalued houses. But there are the way-out pads. One sample: 7-foot 1½-inch Wilt Chamberlain, with a $200,000-a-year salary, advertising endorsements and some investments, has acquired a taste for high living. The former center for the Los Angeles Lakers basketball team has outdone himself in building a bachelor pad atop the Santa Monica Mountains—spending $1.5 million.

37 Is Art Alive
in Los Angeles?

As a cultural center, Aldous Huxley once said at a party, "Los Angeles is a waxworks museum. Everything looks real, then you notice it's a fairly good replica which, however, never fools you."

The city has tried hard, grabbing at culture like a pensive carnivore. In the 1920s the Los Angeles Philharmonic Orchestra went through the right classical scores and in Hollywood, on a spot which had at one time been the site of an Indian village, began to put seats on a hillside. Here it staged pageants and devoted itself to music until "Going to the Bowl" became a social event. It became the fashion for box holders to bring hampers of wine, roast fowl and coleslaw and eat a supper while waiting for the concert to begin. As one of Los Angeles' wine snobs told me, "It was hardly a good place for a good wine. How could you keep it at room temperature?" Yet it has remained a cultural pilgrimage. There were always interruptions by passing planes. I remember one night, as the heavy music of a full orchestra echoed back from the hills, John Barrymore, quoting Mark Twain, said, "Wagner is better than he sounds."

What had begun in the early 1800s as Christmas plays in the Plaza, *The Shepherds* (*Los Pastores*), gave way in the 1880s to show business at the Turnverein Hall, the Grand Opera House, the Merced Theatre and Hazard's Pavilion. The city resented San Francisco as a cultural rival and had an appetite for responsibility.

The Belasco Theatre in the 1920s had an active stock company. And Oliver Morosco is remembered for bringing standard farce and comedy to Los Angeles, but hardly Shaw or Ibsen. That had to wait for the Pasadena Community Playhouse to be created. Under Gilmore Brown, in its last two decades of success, it became a dedicated dramatic school and a theater where the best of European playwrights, as well as such Americans as O'Neill, Elmer Rice and Robert Sherwood, were given professional performances to try and articulate a vague hope that southern California would become a bit of ancient Athens. I got to know the place in the 1940s when a play I had co-authored, *Gauguin,* based on the life of the post-impressionist painter, was presented there with a then obscure actor, Raymond Burr, playing Paul Gauguin. He was close to 250 pounds by the look of him, and gave a fairly interesting performance up until he was to throw himself on a cot, the despairing painter in the South Seas, resigned to failure. As Burr hurled his bulk on to the cot (it being on casters) it took off and continued right through the cardboard wall of the hut.

The Pasadena Playhouse was of international prominence, "the best little theatre in the nation." But in the 1960s, when it needed support to

The Los Angeles Music Center, society's gathering place. Many citizens claim they can't afford to attend. (UPI)

continue, the support was not there. In the end it was shut down after Gilmore Brown's death, and its fate was spoken of as becoming a parking area. No building in Los Angeles County just fades away, it becomes a parking lot.

Dorothy Buffum Chandler had a dream—*and* a successful newspaper behind her to keep it green. She also made the effort to get the culture grabbers and the rich to contribute, and during the 1960s she pushed through the city's Music Center for the Performing Arts in the Civic Center, with a Mall and a series of new buildings, which, while not of an original avant-garde splendor as architecture, served well enough for music, ballet and whatever drama there was in Los Angeles. Mainly, it pleased a social milieu that felt a need for a cosmopolitan atmosphere.

The Pavilion, the first public building in Los Angeles to be named for a living person (when it became the Dorothy Chandler Pavilion), was dedicated in splendid style. *Time* magazine, which had at one period hoped to start a newspaper in Los Angeles and been frightened off by the *L.A. Times'* position, reported the event as a dazzle "of diamonds and décolletage . . . celebrities and just plain millionaires plentifully on hand . . . welcoming the growing edge of another U.S. explosion—culture."

Zubin Mehta, the conductor, rose to promise first-nighters, "This evening we are going to usher in a new era."

The Huntington (one doesn't say museum or gallery) is a series of huge gardens, set up by railroad money of the original robber baron—a museum of fine English paintings. The "Blue Boy" is here, "Pinky," some marvelous Turners and others of the English school. As Helen Wurdemann, director of the Los Angles Art Association, said after visiting it, "You are as likely to find a Picasso here as a loud belch in St. Peters."

The rare book and paper collection at the Huntington has a marvelous set of Rowlandson watercolors, and more rare books than any place west of New York. My favorite spot is the Japanese Gardens, complete with an old bronze bell you can ring, if you care to.

One view of the Los Angeles County Museum of Art: "The building, I

IS ART ALIVE IN LOS ANGELES?

gather, is on a prehistoric burial site. Pitch pits, I believe." (Stanton Mac-Donald-Wright, pioneer modernist painter)

As for the museum's permanent contents, Katherine Kuh of the *Saturday Review* wrote, the pictures "do not add up to a collection." Actually, the museum, as a social gathering place, is a success.

"We are ignored by outsiders who control the museum," said one local artist, expressing what several felt.

"We local artists did not expect the museum to turn into a culture club."

Actually, art is a social success in Los Angeles, the city and the county. Million-dollar collectors with checkbooks exist, ready to buy up art collections, often through some tax reducing schemes. As Stanton MacDonald-Wright put it to me: "This art kick gives people who are low on the social scale a way of being permitted into the better homes."

There is a great deal of the buying of art, and there is an art dealers' street: Los Angeles' 57th Street is La Cienega Boulevard between Santa Monica and Melrose. "Galleries," to quote MacDonald-Wright again, "come, flourish and die like festering lilies of the field. Some dealers are Eastern Europeans, part super-salesmen, part pack-peddlers. Some are atrophied females to be treated with raucous indifference. Salesmanship can be as pushy as a secondhand car salesman getting rid of a dud. And snobbery exploits the foolish rich, from Bel Air through Beverly Hills to Pasadena, who put on their walls some of the second-rate best of big names. There are one or two dealers (not more), experts, knowledgeable, who are sagacious, know what it is all about. But the rest?"

(MacDonald-Wright was outspoken and had high standards, perhaps too high at times.)

One of the shining examples, free of the ruck of commercialism of local art, is the Los Angeles Art Association, a nonprofit organization founded forty years ago to show the work of artists who have no commercial galleries. It has done amazingly well in its present magnificent galleries, which are among the few local works of art in building design. Administrated for the last twenty years by Helen Wurdemann, its director, it continues to stand out like a lighthouse among the dwarf pines on the coast.

POSTURES AND POSES

Los Angeles is not wholly sterile and fashionable to true art. Stanton MacDonald-Wright was still painting at eighty-three (he died in 1973), the last survivor of the Americans who went to Paris in the first decade of the century. He was one of the co-founders with Morgan Russell during 1909–1914 of a new approach to modern color and form in synchronism. Lorser Feitelson and Helen Lundeberg are much admired international artists who pioneered surrealism in the United States and (they are husband and wife) are responsible for the west coast's most important advance in art, the creation of Hard Edge Abstraction painting long before it occurred in New York City. The late Knut Merrild preceded Jackson Pollock in the drip and flow school of freely manipulated paint without brushes. Pollock himself got a great deal of his early training in art in Los Angeles. So a few remarkable talents do keep a region from being benign.

The most interesting tug of war to save something of value has been that contest between the Cultural Heritage Board set up too late (in 1962) and the real estate sharks and historic building wreckers with their bulldozers ready to level everything in sight to raise up some piano-box structure or lay out rows and rows of development of bad taste with barbecue pits known as "ranch style."

The board declared about fifty landmarks, settings and buildings as "historic cultural monuments." These cannot be sentenced to the wrecker's ball, moved or altered without the permission of the board. It's a mixture, a search for assured secure assumptions, of the best and the most foolish. At the top are the amazing Simon Rodia towers in Watts. The city council thought so little of them that it once ordered them pulled down as a hazard. But enough people rallied to save them when the city tried to pull them down in a test run with a tractor and failed. Rodia, a native genius, was an Italian laborer, a bricklayer and cement worker who spent thirty years collecting old beer and soda bottles, broken plates, steel rods, bedsprings, bathroom fixtures. Carefully, over the years, he built a series of magnificent openwork towers out of his junk. They are, and remain, the most original art creation, not only of southern California but most likely in the nation. A visiting London friend said: "They are well

The folk art masterwork built in Watts by Simon Rodia in 1959. The city has been trying to destroy it, so far unsuccessfully. (Wide World)

worth leading an armed party into Watts to view them, a sort of cultural safari." He was aware Watts is dangerous ground for white folk.

Frank Lloyd Wright's Hollyhock House in Barnsdall Park, much restored (noted one contractor's helper: "The only things that held it up were the termites standing on each other's shoulders"), is a good enough example of fine design. The Bradbury Building, downtown, built early in the century, is the most beautiful office building in the state. Pure Art Nouveau, it had been threatened, but still stands, showing what could be done before designers sold out to the cube, the functional box and the idea that a building was created to make interesting shadows for photographers.

Among the treasures also protected is The Thousand-Year-Old Encino Oak, which may be all of a hundred years old. However, most of the splendid ornate Victorian mansions around Bunker Hill, and other places, have been lost. The city catches feverish vibrations of the newest fashions, then overdoes them, and drops them.

Perhaps the only true geniuses among southern California architects were the brothers Sumner Greene and Henry Mathers Greene, who, in their houses early in the century, were inspired by the best of the Japanese classical houses and an Oriental feeling of sensitivity for wood. Greene bungalows still exist, perhaps in some hidden-away street, modified, added to or violated. Nothing as original and as good and easy to live in at modest cost was ever created by any other local architects. The names of Wright (not a Californian), Schindler and Neutra are tossed about when talking about Los Angeles buildings as art. But Wright did his best work elsewhere, and when I interviewed him about a small strange structure of a business building in the shape of an Indian wigwam he did in Beverly Hills, he winked and hinted it was his revenge on Beverly Hills. Schindler was a pioneer in the square box construction. I once spent a year lecturing in a compound he had built on King's Road; it was sad to see neglect and faulty construction (he had been forced to build the place himself) beginning to destroy his fine ideas. Neutra, to whom I also talked (I was planning a series on Los Angeles buildings), struck me

IS ART ALIVE IN LOS ANGELES?

as an inflated ego. He was very shrill against placing any paintings or statues in his houses. "They don't need them, they have *my* forms." The late Agnes Marx once had Neutra build her a set of dining room chairs. They kept falling over backward.

Looking at my notes—too sparse notes, I now see—made when talking to Frank Lloyd Wright, I asked him what was the future of southern California. "Oh, it will become bigger and bigger and extend itself north and south. And soon Los Angeles will begin in San Diego, swallow San Francisco and pave every acre of earth up to the Gold River. The only historic monuments spared will be the rest rooms in the gasoline stations."

BOOK VI

UNDER
THE
TINSEL

38   The Devil in Watts

On August 6, 1965, Los Angeles experienced the worst riots of any American city since the notorious draft riots of New York City during the Civil War. Just a week before I had lectured to the Los Angeles Art Association, "The nonconformist is a member of a permanent revolution. . . ."

The Watts riots alerted the white culture to its mistake of thinking it held its 650,000 blacks under stern control. In 1940 there had been only 75,000 blacks in the county, but the attraction of wartime wages and easier welfare rolls, as well as its appearance as an escape hatch from southern bigotry, soon made Los Angeles a partly black city.

Watts, on a surface viewing, is not a slum. I have visited it often, before and after the riots, to view those amazing folk-art towers raised there by a self-trained Italian artist. There are lawns, the small houses are usually painted, and while a hostile environment, the area is, nevertheless, usually placid. But it is crowded, isolated, with ugly railroad lines bisecting it. It was in need of much renewal.

Watts itself as a community, when its population was mainly white, was not annexed to Los Angeles until 1926. Among its original black settlers had been workers placed there by their employers, the Pacific Electric Railroad. Unpaved, it was known as Mudtown.

August 1965 had been humid and hot, and the police had been troubled by young black gangs harassing, robbing, breaking and entering. Mostly they attacked respectable blacks. Central Avenue was the Main drag, with a plentiful supply of liquor, whores, horse-books. Drugs were available, as well as preachers prophesying moral disintegration. Jobs were few. Dawn saw many of the women leaving in droves, with their cleaning bundles, to ride for an hour or more on buses to the upper-middle-class neighborhoods of the county for housecleaning, cooking and child care. There was an envious animosity of black males to their working women. The token hiring of blacks by business, industry and television had not yet taken place. But for a few light-skinned Negro actors and some publicized singers, the Los Angeles County black was a muscle worker, when he worked. Under such conditions, a minority population—sullen and deep in self-pity, their education dismal, the young people turned off—was ready in the humid August night for trouble in a hostile police environment.

At seven o'clock the police, who had been in the habit of handling and rousting blacks much too firmly, and in some cases, brutally ("We never laid out no rugs for nigger prisoners"), arrested a belligerent drunken black youth. There was trouble, a scuffle, and a mob of blacks gathered

THE DEVIL IN WATTS

around police and prisoner. So the Watts riots began in a pathological situation of overreaction.

It can be clearly stated that the spark was resentment against white repression, prolonged hates on both sides. As the riot spread, a wild current built up—to destroy and burn seemed the simplest thing to do. This was followed by looting—breaking and entering, smashing of storefronts and carrying off of radios, television sets, clothing, food and liquor. A gambit of resistance turned into a madness. Avid expectancy of loot turned to more and more direct action.

By the next morning great fires were burning, "good or bad" blacks were being burned out, along with shops, cars, supermarkets, liquor stores. Fires on 103rd Street were kept going by sniper fire and brick- and rock-tossers, actions that prevented engine companies from getting to the flames. The fire fighters had to withdraw. The mobs looted and surged north like devouring locusts, moving through sixty blocks, fighting police all the way, shooting and rock-tossing, continuing their burning and looting. It was no organized rebellion, merely obscure despair, greed and avarice, "Giving it to Charlie" (the whites).

Gun shops in white neighborhoods had a run on weapons as whole sections of the county prepared, by arming themselves, for a black uprising.

I was on my way to give a lecture in a nearby town and the car I was in passed through streets filled with broken plate glass, smashed shopfronts. A few blocks away I could see flames rising and hear sirens, the sound of shotguns and the bang of gas grenades. When I got to the lecture hall, there were only ten people present, the rest of the expected audience had stayed home and, I was told, their menfolk were arming.

By Friday night, ten o'clock, the National Guard was marching into Watts in full battle gear, moving down Los Angeles streets toward what one officer referred to as "the front." Moving in force, young, unsmiling men, shoulder to shoulder. They began to clear the streets. Molotov cocktails had been used effectively and fires were still breaking out in new sections. There seemed to be a cruel finality in the making.

The black mobs were coagulated into many individual sections, retreating, advancing, some with firearms, all able to run and disperse at any show of strength. Against them were massed the police, the sheriffs' groups, highway patrolmen, state troopers, various law enforcement groups, city marshals, firemen and the National Guard. The blacks were, of course, heavily outarmed, with chemical weapons and military vehicles.

Burning, looting and serious gunfire from the blacks continued. The white lawmen (and black police) returned it with stronger firepower. The city, then the nation, was stunned by the violence of the prolonged outbreak. Decent, hardworking blacks, caught up between the two battling forces, hid themselves or stood by helplessly as they often saw their homes looted and burned by their own kind. Some shops put up signs: THIS IS A BROTHER'S BUSINESS or just BLOOD BROTHER.

A curfew was declared at eight o'clock Saturday night, and all fire crews rode through the district with National Guardsmen carrying loaded weapons. The raucous stutter of tanks echoed in the streets. All day Sunday and into the night, the bloody business of rioting, looting and sniping went on. By Monday, it was clear the black fury, frustration, the senseless, brainless riot was dying down; the vicarious satisfaction of fighting whitey was turning to fear. They were being overpowered by Police Chief William Parker's ability to hit hard and hit in strength. What was left was a burned-out district that could have been a picture of a bombed Vietnam city. The sun rose on smoldering ruins, smashed and looted buildings, the tramp of armed forces and staring faces—sickening spasms of fear apparent—in doorways and windows. Bloodstains showed where thirty-four persons had died in violence.

Much of southeast Los Angeles, drastically altered, lay in ruins from fire and marauding mobs full of rancor and malice loose for six days. Burned-out cars, many turned over, still littered the streets. Public order was being restored by military force. Besides the 34 dead, 1,032 wounded had to be treated. Some dead were never reported, and many hurt people did not come forward for treatment. Of the 952 men and women arrested, 500 were under the age of eighteen, caught pilfering, setting fires. The scars of Watts were visible. The squalor was worse, and

THE DEVIL IN WATTS

the city was filled with harsh dissonances, new fears. Some stores never reopened, other buildings were never repaired, whole sections were razed and lots grew wild grass where once there were businesses and homes.

Some efforts have been made to help Watts and its people recover. Job-training and job-finding services were put forward. Black business was encouraged. The police walked carefully and did little clubbing unless they had to attack hate groups of blacks who set up fortresses and stood dramatic but futile siege. There was a surge toward black history in Los Angeles schools. Black faces began to appear—as sales help—in smart shops, and light-colored blacks were hired for television appearances, mostly in commercials and, if expert on the playing field, as sports announcers. Racial tensions are dormant but are still there. Segregation in southern California still exists but is glossed over by explanations or double-talk. Welfare, child care, family aid, has been increased, but it merely entrenches a Welfare Society deeper into depending, demanding the handout. There is no active war in Watts, but there is no peace. Beliefs and ideologies, marijuana and messiahs mix in despair, confusion.

Watts may be the only major riot that has inspired a tremendous annual festival and celebration. The *L.A. Times* covered this social event:

Up to 100,000 persons are expected to help the black community here commemorate the anniversary of the 1965 Watts riot during five days of events that begin Wednesday at Will Rogers Memorial Park.

The annual Watts Summer Festival will be one of pride rather than despair, according to Tommy Jacquette, festival director.

"We're not commemorating the 1965 violence," he said. "We're celebrating riots in the same manner the nation will celebrate its 200th birthday in 1976. Both had violent beginnings. Now we're working for a better world."

"A Better Watts, A Better World" was the theme of the event.

A black in a writing class I teach at the University of Southern California wrote of it as "the sad perversity of retrospective sentimentality."

39 The Manson Family

W C. Fields said, "I judge a city's standing, yes, by the quality of its murders. The shoddy lower class crimes of late have impinged on the usually high standards of our fair city in the matter of interesting foul deeds ending with a few stiffs. . . ."

The remark was made while the great man was waiting to start a film scene at the old Universal Studios. I was working there to turn the play

THE MANSON FAMILY

Uncle Harry into a motion picture. Fields also felt that giving a poor crime a good name got it more attention than it deserved.

No one ever writes of Los Angeles murders without mentioning Winnie Ruth Judd. She was a most uninteresting woman who chopped up two women friends and put their parts away in trunks in storage. She was locked away for many years, making headlines every time she walked away from the confinement of some institution. The only outré thing the press could hint at about Winnie's crime was that perhaps it was a *ménage à trois* of lesbians. The Black Dahlia was another rather shabby crime that only began to gain impressive press space when some reporter labeled it the Black Dahlia case. The girl who was hacked up was a bar-room tramp and hardly a combination of Mata Hari and Garbo as one was led to believe. Her murder was never solved. A half-dozen confessions a year are still received.

In the 1960s two events brought back the charisma, the quality that Fields missed, to Los Angeles crimes. A little paranoid Arab put an end to Robert Kennedy's fairly good chance of beating Richard Nixon to the White House. It was a murder done directly on live television again (as in the Oswald killing), photographing a homicide. As photo journalism it had stature, containing political overtones involving both the killer and certainly his victim. But the Arab wasn't too interesting and the trial developed nothing dramatic beyond the fact that the gods didn't care much for the Kennedys (*"He* has no respect for money," from a reporter's notebook).

Charles Manson and his harem of shopworn case histories dominated the Los Angeles scene in the late 1960s. The trial was impressive enough to attract worldwide attention. As I sat watching Charlie in court for several days, I was impressed by his stoic aura of confidence and the devotion to him of his tainted girls. They saw in him a combination of the Messiah and a Don Juan crossed with a smear of Krafft-Ebing—incest relationship with a father image. Certainly he was a folk hero to the hippie, the way-out fringe at a time of peace marches, college campus riots somehow interwoven with the drug culture of Tim Leary ("Drop out.

Turn on. Tune in.'') and the rage for the Beatles and the nasal whine of country music.

Charlie was small, delicately built but wiry. He had the face of a fanatic who played it cool, only the eyes like a hawk's seeking to escape from his skull. Not very attractive as a man—most of the time with a heavy reddish beard and long sweaty hair. At other times his head was close-cropped and his face clean-shaven. He seemed to spend his time in his cell redesigning his image. He never lost that confidence in himself that ego gives.

Illegitimate, a dishonest drifter from childhood, Charlie by his middle thirties had spent most of his teens and maturity in legal confinement. He was a steel-hard, full-time criminal bathed in self-pity with a loathing for those who had money, fame and power. When he appeared on the California scene, Charlie was fingering a guitar and humming folk music he had composed. Charlie tried to break into the rock and country music field, seeking a recording. That aspect of his life is not well documented, although the press said he had contacts with Doris Day's son who was involved with music promotion. Charlie reminded me of D. H. Lawrence, who also had a group of worshiping females and, like Charlie, wanted to create a community in some remote spot with himself as philosopher-sultan.

Certainly Charlie went further than just thinking of it. He gathered in a group of runaway girls, middle-class, upper-middle dropouts, part harem, part sadist-dominated cult. A few dim-witted males were sometimes part of the band as they roamed southern California in stolen jeeps and vans, lived in trailers in desert outposts, at semideserted mines and ranches. As a trade, they stole Volkswagens to make over into dune buggies.

The girls scavenged for food in garbage cans of restaurants, and some were not above prostituting themselves when times were hard. A few babies were produced. Charlie, replenishing the earth, began to talk of saving the world when the blacks took over. Like Hitler, his big point was race, and saving it. Often there would be a dozen in the Family, camped out someplace beyond police calls and the square world, making out, listening to Charlie sing his songs, talk of the blacks taking over and his small band waiting to alert the surviving whites, lead them to win the race war that would come. How much of this was blowing grass and alcohol and psychotic dreaming we do not know. The reporting of his ideas may well have built up more than actually existed. Why murder those he wanted to save?

Two cold planned murders were done by the gang (two that we know of). A ranch hand named Shorty was done away with, his head cut off, and in parts he was buried someplace. No remains were ever found. A music man who had some connection with the Manson Family was murdered by a male member of the gang, most likely in a blackmail plot that failed. Police work was casual or lazy at first in both cases.

The Charlie Manson gang came to glory in their *Big* one, the wiping out of a whole party of people, hangers-on to the show-biz world; a hairdresser, a coffee heiress, an actress married to a decadent but inspired Polish director (he had filmed *Rosemary's Baby*). Neither the director, Roman Polanski, nor Charlie Manson was present on the massacre night in Bel Air—an exclusive hillside community—when several of Manson's gang, some of the girls and one man, broke into the fenced estate of the rented house. After some simple torture and tie-ups they executed the director's pregnant wife and some house guests (by knifing) and a stranger departing after a visit to the caretaker's cottage (by shooting).

It was gory enough (one killer wrote PIG in blood on a door). Such was the end of some members of Hollywood's dismally overpublicized glamour set, the kind of names appearing as gossip items in the sleazy film and TV columns of the Los Angeles press.

The crime really shocked the city—a brutal mass slaughter beyond reason or sense. It was not for robbery, though there was some talk later that Charlie had planned to have local blacks be blamed for the murders and so rouse up the racial fires of the city which had been banked since the Watts riots. But this on inspection isn't really a very satisfactory explanation. It was clearly just an orgy of killing for kicks, a hatred of folk who were accepted by established show business people.

As for Charlie, the plain answer could be he just was enjoying seeing how far he could drive his dominated bitches and followers to do just what he asked, no matter *what*. Certainly Charlie was proving to himself he was a sun-drenched California de Sade.

The next step was to destroy a prosperous businessman and his wife in their home—trussed up like Thanksgiving fowl for the oven and murdered, the man having a barbecue fork—available in any respectable home on the coast—stuck into his stomach.

The Manson Family seemed to have no fear of the law, or rather any awareness it was dangerous. But the law caught up to the earlier murders, the stealing of cars to turn into dune buggies. The Family was being arrested on vague charges. Then one of the jailed girls talked of the Family's crimes to a cellmate who reported it, and so the information was promptly put into the hands of the law. The murder indictments brought the Family into the news headlines. Charlie appeared to enjoy it.

The trial of the Manson Family in Los Angeles turned into the typical circus act that played so many courtrooms in the late 1960s. One of the harem girls turned state's evidence. The Family on trial and those members or hangers-on outside began to tune up their acts. The D.A.'s men and some defense lawyers joined the drama, each with his own act. Marchers, banshee howlers serviced the TV cameras. Some shrinks wrote rather poor interpretations of the Manson circle for the press—without actual interviews of the Family—or nodded and scratched their jowls while talking cant on television.

Charlie in the courtroom held center stage. He trimmed his beard, gave himself haircuts, got rid of the beard, grew it again. He shaved his head, scratched a cross on his forehead till it bled. Soon all his Family, in jail or outside marching, were all scratching bleeding crosses on their foreheads. Some of the pickets shaved their heads.

The outcome of the trials was predictable. Charlie and his Family were put away—it was hoped—for many years. Charlie insisted society had made him do it.

THE MANSON FAMILY

Even more newsworthy nationally than the Manson murders was the shootout that occurred in Los Angeles during the summer of 1974 when the so-called "Symbionese Liberation Army," which had kidnapped Patricia Hearst, showed up in the Southland with Miss Hearst in tow. By that time she had renounced her former life and, according to taped messages, had become "a soldier of the army" and been involved in a bank robbery. One of the kidnappers was spotted when he tried to shoplift a pair of socks priced at about 90 cents. To cover his escape Miss Hearst fired an automatic weapon from the getaway car.

Soon the police were closing in on the fugitives and cornered six of them in the black section of Los Angeles in a house—1566 E. 54th Street—where Miss Hearst was thought to be. But by the time police came on the scene she was gone and only other women members of the gang and the black leader and a white man were trapped. What followed was one of the most prolonged shootouts in Los Angeles police history.

Contrary to what was later reported by some, the police did give warnings, did ask for surrender. They were answered by heavy arms fire. When tear gas was tossed in, the fugitives donned gas masks they had brought along. They also had a small armory of weapons and gasoline-filled bottles. An army of police in flak jackets exchanged prolonged fire with those inside the house and most likely one of the Molotov cocktails set the house on fire. No fire-fighting unit could get near the place because of continued arms fire. According to the coroner's report, the black leader, "Cinques" De Freeze, committed suicide. They were all found dead inside of the fire or wounds.

The police, in great danger during the engagement, were at once attacked by liberal organizations, radicals and the Civil Liberties Union for not charming the fugitives out. As for Miss Hearst—Patty to the press— she was reported in a dozen places a day but managed for a long time to avoid capture.

In September 1975 Patty was finally apprehended in San Francisco. After many visits to psychiatrists, official and private, and a costly legal defense, in March 1976 Patty was convicted of a federal charge of bank robbery. She was sentenced in September of that year to seven years in prison (although she would be eligible for parole in eighteen months) and was informed that in early 1977 she would be tried for kidnapping and several other charges her co-defendents Emily and Richard Harris had already been convicted of.

The Patty Hearst saga and its bizarre series of events made front-page news nationwide for months. It also reinforced southern California's strange attitude toward crime which has carried over into the twentieth century. One reporter feels "it's as if it were a spectator sport." All too often, it is.

40 The Amazing Game of Politics

T he late satirist and cartoonist Milt Gross, who in Los Angeles wrote for Charlie Chaplin's films, once told me: "Politics in California is not any more corrupt than in any other state of the Union, which means it's pretty dirty." Much of this corruption was hidden or covered up. Now the average citizen of California, as polls show, no longer regards most public officeholders as trustworthy.

UNDER THE TINSEL

One who knew the dishonesty to be found in the California Legislature from the inside was a man named Arthur S. Samish. I talked to him in San Francisco once when I was working on a genre history of that city. He was solid, fat—close to 300 pounds on the scales—amusing, clownish and *very* smart. He had written a book, *The Secret Boss of California,* and he was.

As a lobbyist Samish had millions of dollars available, as he put it, "to select and elect legislators who voted the way I wanted, and if they didn't, I unelected them."

One man who figured Samish out was U.S. Senator Estes Kefauver of Tennessee, chairman of the Senate Crime Investigating Committee. Kefauver said, in 1951, "Samish is a combination of Falstaff, Little Boy Blue and Machiavelli, crossed with an eel."

In the 1920s and into the 1950s Samish fronted for the liquor industry, breweries, race racks, big oil, cigarettes, bus, trucking, railroads, films and others by his lobbying activities in Sacramento. He controlled funds of $150,000 a year produced by a 5-cent-a-barrel assessment on beer. He testified he spent $953,943 in six years for "public relations." Many agreed he was, in public, modestly quoting a *very* low figure.

Samish was careless in his use of money, including his own. He was convicted in 1953 of evading $71,878 in 1946–1951 income taxes, sentenced to three years in prison and fined $40,000. He served twenty-six months.

A now retired politician told me: "Artie Samish sure knew how to give big-time parties when he wanted us boys from southern California to vote some swindle on the taxpayer. Artie, he had this fancy set of rooms in this posh hotel, see. Near the statehouse. And there it was Liberty Hall *all* the time. Booze, good eating, Havana cigars, card games. And Artie was a great host—all over the place—a big ball of lard laughing it up, slapping your shoulder. And someplace along in the festivities you were told what the oil bastards, the racetrack gang, the booze or railroad boys wanted done to some bill. Most of us did it. We were sorry to see Artie get nicked by Uncle Sam and go to the can. He was never the same when he came out."

Arthur Samish himself felt it wasn't just the prison term that dethroned him, ended his power. It was some direct quotes in *Collier's* magazine from *The Secret Boss of California*. He admitted he had shot his mouth off and was quoted as saying:

I am the governor of the Legislature. To hell with the governor of California. Drop a $2 bill in the Capitol rotunda and you'll start a riot.

Samish died in February 1974, aged seventy-five. A mass for his soul was said in San Francisco at the Saint Ignatius Church. No legislators were listed as attending.

How does Los Angeles react to political corruption? More than Samish, it is Richard Nixon and the Watergate affair that has turned the Los Angeles voter and his family into cynics in many cases when it comes to a respect and a belief in the honor and integrity of the elected official.

The California polls all bear this out. Although one must be sure one is reading a *real* poll and not some special group buying a dream reading that distorts the true facts. One of the most respected is the Caddell Poll, which in February 1974 did interviews with a thousand families asking which California public officials they regarded most favorably and unfavorably.

The big surprise was the result on Tom Bradley, the black mayor of Los Angeles who retired Sam Yorty: Bradley—favorable, 63 percent; unfavorable, 5 percent; no opinion, 16 percent; never heard of him, 16 percent.

No surprise was the result on a native son from southern California: President Nixon—favorable, 30 percent; unfavorable, 67 percent; no opinion, 3 percent.

And this poll was taken *before* it was revealed that while Nixon's legal residence is California, and he voted there, he paid no state income tax and had overlooked capital gains taxes on his various real estate setups in San Clemente. For a long time the Number One best seller in Los Angeles was a book in which Harry Truman said of Nixon: "All the time

I've been in politics there's only two people I hate, and he's one. Nixon is a shifty-eyed goddamn liar, and people know it."

A political friend of mine shook his head when I quoted that line to him. "And in the end people don't care. Dickie will survive, stink and all."

41   Mayor Sam

S am Yorty seemed a bright change from all the other fuddy-dud-
dies, party hacks and chairwarmers who had been mayors of Los
Angeles since World War I. Many of the city and county offices
had been captives of the oil interests, favored contractors, the city's newspaper's endorsements, the fund givers of special interests, ranchers, lobbyists, tourist-trappers and anti-union activities.

Sam Yorty—no one, friend or foe, called him Samuel—had come out of the Middle West in the 1940s, a small figure of a man with a quick smile, a wise eye and an awareness that a person was what he made of himself. A Democrat who at times hardly ever agreed with the party, too cunning a personality to some of the Democrats in power, he ran for public office and became congressman.

In the 1960s and early 1970s Sam Yorty was twice mayor of Los Angeles and wanted a third term. Half clown to many, and an agile tight-rope walker in politics to others, he was in middle age still boyish-looking, trim, neat, his thinning hair with a streak of white in it and a voice with an amused "gee folks" burr to it. He had hoped to be governor, but saw his chances failing.

Like Sam Goldwyn, who was best known for his shattering of the English language (actually the work of press agents and gag writers), of Sam Yorty one could always get a laugh by asking, "Is Sam out-of-town traveling again?" He certainly seemed always to be in Asia or Europe or Latin America, smiling, shaking hands, getting awards.

He was feisty in his relationship with the powers that actually controlled the city, among them the *Los Angeles Times*. Somehow a feud started between them and the paper began to snipe at the mayor. Sam Yorty took them on—a brave thing to do, but it had its advantages. Sam was smart enough to see that the *Times* had given him a great weapon; the game of David against Goliath, and the resulting millions of dollars of free publicity space in the paper. He openly attacked the *Times* as bigoted, against "the people's interest" and the tool of special groups. The *Times* attacked him for slackness in office, the number of city officials who seemed to get indicted for kickbacks, bribe-taking and other hanky-panky, and the many changes in zoning restrictions worth millions to real estate operators. Actually little of this was Sam's doing. The real power lay with the city fathers.

The Democrats disliked the little mayor as he turned more and more toward far-right Republicans, talked of "pinkos" and "liberals" as if they

MAYOR SAM

had laid siege to City Hall. Sam visited the White House, praised and then endorsed Richard Nixon for reelection and hinted, according to some press reports, that he might be offered some cabinet or other official post in Washington.

The *Times* struck with a cartoon by its brilliant editorial cartoonist, Conrad. Conrad did a drawing of Yorty at his desk, on the phone, announcing they had come to appoint him to some high office, while closing in on him were two asylum attendants in white coats with a straitjacket and a net.

Sam Yorty sued the *Times* for a million dollars. But in the end the case was thrown out of court. The infighting and name-calling reached bitter heights.

Sam Yorty had had trouble when he planned to run for a second term as mayor. Not only was the *Times* on his back, but the picture of his new bedfellows, the conservative right-wingers, hurt his image as just a simple man of the people. His comments sounded to many like red-baiting and racism. It appeared that Sam had had it.

His main rival for the mayor's office was a retired black police lieutenant, Tom Bradley, a decent man but low-keyed, mild and lacking political punch and color. Los Angeles likes razzle-dazzle elections. However, when the polls showed Sam Yorty would go down to defeat, he replied with a kind of racial theme: that the white police and firemen would not serve under a black mayor, and that the blacks would be favored over the whites in the city.

The polls showed Tom Bradley well ahead in the race right up to election day. Then in the privacy of the voting booth Sam Yorty was reelected mayor. Los Angeles had drawn back at the last moment from electing a black mayor. The ruins of the Watts riots were still plain to see.

The *Times* continued its attacks on Yorty (it attacked Reagan and Nixon, too, in some of its columns and cartoons, but loyally it always endorsed all Republicans for office during election week).

When Yorty decided to run for a third time as mayor of Los Angeles, he believed a repeat of the tactics that had defeated Tom Bradley before would work again. So there appeared again the advice that a black mayor would not have the police and the city officials behind him. But Yorty's reputation had suffered, and the blacks had become politically more active. Sam was traveling again, and more city officials had been indicted and some found guilty. Even if Sam had had nothing to do with appointing or supporting them, he got the blame, for he had ruled at City Hall in the mayor's office a long time. People were looking askance at his trading of some city shoreland to a big oil company.

Tom Bradley was elected, the first black mayor of Los Angeles. He continued to be a decent, hardworking mayor. Not a very interesting or colorful figure, but after the flamboyant Yorty, who for a time had a radio and television talk show, *The Sam Yorty Show* (even at the end he still held press conferences, but they were no longer rewarding as news), Tom Bradley seemed a nice change to many citizens. And Sam joined the Republican Party.

42 The Rise and Fall of Bart Lytton

The magic spring was guarded by a giant in a deep mountain cave. When asked if one might drink of the spring, one was told, "The price is your right eye. . . ."

—The Eddas

UNDER THE TINSEL

T o meet a legend before he is a legend gave me an insight, almost an excruciating consciousness, of the problems one faces in evaluating Los Angeles. I first met Bart Lytton in the early 1940s. We were both writers at the RKO film studios. We shared a row of dusty offices with Milt Gross, the great satirist of the twenties, whose "Nize Baby," drawings and texts, had been the delight of millions of readers of the *New York World,* and with Jed Harris, another great light of the same period, whose fame as a producer of such plays as *The Front Page* had made him the wonder-worker of Broadway. An odd man. Milt called him "the walking Rorschach test."

Both Milt and Jed were lost geniuses in exile who were attempting to remain in Hollywood—that elephants' burial ground of great talent just too big for the setting: the Hollywood studios at this period were at their most banal. Both men were to leave brilliant fiascoes. Bart was young, bouncy, fun, yet I sensed an incomprehensible uneasiness. The four of us formed a sort of outlanders' group—New Yorkers transported "to the caves of Ali Baba" (Jed Harris).

Bart was to become a multimillionaire banker, creating a savings and loan empire in the 1950s, the fifth largest such association in the nation, one with assets of three-quarters of a billion dollars. For twelve years as the creator of Lytton Savings, he would flamboyantly rule and amaze banking circles with his mania for publicity and success. Then he was destroyed after a sixteen-hour nonstop effort, an all-night conference with his creditors. Fourteen months later, Bart was dead. Some said of a heart broken by the disaster that had struck him—some hinted he had removed himself from the scene. In a rare pensive moment, he had once quoted to me a line he attributed to Yeats:

> We live each other's death
> and die each other's life.

But that was all in the future. Bart was not a very good screenwriter and he jested about his failings and his films—*Hitler's Mad Men, Bowery to Broadway, Follow Your Heart.* We became good friends, for he was an amazingly likable man, once one recognized that behind the public ego, the brazen public stunts, was a sensitive rather frightened person caught in a clash of aspirations. We remained good friends—I saw a great deal of him on his way up, and observed him in his decline. It was some decline, but an anguish that he could still announce as meaning merely that, "Well, perhaps the relief chauffeur will have to go."

His estate, once estimated at $50 million, was, when he died, worth $1,334 and a few cents. If we have not lost most of our capacity for wonder, we can ask of Bart Lytton—was it perhaps that his destiny was created by his strange childhood? His father, a lawyer in Youngstown, Ohio, was mysteriously murdered when Bart was three. The crime was never solved. His stepfather was a well-off doctor in New Castle, Pennsylvania, but Bart seemed in the way. He always bragged about being sent away from home. "My parents always belonged to the best country clubs . . . I went to Staunton Military Academy with Barry Goldwater. . . ."

He dropped out of college in 1934. The family refused to support him and he, robust, sanguine, expansive, became a reporter at $15 a week. He had met a girl named Beth. The story goes that her last name was Lytton and Bart took it as his own.

As a free-lance writer with no subtlety or sense of style, he managed to save enough to get them to Hollywood and a job at RKO. He was impressive, handsome as a patrician Caesar of the second rank. He left the studios in 1945, aware that he would never be an important screenwriter.

When another screenwriting job was offered, he always said, to get it, he had to join the Communist Party of America and carry a card. There is a myth that in the forties to get, and hold, a job in films, one had to be a Communist Party member, as the Marxists had infiltrated as a power in all the major studios. This is sheer nonsense, but still believed by many. There were one or two party members, Marxist enclaves in fairly high places, but never on top as studio bosses. I knew of no really talented writers who were called party members, but for Albert Maltz. Actually, Bart had a vulnerability for any group that let him talk. He was romantic and being a Communist was a sort of status then, in some circles. Bart was to explain, "I quickly became revolted by the party's extralegal maneuvers and its complete disregard for the individual, and when I voiced these criticisms, I was expelled 'as an agent provocateur,' 'an FBI informer' and 'an enemy of the people.' "

He certainly testified in Washington before the Un-American Activities Committee against Hollywood party members. But there is big doubt that he was ever an F.B.I. agent. He testified out of fear, and a horror of the possessive strategies of Soviet evil; the rigged Stalin trials in Moscow. "When I was kicked out of the Communist Party, Hollywood blackballed me. I couldn't get any writing job. I finally went to work as a men's clothing salesman for $8 a day. I had an aunt in the mortgage business and when she saw how miserable I was doing, she offered me a job. I grabbed it and found I had a talent I hadn't even been aware of—making money with money. I stayed with my aunt . . . then opened my own mortgage company. With the profits from that, I moved to Las Vegas in 1954 to get into another branch of the money business—savings and loans. I used $15,000 of my own money, borrowed $30,000, took in two partners for $5,000 each and bought the First Western Savings and Loan Association. The next year, I bought another S&L in Vegas and one in Albuquerque."

With the profits from Nevada and New Mexico, Lytton turned to Los Angeles. In 1956 he bought Canoga Park Savings and Loan Association for $280,000, assets $1.4 million, and changed the name to Lytton. In three years Lytton's company had assets of $72 million. By 1962, $333 million, in 1967, $762 million.

But to Bart money was a load on his shoulders—it was an obsession—to show it off—to get it talked about—and to spend it. I used to sit some afternoons in Bart's private inner suite in his peppermint candy-colored bank building—he in his shorts, showing me his collection of shirts on shelves, cuff links, ties, hand-sewn shoes. He had hired Clark Gable's former valet, and would introduce him as a celebrity. Bart was happy as a kid with a new red wagon. I envied him—not the haberdashery, but the ability to take pleasure in material objects. I liked him best when there was just the two of us. "Only the artist and the criminal have the full power to express themselves. I'm an artist in money."

Bart could in public be a curiously aggressive figure. Brazen, loud-talking, amusingly bright and enough of the writer remained for him to get off quotable remarks to reporters who respected a guy who had made it big.

He was envied and hated by the town's bankers.

Yet these men protected Bart—even if only to keep a scandal from breaking, the public from hearing about his past. None of the Los Angeles newspapers ever brought up his Communist past, never in all the stories they wrote—and they wrote a lot. He was a good advertising account. The bankers offered him no help when he began to slide toward the skids. "Too flamboyant . . . too egotistical . . ." they told each other in their exclusive anti-Semitic clubs, or at the Hillcrest Country Club of which he was a member. He ignored the rules of the smug orthodoxies of banking.

Bart gave marvelous parties—the kind of parties people think of as "Hollywood parties:" In truth, real Hollywood parties are dull and trashy, overloaded with liquor and boring people boring each other and getting their names repeated and repeated in gossip columns. Bart's parties were much different. He had a genius for collecting interesting people, and the most interesting visitors. I remember a Nobel Prize scientist: "The universe is nothing, a mess of gases and rock." Bart was a good host and served marvelous gourmet food. His gardens would be covered by tents for a festive night, and two, three hundred people served, amused, entertained. He seriously collected the art of the best modern southern California painters (later it was discovered that Lytton Savings and its stockholders owned them, *not* he personally).

Bart hired Mort Sahl to broadcast television political news from his offices. When Mort tried to switch the show's slant toward Adlai Stevenson,

Bart moved in on camera and told Mort, "I'll not have this show turned into a rally for *one* man."

Mort replied, "Get off camera and stop trying to censor me."

"This is my show! I'm paying for it. . . . say whatever you like. But by God, I have a right to respond!"

Southern California loved the public prime-time brawl on live television. Mort frowned but stayed with the show. *Newsweek* ran Bart's picture with Jackie Kennedy. Bart took on militant blacks and hippies in TV debates. He talked back to boss Jesse Unruh of the Assembly (whose own fall from power in the 1970s was to be nearly as complete as Bart's). Unruh said, "Bart is a mad genius in equal parts."

Bart wasn't mad, just charmingly a bit paranoiac. Deep down he was a skeptic. Hysterical at times, hallucinated—but not mad. I attended his New Year's parties when I was in town, events which he gave for old friends, not the big shots, the studio or TV stuffed shirts, or what passed for society in Los Angeles. ("Barbary Coast whore to Pasadena Kennel Club in two generations.") It was on New Year's nights among people he had known—aging screenwriters, a bit shabby; playwrights who hadn't made it big, often modest people he really enjoyed being with. Here one saw him at his best, felt his affinity with humanity. Still talking, but not as much or as loud. I remember the last New Year's night I went to a Bart Lytton party. We sat and smoked in a side room of his Malibu beach house, once owned by Louis B. Mayer, as guests waited for midnight.

"What do you think, huh? What do you think?"

I asked, about what?

"Everything. I have this feeling like a kid's crazy wonder—want to do things—to piss in the open air on dead leaves, and watch the stars. At times like this, when I'm with people I knew when I first hit this town, then I sense the rest isn't all real. . . . I know I overact. I overreact. It's as if I'm wound up like a tin alarm clock they used to sell—the spring tight, and I don't want it to snap or run down, like one of those sidewalk toys that out of power fall over on their ass."

THE RISE AND FALL OF BART LYTTON

And then it was midnight and no one knew all the words of "Auld Lang Syne."

Unlike most people who liked Bart (and many people did like him), I didn't give him advice or tell him to simmer down. He seemed, that evening, sad and brooding, yet pleased he was with people who liked him, didn't envy him (to envy him, knowing the facts, would have been true sadness). Bart spoke of the insults he still took from Los Angeles Marxists and fellow travelers. He seemed calmer, more controlled. Perhaps I had the hope he would slow down. There were hints he was in trouble, Lytton Savings facing worried creditors, but I put it down to enemies.

By the spring of 1968 he was bobbing in a sea of trouble, going down for the third time. There was talk Lytton Savings held more than $70 million to $80 million in uncollectable mortgage loans on newly built, unsold tract properties. A depression had hit the California building industry.

Bart went to Wall Street for help, and to extend his loans. They made hard terms. It came down to him to find $3 million to carry Lytton Savings through a hard few weeks.

But . . .

What I now set down I got in a long conversation with a man who was close to Bart, day by day over a long period of time. He was not a banker, but was involved in one of Bart's nonprofit projects. He told me, "Bart had the promise of the three million that perhaps could have saved him. Some of the Los Angeles groups notified the Wall Street people and put on the pressure. Bart did not get the loan."

As Bart saw it:

"It was the fastest growing financial institution in the history of mankind. Grew too fast. We had to borrow money to maintain the growth. When money got tight and the housing boom crashed, we couldn't meet our obligations. We lost $14 million in three years. We kept waiting for the tight money to ease up because we knew when that happened, we'd be OK . . . it happened too late. Our stock dropped from a high of $28 a share in 1964 to $4.60 a share in 1966. Ninety days after I lost control, all S&L stocks jumped more than 100 percent. Lytton went as high as $14. If I could have hung on till then, I'd have been a hero."

Bart Lytton couldn't hang on. He was feared, hated by the conservative financial establishment. Most reveled in his fall. He went to them for aid and they refused.

Did they also kill the Wall Street loan? I do not know. What is true is that Bart lost control to new management. They, to keep public confidence and not cause a run on the association, gave Bart a highly paid consultant's role for ten years. Before the fall, as chairman of the board and president, he may have paid himself a salary of millions a year.

His personal assets had been variously reported as $25 million to $50 million. Whatever they were, all went in attempts to bolster up Lytton Savings.

Once he had been called the tiger of the industry. Now did he miss wealth? He felt one of the "freedoms of wealth is the privilege of speaking one's mind. I say what I think and I do what I want. The petty pleasures of group concordance disgust me. That's why I have that Emerson quote hanging in my office—'Whoso would be a man must be a nonconformist.' "

With Lytton Savings lost (it became Great Western Savings), he gave a huge party for the saving association's employees. Two hundred guests ate and drank. He admitted he was "a loser for the first time in my life." Hardly true—there had been earlier defeats—as a reporter, as a screenwriter, perhaps other things. He remembered when he had entertained in his house and gardens John Kennedy, Baron Edmund de Rothschild and a whole group of touring Russian composers, including Shostakovich and Khachaturian, or when he had mounted a huge Los Angeles Music Festival.

The last time I saw Bart at Lytton Savings was when he planned a project in a museum of film history he had set up in part of Lytton Savings, a project to do a documentary motion picture on the contemporary scene. The first section actually shot featured a round-table discussion by

THE RISE AND FALL OF BART LYTTON

Clifford Odets, Jean Renoir and myself—a playwright, a film director and a book author. Herbert Klein, a very excellent director, got us all together and shot several hundred feet of film. Perhaps we said something of value about Los Angeles and its endeavors, its aspirations. The film was never finished. Bart's decline came about around this time. The film footage is someplace in storage. Herbert Klein, at present working on a huge documentary about the masters of modern art, told me he had no idea where the footage was. He added, "To the rest of the nation Bart may not have seemed real. He was like so many of the men who created modern southern California. They are all like characters from the novels of Balzac, and who got trapped in the wrong time machine."

43 High Rise and Freeways

In the 1960s a cult predicted that all of the Los Angeles area would tilt into the ocean, "with the death of millions as sure as God stack-bombed Sodom and Gomorrah." Or read:

HIGH RISE AND FREEWAYS

> THE LAST DAYS OF THE LATE, GREAT STATE OF
> CALIFORNIA. By C. Gentry.
> Affectionate "farewell" to California as the greatest earthquake
> in history strikes and 15 million people with most of the state
> slide into the Pacific—is the Golden state doomed like
> Pompeii?

Most of the cult members, after some virulent verbal abuse, left for safer ground, but Los Angeles did not destruct, although there is a conscious premonition that slow death might be in the air, the result of the dreadful brown-orange haze called *smog* that hangs over the city.

Los Angeles has no practical, adequate transportation system, so most families have two or more cars, and 4 million are in movement every day. Weekends there are added out-of-towners coming to the big city for a visit. Overhead more than 1,000 jets a day come and go with open exhausts. When asked, "Is Los Angeles good for allergy?" one chest and throat doctor replied, "Very good. For *me*. I own six apartment houses."

Eye damage and emphysema are directly blamed on smog, and plants and crops suffer but are not vocal about it. As far away as Arrowhead Springs high in the mountains, great pine trees are dying of air pollution wafted to them by Los Angeles. Antihistamines are gobbled up like Girl Scout cookies.

Sometimes in the fall and at the start of winter, strange hot winds come from the desert, blow as regularly as the *touristas'* trots below the border. Winds called Santa Anas blow steadily and press down on the city. Then smog is pancaked out to the surrounding beaches and coastal cities, so that the landscape takes on the appearance of a bloodshot eye.

Control of auto-produced smog in the future is a reality as to law, but no one knows if the gadgets to be used will actually work. The Detroit car makers and giant oil companies drag their feet in hostility. They make a laborious charade of complying. The oil companies in southern California, mainly interested in driving out the small independent dealers, went so far as creating artificial gasoline shortages and issuing propaganda for the Arab cause in the Middle East (1975).

All of this overuse of the car, the desperate need for transportation,

A blanket of smog drapes Los Angeles in a typical scene. (Wide World)

A four-level interchange freeway in Los Angeles, one part of the massive system
of roads that is overcrowded, often to the point of becoming a solid traffic jam.
(UPI)

has caused the building of huge freeways, six to ten lanes of murderous traffic, roadbeds crossing and recrossing at various levels, cloverleaves, exit and entrance ramps in layers like a Brown Derby club sandwich. These, photographed from the air and at various angles, have created images stolidly indifferent to men, images that seem out of H. G. Wells' *The Shape of Things to Come*. Actually, traveling on them in clouds of deadly exhaust, fogs of dismal fumes, one notices barriers of heavy steel mesh and cement-block walls that separate the traffic moving in opposite directions. These are often torn to bits for hundreds of feet, or the blocks are crushed and broken. The repairing of these walls costs $500,000 a year. It is a recurring destiny, usually a few times a month for a drunk, or some befuddled runaway wanderer will go the wrong way, use an exit for an entrance, and at fifty to eighty miles an hour turn himself into as deadly a death weapon as a berserk Sherman tank.

Even if accidents are avoided, it is no pleasure to ride the various lanes going your way, as speed freaks, or oldsters who creep along, try to work out a traffic program. Several times I have been a passenger in cars that were given traffic violations for "going too slowly" in the middle lane at sixty miles an hour. There is no adjustment to safe car travel in Los Angeles.

The result of such an auto culture as in Los Angeles has brought a plague of secondhand car dealers. Their ethics, some buyers insist, are just to the left of Attila the Hun. Acts close to piracy are reported of some legitimate dealers whose sales methods and repair services would have charmed Captain Kidd. Feeble efforts have been made to do something about the gouging of the southern California motorist by car dealers and repairmen. But as with all of California's habitual exploiters—some television repairmen, undertakers, loan companies, unions, banks, medical associations—all have their powerful lobbyists and feeble, greedy legislators who often step away from any tight control of bad business habits.

The automobile business in its privileged position has caused the destruction of many still fine buildings, only a generation or so old. The wrecker's ball is always busy knocking down whatever stands in the way of producing more parking lots. As with strongly held taxi franchises, parking lots are a lucrative business, given to certain favored firms. Some parking lots of some eating and amusement places are said to be controlled by local Mafia types who pay certain restaurants thousands of dollars in advance for taking over the parking rights even, at times, before a new eating place opens. Then all tips must go into the kitty of the boss. Woe to a parking-lot boy who is suspected of pocketing a few bits.

There is a story of a customer who walked into a Jewish delicatessen in the Jewish neighborhood of Fairfax Avenue. "You got a parking lot?" asked the customer. Answered the owner, "Look, if I owned a parking lot, would I be in the delicatessen business?"

What is said of this city in transit?

As a female resident of Los Angeles sees her city:

"It's like a multidivided cell; everybody is in their own cell sac and they don't know about the other cells. I don't think they're disinterested in each other.

"People out here do everything a little faster. They get married and divorced earlier and remarry more quickly. From what I've heard it's a rotten town for wives of important movie men, unless they're clever about working themselves into scenes . . . or unless they take an active part in their husband's business."

"Take an opium eater's dream to Los Angeles, and they will realize it for you; the more it costs, the more they will believe in it. You can have a real Polar expedition, a real volcano, a reconstruction of the Roman Forum on the spot; anything you please, provided it is enormously costly. . . . Oh, those scenes of Oriental voluptuousness as imagined by a whaler's cabin boy! They would make a monk of Don Juan. . . ."

So wrote George Bernard Shaw. He had visited Los Angeles in 1933—and had lunch at M-G-M studios with Charles Chaplin, Marion Davies, Louis B. Mayer and Clark Gable.

Talking to the average citizen about earthquake danger—meaning people I met and interviewed (after all, who would admit to being

Culture comes to M-G-M: The frightened-looking people lunching with George Bernard Shaw in 1933 are Charles Chaplin, Marion Davies, Louis B. Mayer and Clark Gable. (M-G-M photo)

average?)—I came to the conclusion that in Los Angeles—earthquake country—no one really cares for what the scientists claim as the origins of quakes. All had experienced some minor shocks; a few of the elderly remembered some stronger tremors. As for predictions of some monster quake to strike Los Angeles, mostly I got a shrug of the shoulders or a disbelief in science as voiced by one acid-tongued woman: "Why, if they're so goddamn sure about things, can't they predict the weather right?"

John A. Blume, president of an engineering firm, discussed the physical and economic wreckage expected in the wake of a large 1906 type earthquake in a major city. "Such a temblor if it struck would do between $10 billion and $20 billion property damage, kill between 2,000 and 5,000 people during the early morning hours, between 10,000 and 20,000 people if it hit during a rush hour."

Scientists see the San Andreas Fault as only one of several great earth fissures in the state, with many minor connecting faults crisscrossing the state, so that California would appear to be bored through with many dangerous underground threats.

About all that has been done concerning this officially is to insist that the high-rise office buildings, luxury apartments and public structures adopt "earthquake proof" construction. This may merely be a term like "fireproof" which often isn't. No disaster has yet tested any of the new thirty- to forty-story buildings—not in any major quake. There are those who fear the worst after observing the great fire in 1974 in a Brazilian high-rise building, where hundreds were trapped in a blazing horror on its top floors, and more than 200 deaths resulted. They see the possibility of the modern Los Angeles high rise becoming a huge death trap if a quake should cause a fire in some lower stories. With elevator service knocked out and stairwells jammed or destroyed, thousands could perish even if the structures still stood.

So Los Angeles sits—or rushes about—on an unexploded time bomb. After more than thirty years at living here, when my windows rattle and cherished objects on shelves begin to dance, I merely count the seconds,

HIGH RISE AND FREEWAYS

three or four, and if the St. Vitus shakes don't continue, I go on with whatever I am doing. If I'm in bed at the time, and I feel a vibration through the house, and the bed begins a kind of waltz on its thin legs, I merely stay where I am and wait for the tremor to pass. I have discovered by checking around that most citizens of Los Angeles follow my procedures.

In 1971 when the last large quake hit the city area—a Richter reading for the main shock was 6.6—the shaking was heavy enough for those of us who lived twenty miles away, quake dwellers of many years standing, to realize it was a big one. The greatest damage was in the San Fernando Valley, where a big but poorly designed veterans hospital collapsed from its foundations and bridges over many of the eight-lane freeways fell down. In sixty seconds, $553 million in damages was suffered, mostly in public buildings. It was also feared that had the Lower Van Norman Lake Dam, close to collapse, actually failed, the "San Fernando earthquake might have become infamous as the deadliest in United States history" (The San Fernando, California, Earthquake of February 9, 1971, Geological Survey Professional Paper p. 33). More than twenty cloverleaf overpasses collapsed. Seventy persons died. But Californians simply take this in their wobbly stride.

44 A Bird's-Eye View

One of the reasons people take such an interest in southern California is that it has more coverage by reporters, cameramen and gossip columnists than any other American city but Washington, D.C. More lies are written about the district, more legends and myths engendered than in anyplace other than ancient Greece. It is mainly so because the now nearly dead film industry created a dreamboat version of life, and its great stars were given pasts right out of opium smokers' dreams. Television is now 95 percent created here, and cults, murders, riots and politics seem daffier under the strong sun.

Let us look at the towns that exist only because their lifelines are attached to Los Angeles.

I live on a four-acre mountaintop, have five deer in residence, a fox, raccoons, a red hawk and marvelously colored lizards; yet I am inside the Beverly Hills city limits. It takes only a minute and a half down a winding mountain road to reach Sunset Boulevard. When I came to Beverly Hills more than thirty years ago it was a village of about 36,000 people. It still is. But it has become a smog trap, and along Wilshire and its crossing streets it is Fifth Avenue at rush hour. More and more great department stores and fancy shops have crowded in—Saks, Magnin's, even a Pucci. Banks and insurance companies have erected high-rise buildings and moved their staffs out—buildings hardly fitting in design for more than piano boxes and bookends. So, while the resident population hasn't moved much, the business district is a snarl of traffic, and zoning laws seem to have a way of being bent.

Beverly Hills, which in 1920 was a mere desert until good hard salesmanship sold it as exclusive, grew so fast that pictures taken of it ten years apart look like different places. It is the real estate agent's dream. Values are ridiculous. In 1941 you could have bought most of the houses on Elm Drive, the 600 block where I lived for twenty years, for from $16,000 to $22,000 each. In 1960 these houses were selling for $100,000 and more. Today the asking price is up to $200,000. It must be kept in mind these are the same houses, some fifty years old. There are no lots for sale on most streets, so if you want a new house in Beverly Hills, you buy an old one and tear it down and build again. I have counted eight such jobs in the last two months. Warning: The *only* part of Beverly Hills worth living in as a social asset is *south* of Wilshire. To buy *north* of Wilshire is to be at once known as a fool or a slum dweller.

Taxes have becomes murderous. In ten years a house went from $1,200 in taxes to $4,300—and still rising.

UNDER THE TINSEL

The average Beverly Hills house needs the services of a gardener, a pool man (two weekly visits each), a housekeeper, a plumber on call, and sometimes a maid and a cook. I am on speaking terms with five butlers, none of whom I could have afforded. If one can pay the price, Beverly Hills is the best living in the world. I can't afford it but I stay.

To the west of Beverly Hills is Bel Air, much more fashionable than Beverly Hills in the last few years. It has gates and is still wild in spots. And here a house and grounds can cost from $300,000 to $1 million or $1.5 million. It has tennis courts in greater number than Beverly Hills.

Beyond Bel Air is the University of California at Los Angeles, a huge factory of more than 40,000 students. I have taught there and found it a kind of jungle, with everyone fighting for position, politics in all places and the resulting students of all kinds, from hippies to dullards. Visiting professors I have talked to were not much impressed by UCLA's methods. I live here, so don't ask me.

Beyond the college lies Brentwood, a middle-class section of the city. Charming, once cheap to live in, now costly to exist in. The college itself is in a section called Westwood, which was once a fine little village to shop in. It is now a madhouse of high rises and department stores; its only healthy sign was that a big Sears store left, finding it not the gold mine it had expected.

Beyond Brentwood one comes to Santa Monica, the waterfront— again, overbuilt and a mixture of shacks, new high rises, hamburger grease pits, fast food (bad), old hotels and new ones of poor design. The biggest thrill in Santa Monica is the Port-O-Spain building, a tall edifice in which the elevators climb the *outside* of the building, clinging to one wall, and the sight is well worth seeing, if the smog will permit.

The coast highway runs past Santa Monica and is usually open except when the high coastal cliffs decide to fall down and block it. These cliffs— 300 or 400 feet high—are made of decomposed granite and they have been eroding for ages. In the wet season, a house or two can come down with a section of cliff, but warnings are given in time. People still live up there with part of their yards hanging over in space.

Up the coast a few miles is Malibu. This is the "in" place, with a private

A variation of the many "stilt" homes built on the many hillsides surrounding Los Angeles. The houses here are in the Coldwater Canyon area and command a sweeping view of the San Fernando Valley. (UPI)

gateman. Actually it is a kind of low sandbar, not very interesting as a sight, and there are a dozen better spots to build a beach house. But the fashion for some time has been to say, "my Malibu beach house." Motion picture and TV actors swarm there, rich tax lawyers, retired industrialists turned art collectors. Giving their names means nothing, for the population changes as success or failure brings one in and washes another out. Bart Lytton used to give marvelous parties there. But I've been to some bummers there too. The parties to avoid are the ones listed by gossip columnists as "A parties." These are merely egotistical admiration societies of rather dull people who are powers in films, TV and radio, agents, and women on the market, or swinging, or just divorced. It may sound interesting, but it isn't.

Huntington is John Birch country, "right wing and square," money and class without any flashy settings. No "A party" person would be invited here. Here the food is of the best, the politics high Tory, the décor genteel.

Laguna, on the highway south of Los Angeles about thirty miles, is a kind of California Coney Island *and* Cape Cod combined. It has an art colony that has not accepted anything painted since 1900 in the modern style. It sells hundreds of paintings of waves, sunsets, rocks, boats and beach scenes. Once a year it has a festival called "Living Pictures," a series of still lifes is created of master works by Degas, Rembrandt, El Greco, Winslow Homer and other old favorites. Real people take the part of the figures against painted props. Nobody on stage moves for a few moments and the applause is long and strong. I was told (but don't believe) that one old lady said: "The colors are better than the original."

The beaches are marvelous all along the coast and of course overcrowded, packed with humanity. On weekends parking spaces and stretching-out spaces on the sand are gone by about eleven o'clock. Muscle Beach is in Santa Monica, a popular spot for exhibitionists, musclemen working out, balancing acts and just watching. It is also a homosexual area open to professional studs and closet queens looking over the scene.

San Francisco is much more of a homosexual parading ground, but Los Angeles is a good second. Gay bars stud the whole county and by now they are usually not molested by the police.

Surfers enjoy the coast, and the scuba divers too. The divers sometimes get caught in the kelp and drown. The life of the beach boys (and girls) seems only to consist of sitting on the sand, getting darker and darker like a good pipe and talking a jargon of their own.

Motorcycle gangs are usually lower-middle-class dropouts and the best known, Hells Angels, gather around San Francisco. The Los Angeles gangs mostly roar about, but are not as deadly as the northern groups.

I have tried in this chapter to give a kind of bird's-eye view of Los Angeles and its surrounding towns—and the people in them that make up its sports, its way of life. In a way I want to prove Fred Allen, the Plato of radio, wrong in his statement quoted at the beginning: "It's a great place to live if you're an orange."

What is Los Angeles like to a circling sea gull? Seen from the air, one is struck by the orange-brown mist on the horizons that look like fringes of Hell. But on a fairly clear day flying in from the east one passes the dark outlines of mountains, then a stretch of desert and soon lines of roads, more roads, then super-highways and at last the green groves of oranges and lemons, the cubist shapes of fields laced with the silver sprays that water this dry land. It only rains a few days in the fall. Nine to ten inches is often the yearly score.

Then appear houses, first scattered, then in clusters on hillsides, along canyons, factories too, stadiums and playing fields *and* swimming pools— bright blue coins blinking in the sun. The freeways grow thicker, the houses closer together and that dry concrete ditch *is* the Los Angeles River. If the flight is a bit to one side there are the green acres of Forest Lawn, the most famous (or notorious to some) burying ground on earth. We fly on to find the city surrounded by sections called San Fernando, Northridge, Long Beach, San Pedro, and if the plane is turning

The city of Los Angeles as it appears to the visitor flying in on a smogfree day. The San Gabriel Mountains form the backdrop. (Wide World)

southward back to sea, below is Balbo and its yacht harbor, Newport, more boats and waterfront homes, so crowded that it's hardly worth taking to the open water.

The city itself appears at last, squares and squares of a city that first followed cattle trails and then spread.

International Airport is huge, keeps nibbling away to expand, but is already at Palmsdale. It is not as badly handled as Kennedy in New York, but weekends one can hardly get in, and often doesn't.

Getting away from the airport, about ten miles from the city, is done by taxis, buses and private cars. The taxi situation in Los Angeles is bad. Yellow Cab, up to this year, had all of it for its own, never fully gave the proper service. Distances are vast and nearly everybody owns a car.

Riding through the fringes of the city to reach its heart one passes a dozen main streets of little towns, all alike, all having the same Radio Shack store, Sears, Grants, Pennys, Wards, K-Marts and branches of L.A.'s big stores. All film houses show the same films; it's called "a saturation run," some say "so no one can warn anyone else to stay away."

Close up the city is clean, bright—lawns and trees (many palms line the streets). Even the slums are fairly decent-looking, the misery hidden away inside. Graffiti is not yet the poxed curse it is in New York, but the game is spreading. There are special crews who go about painting it out.

45 Only an Intermission

At this point I bring to a brief recess the progress of a city of resiliency but little restraint, backfield always in motion. There is no end yet in sight to the theme of this book, the saga of a devouring giant. I have chosen to include the career of Bart Lytton who personified in its most dramatic form a creative force, the type of dreamer who made the city. That he failed grandly in the manner of Greek trag-

edy is only fitting. So did H. Gaylord Wilshire. ("Southern California will
be the most thickly settled part of the American continent.") All of the
men in the Los Angeles story who became part of its history were in
some way affected by the air, the sun, the opportunities of southern California—the Spanish soldier, José Vicente Feliz, the bandido Tiburico
Vasquez, "Don Benito" Banning, Downey, Otis of the *Times*—all were
men who wanted to fulfill their desires, swallow perhaps more than their
share.

A greed that made the city—what else gives it its strange beat? Not that
note of a different drummer, but the hum of dangerous traffic, the snort-
ing bulldozer destroying the landscape. The idea is that what represents
progress, sanctions everything. Even the bandido Vasquez saw himself
not as a mere highway hoodlum; he dreamed as large as any of the city's
builders. He wanted to create a revolution and lead the Chicanos to take
back southern California from the Yankees of the Estado Unidense.

The city is always changing, so there can be no final summing up. It is
still moving, grabbing off a bit of shoreline here, taking some area for a
park, condemning paths for more freeways. It pretty much controls the
state politically (so say the canny lobbyists). It leads in banking, insurance, in freight loading, shipping, fashion designing, television production, new godheads and minorities. Once it looked over the land mass it
desired. Now it moves *upward,* its high-rise structures are being built near
a great underground crack, a fault in the earth that once leveled San
Francisco but does not worry Los Angeles. Up go the towers of commerce, the condominiums, while pushing up land values, north, south,
east (west is the ocean and there its interests for conquest eye Japan and
China).

A recent survey revealed that the tall buildings have renting problems,
there is a scarcity of tenants, but this does not stop the expansion upward, without solving the glut of traffic problems created at the ap-
proaches of these huge new developments.

And what of population growth? There are those heretics who hint Los
Angeles would be forced to throw up, like a dog its dinner, a great deal of

the state it had swallowed too quickly. But the city disputes the figures of the State Department of Finance that more than half of the southern county's seventy-seven cities have lost population since the April 1970 federal census. Los Angeles' population, the state experts say, has dipped to 2,777,800, a loss of more than 32,000 in three years. In 1976, for the third straight year, the upstate gloom-grunters insist, Los Angeles County—once the nation's fastest growing—will lose 40,000 residents, according to their estimates.

Can it be that newcomers are no longer converging on the five-county Los Angeles area, the sixty-mile southern California area around Los Angeles? Fewer people are moving into the area, and population is increasing at its slowest pace in years. The busy urbanized five-county area around Los Angeles measured the region's economy—Los Angeles County, Orange County, most parts of Riverside, San Bernardino and Ventura counties. Leaving, says one survey, will be the most needed citizens.

Silly talk, manipulated figures insist Los Angeles' boosters. There still will be an increase of nearly 57,000 persons in the five-county area's total population, the surplus of births over deaths—short of the record 344,800 in 1956, but still a plus growth.

The state, that part of it not yet in the grip of the city's expanding interests, disagrees with Los Angeles figures as to its population count.

Estimates by the Los Angeles Area Chamber of Commerce's Research Department put Los Angeles County's population at 7,220,000. The state insists it should be 6,967,000, a difference of more than 250,000. The Chamber also estimates the city's population at 2,860,000, substantially higher than the state figure of 2,777,800. Most of the people who have left Los Angeles County, plagued by smog, high rent and land values, crime and traffic, are moving to less congested areas of California as well as to Orange and San Diego counties.

And what are Los Angeles' hopes of conquest beyond the state? Los Angeles has always had national aspirations. A movie actor made governor became serious about becoming President of the United States. Its great plane-building facilities dominate the future of air and space travel, design and production. Its brains set a landing on Mars. It is nearest to the trade-hungry People's Republic of China, to the rising world power of an exporting-importing—mad Japan again on the march, seeking raw materials. Waiting are the underdeveloped eastern frontiers of the Soviets; contracts already exist with Los Angeles firms to explore Siberian gas, oil, other resources. Plans are on the drawing boards to build great factories and facilities.

A fanatic would shout: "Today California! Tomorrow the world!"

But they were in many cases fanatics. The mission fathers from Father Junípero Serra on; the ranchers, the dons—Pico, Noriega, Coronel, Luzo—the handful of Americans who took over California, Stockwell, Frémont. And those who brought water to this desert first from the hills, then from a thousand miles away. If Bart Lytton was their Don Quixote, he was just filling a role that so many other shakers and messianic movers of Los Angeles had played before him.

Was it all worth it? Writing more than forty years ago, Robert Whitaker wondered:

I have been privileged to live in one of the fairest and kindliest of all the regions of the earth. California is, indeed, a marvelous land, beyond anything the passing tourist can ever know, and many of its people are among the choicest fruits of human evolution. All of this only accentuates the bewilderment and bitter disappointment which must be felt by any thinking man at the social barbarism of California . . . our ignorance, our intolerance, and above all our complacent social inertia.

There is a strange loyalty to the rhythmic flow of life in southern California. It is, for me, best expressed by my daughter, Joan. When she was a child, someone asked her where she came from. She answered, "I was born in Los Angeles at the age of six."

The true Los Angeles philosophy.

Los Angeles Chronology

1500   An estimated 300 to 500 Indians were living in Los Angeles County.

1542   Admiral Juan Cabrillo entered Santa Monica Bay, naming it "Bay of Smoke" because of Indian campfires.

1769   August 1. Father Crespi made the first historic mention of the future site of Los Angeles in his journal.

LOS ANGELES CHRONOLOGY

1781	September 4. Forty-four men, women and children founded El Pueblo de Nuestra Señora la Reina de los Angeles de Porciuncula, which they called El Pueblo for short.
1781	Charles III of Spain gave royal approval for the maintenance of the Pueblo de los Angeles.
1781	Los Angeles ordered by Spain to aid the American colonists fighting for freedom from England. No records exist to verify whether or not they complied.
1782	March 18. Father Junípero Serra visited Los Angeles to condemn moral conditions in the pueblo.
1786	Landholdings officially turned over to the settlers by the missions.
1790	The population was recorded as being 139 people broken up into 28 families on 29 farms.
1800	Spanish California consisted of about 1,000 settlers, soldiers and missionaries and 13,000 Indian "converts."
1810	Christmas plays, among them *The Shepherds* (*Los Pastores*), given in the Plaza.
1818	The new Plaza was begun and a church was raised.
1822	April. The city swore allegiance to Mexico, which declared its independence from Spain.
1826	November 27. Led by Jedediah Smith, seventeen American fur trappers and mountain men appeared at the Mission San Gabriel, staying six weeks before leaving to trap beaver in California streams.
1830s	Packtrains and traders reached Los Angeles from Santa Fe, New Mexico.
1837	In a civil war, troops from northern California seized the city, took prisoners and marched out again.
1839	Governor Alvardo exiled all Americans who were not naturalized citizens.
1841	November 4. John Bidwell succeeded at leading the Workman-Rowland party, one of the first California-bound emigrant wagon trains, to Los Angeles by going through Santa Fe.

LOS ANGELES CHRONOLOGY

1842   Gold discovered north of Mission San Fernando. Miners trekked from Sonora to Los Angeles for the diggings.

1843   American armed forces, acting on a rumor that the United States was at war with Mexico, seized some towns and Commodore Thomas Jones, U.S.N., came to Los Angeles to apologize.

1844   El Pueblo de los Angeles became the capital of Alta California under Governor Pio Pico.

1845   A Californian civil war ended in the battle of Cahuenga in which one horse was killed and one mule wounded. Governor Pico ruled a united California.

1846   May. War between the United States and Mexico broke out. California was one of the main prizes expected.

1846   August 13. Major John C. Frémont and Commodore Robert F. Stockton invaded Los Angeles.

1846   September. Angelenos rose against the American garrison and forced it to surrender.

1847   January 10. After a native revolt, the Americans regained the city.

1847   January 13. An official document of capitulation, the Treaty of Guadalupe Hidalgo, was signed giving California to the United States.

1847   July 4. The American Fort Moors was dedicated in the city.

1849   The first accurate maps of the city were drawn by Army officers. Los Angeles covered twenty-eight square miles.

1849   November 13. The California state constitution was approved by the voters.

1850   April 4. Los Angeles was incorporated as an American city.

1850   In Los Angeles County 8,300 residents were counted, half categorized as "domesticated Indians." In the city, 3,530 people lived in 518 dwellings.

1850   September 9. California entered the Union.

1851   Chief Antonio Garra of the Cupeño Indians organized a revolt against the whites in which five sheepherders were killed. Garra was executed by a firing squad.

1852   The rancheros failed to get justice under the Land Act of 1852, as later American courts found most of the original land grants "abominably flawed."

1853   A Vigilance Committee called the Los Angeles Rangers was formed in the El Dorado Saloon on Main Street. In the following two years they executed twenty-two men.

1854   An average of one violent death a day occurred in the city during this year.

1855   Mayor Stephen G. Foster resigned his office to join a lynch mob, resuming his duties after the hanging.

1855   July 11. An earthquake damaged almost every dwelling in the city.

1857   The gold rush petered out and an economic panic resulted.

1859   A southern California separatist movement declared that the southern part of the state had become part of the Territory of Colorado, but the Civil War prevented making this a legal move.

1860   Abraham Lincoln carried California in his presidential election.

1861   The Chinese population consisted of twenty-one men and eight women, most of whom lived in Nigger Alley (Calle de los Negros). Jacob Frankfort was the first Jew on record in Los Angeles, followed by the Newmark brothers, Harris and Joseph.

1862–1864 Great droughts destroyed much of the cattle-raising industry.

1863   Smallpox exterminated most of the Indians on southern California reservations.

1863   Judge Hastings went to Richmond to offer his services to Jefferson Davis. He failed to raise a regiment of Los Angeles rebels for the South.

1868   Phineas Banning obtained a charter to build the Los Angeles & San Pedro Railroad, a twenty-mile line running to the harbor. It was the first rail line in Los Angeles County.

1868   Ulysses S. Grant received 748 Los Angeles votes for President against "Rebel" Seymour's 1,236, but Grant carried the nation.

1869	February. The first bank in town was opened by John Downey and J. A. Hayward.
1869	The land boom put 20,000 acres under cultivation as farms and orchards.
1869	A boom in raising silkworms became a mad speculation in silkworm eggs, soon selling for $12 an ounce. The boom failed with 100 million unsold silkworm eggs on the market.
1869	The Wells Fargo Express boxes were robbed from a stagecoach just outside the city.
1869	Two hundred boxes of oranges were shipped by boat to San Francisco.
1870	This was a year of thirty-five lynchings and forty legal hangings in Los Angeles.
1870	Los Angeles County was producing one-sixth of America's wine. Oranges brought in $10 a tree. There were 34,000 bearing trees.
1871	A railroad bill was in Congress stipulating that a rail line south from San Francisco would pass through Los Angeles.
1871	The Farmers & Merchants Bank opened.
1871	The county was producing a yearly million and a half pounds of wool; speculators were paying 20 cents a pound to warehouse it while waiting for a rise in price.
1871	October 23. A race riot against the Chinese began. Nineteen men (and boys) were beaten to death or hanged by mobs of white men.
1872	Australian shipments destroyed the Los Angeles wool speculators' dreams and they failed to sell wool at even 12½ cents a pound.
1873	The last free Indians, the Modocs, were hunted down in the lava bed near Tule Lake. Only 20,000 Indians remained in the state.
1874	The famous bandido Tiburico Vasquez began to operate around Los Angeles. Captured, he became a hero in the city jail.
1875	Tiburico Vasquez hanged at San Jose.
1876	Sixty-five thousand acres of fruit trees counted in the county, and more planting continued.

LOS ANGELES CHRONOLOGY

1877   A great drought killed hundreds of thousands of sheep.

1880   Los Angeles Athletic Club founded with forty-one members.

1880–1890   The city had theaters to please all tastes: the Grand Opera House, Hazard's Pavilion and Turnverein Hall.

1880   Robert Widney helped found the University of Southern California.

1880   Sheriff Billy Rowland, who captured the bandido Tiburico Vasquez, started his last term as sheriff.

1881   Harry Chandler arrived in Los Angeles from Landaff, New Hampshire. He was to become publisher of the *Times* on General Otis' death.

1882   Helen Hunt Jackson published *Ramona,* which became a yearly pageant in southern California.

1882   Robert Widney formed a company to bring the first electric lights to Los Angeles.

1883   The most famous California train wreck occurred in the Tehachapi Mountains, killing nearly a hundred people, many from Los Angeles.

1885   The Santa Fe put a second transcontinental rail line into Los Angeles.

1886   Harrison Gray Otis came to Los Angeles and took over a small newspaper called the *Los Angeles Times*. He soon became the political power of the county.

1887   Los Angeles County real estate transactions totaled more than $100 million for the year.

1887   A land boom raised the price of city lots 500 percent.

1888   The real estate boom collapsed, leaving huge losses and many bankruptcies.

1890   July 1. Flag of the City of Los Angeles designed.

1892   Oil was discovered on West Street in Los Angeles. E. L. Doheny and C. A. Canfield made the first major discovery after digging 160 feet.

1893   The national financial panic hit Los Angeles. Widney's University Bank of Los Angeles failed.

LOS ANGELES CHRONOLOGY

1895   December 21. H. Gaylord Wilshire filed a subdivision called the Wilshire Tract with a wide street named Wilshire Boulevard.

1896   William Jennings Bryan carried Los Angeles against William Mc-Kinley in the presidential election.

1897   California became the number three oil producer in the nation, with 1.3 million barrels a year.

1897   The first golf course was opened on a vacant lot; tin cans were used for sinking putts.

1898   The city bought the water rights from a private company for $2 million, but knew it would have to seize water from the Owens Valley.

1900   Carrier pigeons were used to communicate with Catalina Island.

1900   Los Angeles had a population of 102,479.

1900   Seventy-one producing oil wells were brought in on the Rancho La Brea.

1901   Fossils of the saber-toothed tiger were first scientifically observed by the Union Oil Company.

1902   The first all-movie theater, the Electric Theater, was opened on South Street.

1902   Henry Huntington set up an interurban trolley system that led to the famous Big Red Cars line.

1904   The first films of the city were taken in Chutes Park.

1905   A genuine saint, Mother Cabrini (Saint Frances Xavier Cabrini), visited Los Angeles and enjoyed the climate and scenery.

1905   The population was 150,000 and tourists (a word invented in California) kept coming in droves.

1906   Beverly Hills was founded on what was once a Spanish land grant.

1906   Old clothes, relief food and other aid was sent to San Francisco after its great quake and fire.

1907   The first one-reel movie drama, *The Count of Monte Cristo,* filmed.

1908   Los Angeles went after the water of the Owens River east of the

Sierra Nevada. In the next five years, city engineer William Mulholland would built an aqueduct of 200 miles to Los Angeles, bringing disaster to the Owens region and scandals of speculation to private groups benefiting by the project.

1909   The harbors of Wilmington and San Pedro were annexed to the city.

1910   Harrison Otis of the *Times* helped form the powerful anti-labor Merchants and Manufacturers Association to fight craft unions.

1910   Hollywood was consolidated with Los Angeles.

1910   Boosted by the *Times*, Los Angeles became a non-union town. An ordinance was pushed through forbidding picketing.

1910   October 1. Just after midnight, dynamite blew up the Times building, killing twenty-one people.

1910   A reform ticket elected Hiram Johnson governor after his attacks on the corrupt Southern Pacific Railroad and the dishonest Republican Party of the period.

1911   June 26. John Guy Monihan led forty people in eleven open cars across the United States from Atlantic City to Los Angeles, a distance of 4,370 miles. They reached their destination on August 10.

1911   The state flag of California was adopted.

1911   Clarence Darrow was hired to defend the McNamara brothers, J. B. and J. J., the dynamiters of the Times building. They confessed to the crime and Darrow was indicted for bribing the jury. He was later found not guilty.

1912   Teddy Roosevelt and Hiram Johnson joined with the new California Progressive Party to run for national office. They split the Republican Party, leading to the election of Woodrow Wilson as President.

1912   Emma Goldman, famous anarchist and women's rights advocate, was brutally beaten and run out of San Diego along with Ben Reitman. They sought refuge in Los Angeles where Emma attracted large crowds to hear her lectures on free love, Ibsen and Nietzsche.

1912   The first gasoline station in the city opened with gas selling for 8 to 10 cents a gallon.

LOS ANGELES CHRONOLOGY

1913	The discriminatory Alien Land Law was passed, which was enforced mainly against the Japanese-Americans.
1914	Completion of the Panama Canal gave Los Angeles and southern California a cheap shipping lane for its products.
1915	San Fernando Valley was annexed to Los Angeles. In the next four years Huntington, Palisades, Griffith Ranch, Fort MacArthur, Harbor View and several other communities would also become part of the city.
1914	D. W. Griffith produced and directed the film *Birth of a Nation,* signaling the end of the nickelodeon era.
1915	The San Diego Exposition started a fad for Spanish styled buildings and Los Angeles had a revival of the style through the 1920s.
1916	The German Zimmerman Telegram decoded by the British showed that the Germans were planning to have Mexico invade the United States to regain California. There was no invasion.
1916	The Pasadena Playhouse under Gilmore Brown brought great drama and a dramatic school of theater to southern California.
1917	Los Angeles passed San Francisco in population.
1917	The Southwestern Shipbuilding Company Terminal Island had a wartime contract for twenty-three 8,000-ton ships for the Emergency Fleet Corporation. It could build a ship in seventy-seven days.
1917	Los Angeles County regiments were in training at Camp Kearny for going overseas with the A.E.F.
1918	November 11. Armistice signed as Los Angeles went wild. The biggest celebration was held at Hazard's Pavilion.
1918	The Fatty Arbuckle case led to Will Hayes' appointment as tzar of film-making and morals.
1919	A repressive Criminal Syndicalism Act was passed in California, resulting from fear of radicals, the 1917 Russian Revolution and the I.W.W. (Industrial Workers of the World), a militant "working stiffs" union.
1920	The L.A. Metropolitan Water District reached for the water of the

LOS ANGELES CHRONOLOGY

Colorado River; by 1976 75 percent of southern California's water would come from the Colorado.

1920s   The Hollywood Bowl was built on a former Indian campsite.

1920   One hundred thousand automobiles were registered in the city, most of them Henry Ford's "tin lizzie" (the Model T).

1920   Donald W. Douglas started the first plane fuselage plant on Pico Boulevard.

1922   Sister Aimee Semple McPherson appeared in Los Angeles to preach the Four Square Gospel.

1922   The Rose Bowl was constructed in Pasadena.

1922   Noted movie director William Desmond Taylor was mysteriously murdered in his residence in a case which became the most famous unsolved crime of its era.

1922   Wilshire Boulevard became a six-lane thoroughfare and a single lot along it sold for $54,000. But Gaylord Wilshire no longer controlled it.

1923   The Los Angeles Harbor became the largest American oil terminal.

1924   The city had a population of one million and 49,000 real estate agents. One hundred and fifty miles of new streets had been added.

1924   Southern California's trolly system ran on 1,164 miles of track and carried 109 million people. Some of the major automobile manufacturers were to buy up the lines and replace them with buses.

1925   Sister Aimee, collecting $1 million in offerings, built the 5,000-seat Angelus Temple.

1927   Warner Brothers made a part-talking and singing movie called *The Jazz Singer,* thereby ending the silent film era.

1927   September 7. H. Gaylord Wilshire died in New York, facing court actions for unscientific medical claims of a quack invention.

1928   The Boulder Canyon Act and the Hoover Dam (begun in 1931) helped create the Metropolitan Aqueduct, which added more water to Los Angeles' growing needs.

LOS ANGELES CHRONOLOGY

1928	Christine Sterling began to restore Olvera Street, returning the Plaza to its original 1818 state as a historical monument.
1929	E. L. Doheny, Jr., son of the man involved in the Teapot Dome scandal, was murdered by his male secretary.
1930	The La Follette Committee found Los Angeles had "an unhealthy balance of economic power and position dominated by the attitudes of industrial autocracy."
1930–1940	Richfield Oil went into receivership. Guaranty Building & Loan failed. Pacific Mutual was liquidated. Julian Petroleum was looted.
1931	September 4. The city flag was at last adopted by Ordinance No. 70,000.
1931	The Wickersham Commission reported on very brutal police action in L.A. and that anti-labor forces were active among big corporations in disregard of constitutional rights of the citizens.
1932	Louis Adamic reported that there were 15,000 arrests on phony vagrancy charges as the depression progressed and that the unemployed were rousted by the police.
1932	William Gibbs McAdoo was elected to the U.S. Senate from California and received a great deal of federal patronage for the state.
1933	The Great Los Angeles County earthquake, centered at Long Beach, caused much loss of life and property.
1937	Four thousand five hundred factories were listed as industry and grossed $172 million a year. The petroleum industry was nearly double that figure, but citrus and other fruits were still far ahead in earnings.
1938	Franklin Roosevelt granted huge government orders to the local plane industry to build 60,000 aircraft.
1938	Earl Warren was elected governor.
1939	Los Angeles was second only to Detroit in assembling autos. Social welfare schemes flourished: the Townsend Pension Plan, Mankind United, the Decimo Club. Upton Sinclair ran for governor on EPIC (End Poverty in California). He was defeated by biased media reporting and by fake newsreels which showed armies of "tramps" invading the state.

LOS ANGELES CHRONOLOGY

1940	Japanese-Americans accounted for 2 percent of the L.A. population.
1940	Los Angeles population reached 1.5 million, making the city the fifth largest in the U.S.A.
1940	The Mexican-Americans became the largest minority group.
1940	Los Angeles supplanted the San Francisco Bay area as the industrial giant of the west coast.
1941	December 7. Pearl Harbor was attacked. Los Angeles feared Japanese plane and submarine attacks.
1941	Wartime production values had grown to $5 billion.
1942	March. President Roosevelt authorized the placement of 110,000 Japanese-Americans in detention camps.
1942	William Faulkner came to Los Angeles to write the screenplay of *Stallion Road,* which starred Ronald Reagan.
1942	A youth, José Diaz, was found dead in a puddle called Sleepy Lagoon. The police arrested and held twenty-three Chicanos on no clear evidence. Seventeen were convicted but these convictions were later reversed.
1942	The Zoot Suit Riots broke out between the pachucos (young Mexican-Americans) and sailors in various dance halls. Mexican American youths were beaten by white mobs, while the police did very little but arrest Chicanos.
1944	Harry Chandler died. Norman and Dorothy (Buffy) Chandler took over the *Los Angeles Times* publishing empire.
1945	World War II brought such famous exiles as Bertolt Brecht, Lion Feuchtwanger, Thomas Mann, Franz Werfel, and Max Reinhardt to Los Angeles. Igor Stravinsky, Aldous Huxley, Jascha Heifetz and Artur Rubinstein came for the climate.
1945	Los Angeles became a major armament center with jet aircraft plants.
1945	Aimee Semple McPherson died of sleeping pills.
1946	The L.A. Air Pollution Control Board was set up to fight smog.

LOS ANGELES CHRONOLOGY

1953   Los Angeles plants started work on the ICBM (Intercontinental Ballistics Missile), boosting the number of jobs available in the county.

1954   Smog was so bad several times this year that all air traffic had to be shifted to Burbank Airport.

1956   Signal Hill, the great oil field, was declared depleted.

1960   Only 49,000 citrus trees were left in southern California. Thirteen years before there were 135,000.

1960   In ten years Los Angeles had grown by a million persons. In ten more years it would increase by a half million.

1962   Richard Nixon, defeated by John Kennedy, tried for the governorship of California against Pat Brown and lost.

1965   August 6. The Watts riot broke out. Fire, street fighting and looting reigned; in six days 34 people were killed by gunfire, more than 1,000 were wounded and 950 arrested.

1965   Two hundred and sixty acres a day were turned into building tracts as farming fast disappeared from Los Angeles County.

1967   Seventy percent of southern California aerospace personnel were employed by Lookheed in the San Fernando Valley.

1968   Robert Kennedy was assassinated in a Los Angeles hotel ballroom in full view of television watchers.

1971   An earthquake of sixty seconds resulted in a half billion dollars' worth of damages, including the destruction of twenty highway overpasses and a veterans hospital.

1971   April 19. Charles Manson and three girls of his murderous "Family" were sentenced to death for some of the most brutal cult killings in Los Angeles. The death sentences were never carried out.

1971   The great Bel Air fire destroyed eighty-four luxury homes. Seventy-five fire companies were coordinated to fight the raging blazes, aided by chemical and water-drop planes.

1973   City Attorney Burt Pines pointed out the success of obscene films in the city. *Deep Throat* grossed $3.2 million in an eighty-one-week run.

1973   Sam Yorty was defeated by Tom Bradley, the first nonwhite mayor of Los Angeles.

1973   September 26. The saber-toothed tiger (*Smilodon*) was named the state fossil.

1974   The Teamsters and Caesar Chavez's Farm Union engaged in a bloody conflict to control the migrant farm workers. The farmers enjoyed a 43 percent increase in income this year.

1974   A test count showed that southwest Los Angeles' 10th District was about 50% black, 12% Asian-American, 20% Jewish, the remainder minorities: Mexican-American, American Indian, other Caucasian.

1975   Frank Lloyd Wright's Hollyhock House in Barnsdall Park was fully restored.

1975   The county had forty-four square miles of parking space. With poor mass transportation, travel was mostly by car.

1976   The International Airport handled more than 1,000 jets a day—and was obsolete.

1976   June. J. Paul Getty, the world's richest man, died at eighty-six. He left a request to be buried on the grounds of his $20 million private museum in southern California.

1976   A survey showed that 4.4% of the people of L.A. owned 60% of its corporate stocks, 77% of the state and local bonds, 33% of the personal cash, 25% of the real estate and 40% of the noncorporate business assets.

1970s   The state passed an uncontested divorce law enabling adults to obtain a divorce simply on the grounds of disagreement, a liberal abortion law and a law legalizing sex acts done in private between consenting adults. A state law called the Coast Line Amendment returned 1,000 miles of coast to public use. The Patty Hearst kidnapping and following trials were voted the most followed L.A. news events of the decade.

Selected Bibliography

Ayers, Colonel James, *Reminiscences of Early California,* 1922.
Bancroft, Hubert Howe, *History of California,* 1884.
Beers, George A., *Vasquez or the Hunted Bandits of the San Joaquin,* 1875.
Bell, Horace, *On the Old West Coast,* 1930.
———, *Reminiscences of a Ranger,* 1927.
Bogardus, Emory F., *Mexicans in the United States,* 1934.

SELECTED BIBLIOGRAPHY

Bolton, Herbert E., *Fray Juan Crespi 1769–1774,* 1927.

Bonelli, William G., *Billion Dollar Blackjack,* 1954.

Chapman, John, *Incredible Los Angeles,* 1967.

Cleland, R. G., *From Wilderness to Empire,* 1947.

Dana, Richard Henry, *Two Years Before the Mast,* 1909 edition.

Dumke, Glenn S., *The Boom of the Eighties in Southern California,* 1944.

First of the Ranchos, 1927.

George, Henry, *Progress and Poverty,* 1929 edition.

Graves, Jackson A., *Seventy Years in California,* 1927.

Guinn, James M., *History of Los Angeles from Earliest Days to the 19th Century,* 1901.

———, *A history of California and an Extended History of its Southern Coast Counties,* 1907.

———, *History of California and an Extended History of Los Angeles,* 1915.

Hancock, Ralph, *Fabulous Boulevard,* 1949.

A History of California—Spanish Period, 1921.

History of the Pacific States: Vol. XIX, 1892.

Illustrated History of Los Angeles County, 1889.

Indians of Los Angeles County, 1926.

Johnson, Paul C., editor, *Los Angeles, Portrait of an Extraordinary City,* 1968.

Jackson, Helen Hunt, *Ramona,* 1915 edition.

Josephson, Matthew, *The Robber Barons,* 1934.

Layne, J. Gress, *Annals of Los Angeles,* 1935.

Lewis, Oscar, *The Big Four,* 1948.

Los Angeles County Museum, *Los Angeles, 1900–1961,* 1961.

MacKay, Margaret Gilbert, *Los Angeles Proper and Improper,* 1938.

Mayer, Robert, *Chronology and Documentary History of Los Angeles, 1542–1970,* 1974.

Mayo, Morrow, *Los Angeles,* 1932.

McGroarty, John Steven, *Los Angeles from the Mountains to the Sea,* 1921.

McWilliams, Carey, *Southern California: An Island on the Land,* 1946.

Meyers, Gustave, *Great American Fortunes,* 1910.

SELECTED BIBLIOGRAPHY

Moody, John, *The Railroad Builders,* 1919.

Mowry, George, *California Progressives, Berkeley and Los Angeles,* 1951.

Nadeau, Reni A., *City Makers,* 1948.

———, *Men Who Transformed Los Angeles, 1868–1876,* 1948.

———, *Los Angeles from Mission to Modern City,* 1960.

Newmark, Harris, *Sixty Years in Southern California, 1853–1913,* 1921.

Nordhoff, Charles, *California for Health, Pleasure and Residence,* 1873.

Perry, Louis B., and Richard S., *History of Los Angeles Labor Movement,* 1963.

Phelps, Alonzo, *Contemporary Biographies of California's Representative Men,* 1882.

Rice, Craig, editor, *The Los Angeles Murders,* 1948.

Riegel, R. E., *Story of the Western Railroads,* 1926.

Salvator, Ludwig Louis, *Los Angeles in the Sunny 70's,* 1885; translated by Wilber, Margaret E., 1929.

Sawyer, Eugene T., *The Life and Career of Tiburico Vasquez,* 1875.

Schlessinger, Arthur M., *Rise of the City 1873–1898,* 1933.

Seitz, Don Carlos, *The Dreadful Decade, 1869–1875,* 1926.

Spaulding, William A., *History and Reminiscences of Los Angeles,* 1930.

Steffens, Lincoln, *Autobiography of Lincoln Steffens,* 1931.

———, *Letters of Lincoln Steffens,* 1938.

Stewart, George, *The California Trail,* 1962.

Turner, F. J., *The Significance of the American Frontier,* 1893.

Vickery, F. P., *Geology County,* 1928.

Walker, Franklin A., *Literary History of Southern California,* 1950.

———, Hayes, Benjamin, and Widney, J. P., *Historical Sketch of Los Angeles County,* 1876.

Warner, J. J., *Historical Sketch of Los Angeles,* 1876.

Wells Fargo and Company, *Robbers' Record,* 1885.

Wester, Dixon, *The Saga of American Society,* 1937.

Weymen, Walker, editor, *California Emigrant Letters,* 1952.

Willard, Charles, *A History of Los Angeles,* 1901.

Williams, Liza, *Up the City of Angels,* 1971.

SELECTED BIBLIOGRAPHY

Wilson, Albert J., *History of Los Angeles County,* 1880.

Workman, Boyle, *The City That Grew,* 1935.

Early Newspapers: Helpful with local color, letters to the editor and the checking of dates were incomplete files of the following:
Bakersfield Weekly, Southern California; Los Angeles Daily Express; Los Angeles Daily Herald; Los Angeles Daily Republican; Los Angeles Daily Star; Los Angeles Free Press; Los Angeles Monthly Real Estate Advertiser; Los Angeles Weekly Mirror; Los Angeles Weekly Republican; Saturday Night; Weekly Southern California.

Other newspapers: The city once had several competing newspapers, which made for a stronger, fuller coverage of news and local history: *Hollywood Citizen, Hollywood Citizen News, Los Angeles Evening Express, Los Angeles Examiner, Los Angeles Herald, Los Angeles Herald Express, Los Angeles Mirror-News, Los Angeles News, Los Angeles Times.*

Magazines: Some magazines long since gone, others current: *American Mercury, The Argonaut, Coast, Everybody's, Fortune, Hearst's International, Heritage, Holiday, Horizon, The Lark, Literary Digest, Los Angeles Magazine, McClure's, Overland Monthly, Pacific Monthly, Review of Reviews, Westways.*

Index

Page numbers in italics indicate illustrations.

INDEX